D1232081

Forest & Garden

Forest &Garden

Traces of Wildness in
a Modernizing Land,
1897–1949

MELANIE L. SIMO

UNIVERSITY OF VIRGINIA PRESS
CHARLOTTESVILLE AND LONDON

Publication of this volume was assisted by grants from Furthermore, the publication program of the J. M. Kaplan Fund; the Graham Foundation for Advanced Studies in the Fine Arts; and the National Coalition of Independent Scholars

All photographs by author unless otherwise noted

University of Virginia Press
© 2003 by the Rector and Visitors of the University of Virginia
All rights reserved
Printed in the United States of America on acid-free paper

First published 2003

9 8 7 6 5 4 3 2 1

LIBRARY OF CONGRESS CATALOGING-IN-PUBLICATION DATA

Simo, Melanie Louise, 1949–
    Forest and garden : traces of wildness in a modernizing land, 1897–1949 / Melanie L. Simo.
        p.   cm.
    Includes bibliographical references (p.   ).
        ISBN 0-8139-2159-7 (cloth : alk. paper)
    1. Landscape architecture—United States—History. 2. Landscape change—United States—History. 3. Nature—Effect of human beings on—United States—History. I. Title.
        SB470.53 .S56 2003
        712'.0973—dc21

                                                        2002010189

Frontispiece: *Landscape* (etching/engraving by Brian Muchow; courtesy of the artist)

To Brian,

who once led me out of the forest
and into the garden

Contents

Illustrations

Preface

Its arrival is the coming of a wise and intelligent and entertaining friend, who enables us to live more happily because more harmoniously with nature.

How often, I wondered, could this be said of a publication today? The writer was referring to *Garden and Forest,* a unique magazine dedicated to raising environmental awareness during the so-called Gilded Age.[1] From 1888 to 1897 this "Journal of Horticulture, Landscape Art and Forestry" had served as a forum for distinguished writers, scientists, artists, nurserymen, and government officials, including the foresters Bernhard Fernow and Gifford Pinchot, the landscape architects Frederick Law Olmsted and Charles Eliot, the historian Francis Parkman, and the architecture and landscape critic Mariana Griswold Van Rensselaer. Their language was direct, their tone often engaging, sometimes urgent. At a time when professions and specializations were beginning to crystallize, amateurs still contributed articles and queries to *Garden and Forest.* William A. Stiles, the managing editor, and Charles Sprague Sargent, director of the Arnold Arboretum, who had the final say, kept the publishing experiment alive. And high praise flowed in from London, Paris, New York, Chicago, and many other cities and towns.

But the experiment ended soon after the death of Stiles, in October 1897. A terse announcement that December revealed that *Garden and Forest* had relied on subsidies for ten years. Publication would now cease, as there did not seem to be enough people in the United States willing to subscribe and make the journal pay for itself.[2]

Perhaps the business instincts of Sargent and his colleagues were sound. Within a few years—by 1900—both the foresters and the landscape architects in the United States had organized their own professional associations. Soon each group would have its own journal. Professional schools and academic departments for each would appear. Meanwhile, *Country Life in America* (established in 1901) and other magazines would appeal to widening circles of amateurs.[3] It is a familiar story, the progressive breaking down of complex wholes into manageable (or profitable, or analyzable) parts. In time, special tools and new words allowed people to discuss increasingly finer distinctions among increasingly fewer people. The sum of human knowledge around the globe vastly increased. But what of human wisdom? Was all this specialization and separation inevitable? Or did we take a wrong turn somewhere?

These thoughts would not go away as I turned to some unfinished work at hand. A book that the landscape architect Peter Walker and I had written—*Invisible Gardens* (1994)—had linked the social and artistic aspirations of mid-twentieth-century landscape architects in the United States with those of Olmsted, the generally recognized "father" of their profession. To keep the book reasonably short and maintain a focus on modernism, we had deliberately omitted discussions of a few generations of landscape architects whose work in the early twentieth century did not seem to contribute significantly to the modern movement in the United States. The approach seemed logical. Then, too, what those modernists were able to achieve in the American landscape was remarkable, sometimes beautiful and immensely satisfying. Still, we had left a gap in time. It was a time of critical transitions in American history, when individuals' sensibilities, purposes, and ideals were altered by complex forces that we commonly refer to as urbanization, professionalization, specialization, the rise of science and technology, and the closing of the American frontier. All that was part of the intervening terrain between the Victorian era and mid-twentieth-century modernism.

Some years after *Invisible Gardens* appeared, two invitations to write a centennial history of landscape architecture led me toward new perspectives on the generations of professionals who had, for one reason or another, resisted or ignored the modern movement.[4] I was intrigued and moved by their struggles to make transitions between two ways of life and ways of knowing—one slower paced, rooted in country matters, the other accelerating in pace, rate of change, and flight to the city. I noticed, too, these landscape architects' affiliations with horticulturists, geologists, foresters, and painters of the old school—Corot and Constable, perhaps, but not Cézanne.

In time, some things stood out as if in a new light. The landscape architecture textbook brought out in 1917 by the Harvard professor Henry Vincent Hubbard and the Harvard librarian Theodora Kimball, for instance, no longer seemed dispassionate. For among their leisurely reflections on texture, scale, form, and color in landscape design were references to "the blind destructive forces of man's enterprise" and one remark worthy of Jack London: that "even modern city-bred men should find something in wild nature which seems to fulfill and complete their being."[5] Then, too, a focus on the spirit or soul of the landscape in early-twentieth-century works by the landscape architect Frank Waugh no longer seemed anachronistic. As late as 1932, Waugh, head of the Division of Horticulture at Massachusetts Agricultural College (now the University of Massachusetts at Amherst), was in charge of studies in landscape architecture, pomology, floriculture, vegetable gardening, and forestry.[6] This was a fairly large domain, uniting the interests of science and art, reason and emotion, utility and beauty. Did Waugh and his colleagues ever transcend the walls of their separate disciplines, I wondered, and communicate with one another?

In any event, *Forest and Garden* came into being as an effort to recap-

te-nineteenth- and early-twentieth-century milieu, in which
scape architects could still talk with foresters and horticultur-
mon ground. The book follows some friendships and pro-
changes among landscape architects and foresters in partic-
cognizes their common concerns over the waste of natural
resources and the need to preserve some remote, wild, and extraordinarily beautiful landscapes. But equally important are the relations of
city and country, cultivation and wildness, and the overlaps between
them. It is an intricate story, open to contributions from novelists, essay-
ists, architects, poets, ornithologists, nature writers, and others who were
alert to traces of wildness wherever they happened to appear.

The primeval wilderness—which some people now believe to have
vanished from the planet Earth—is a recurring interest in the story. But
the main interest, the heart of our quest, will be traces of wildness (a
quality, not a terrain), along with experiences of freedom, abundance,
the sense of being alive, the feeling of being connected with something
elemental—with the spirit of a place, perhaps, or with the entire universe. These things tend not to be discussed in our time as they were a
century ago, often in poetic language with religious overtones, without
irony or defensiveness. Now our public lives are largely secular, prosaic,
tamed if not civilized, and insured against risks of all kinds. And yet the
call of a loon, the smell of mesquite, a clump of wildflowers thrusting up
through the crack in a sidewalk, or a monarch butterfly hovering about
the humble allium flowers in a backyard garden all suggest traces of
wildness still within our reach.

The search for overlaps between wildness and cultivation will lead
to some out-of-the-way places that may be teeming with life—a sun-
dappled stream winding through town unnoticed while all the buildings
face the street; or a somber swamp lying hidden by trees and billboards
along a suburban highway. Among people and institutions of opposing
views—John Muir and Gifford Pinchot, the U.S. Forest Service and the
National Park Service—there will be some notable overlaps. The historical development of an institution or a group like the Wilderness Society will be touched upon. But what we want to uncover, in the end, are

not institutional or general views but personal feelings and perceptions, of the land, its uses, its beauty, its fate. *why? are these persons, feelings more important?*

Forest and Garden was never meant to be comprehensive. It is not exhaustive in its treatment of any single place, person, idea, or piece of writing. Nor does it venture into the ongoing debates about wilderness preservation, environmental justice, social justice, and related issues, timely and compelling though they certainly are. This is mainly a study of mere traces of wildness, a selective and personal study that focuses on concrete things and firsthand experiences. Abstract concepts and analytical or theoretical frameworks are absent for the most part. Instead, each chapter reads as a narrative, a story. More about the cumulative meaning of these stories appears in the introduction, after a discussion of forests, gardens, and other landscapes as viewed by some influential figures at the end of the nineteenth century. The book ends about midway through the twentieth century, with a consideration of two works that appeared in 1949—Jens Jensen's *The Clearing* and Aldo Leopold's *Sand County Almanac*. Each is a unique expression of something that may someday be rare—a love of the land.

"traces of wildness"

✓ She's upset by the professionalization
of nature - prior to 1900, people talked
(jobs within) to each other, there were shared experiences
across fields

✓ people's feelings of wildness, sense of place
✓ common ground needed" - less popular writers
advised it, she'll focus on them here

Acknowledgments

Writing in solitude I pause, gaze at the pages before me, and know that they could never have been written or become a book without the help of many people and institutions. Among the people are former teachers and students, colleagues and critics, family and friends who said or did something to open a door that let in light, perhaps, or framed a view. Among the institutions are schools, universities, and museums here and abroad, large and small. Unable to acknowledge all, I mention some and hope that a part may stand for the whole.

Three grants, for research, travel, and writing, have supported this book. One, from the Graham Foundation for Advanced Studies in the Fine Arts, was awarded under a special focus initiative, "Sensitive Utilization of Natural Resources."

Another grant came to me, via the University of Virginia Press, from Furthermore, the publication program of the J. M. Kaplan Fund.

A third, the National Coalition of Independent Scholars Grant 2000, was awarded by a young, very promising organization of which I am honored to be a member. To all the people who in some way made these grants possible, my sincere thanks.

Many individuals allowed me access to manuscript materials and images within their institutions. Here I would like to thank Philip N. Cronenwett, Special Collections Librarian, Dartmouth College Library, for permission to quote and paraphrase manuscript materials from the MacKaye Family Papers and the Sally Carrighar Papers; and for qualified permission to reproduce some previously unpublished passages and the image of the title page from the original manuscript of Henry Beston's *Outermost House*. I also extend my thanks to Brent K. Wagner, Archivist/ Librarian of the Western History/Genealogy Department of the Denver Public Library, for permission to quote and paraphrase manuscript materials from the Arthur H. Carhart Papers, the Aldo Leopold Papers, and the Wilderness Society Papers; to Harley P. Holden, University Archivist, Harvard University Archives, for permission to quote and paraphrase from manuscript materials and Harvard College *Class Records;* to Mary F. Daniels, Librarian, Special Collections of the Frances Loeb Library, Harvard University Graduate School of Design, for permission to quote and paraphrase from rare and manuscript materials; to Michael Plunkett, Director of the Albert and Shirley Small Special Collections Library, University of Virginia Library, for permission to quote and paraphrase from the Walter Prichard Eaton Collection; to Nicolette Brombert, Curator of Photographs and Graphics, Manuscripts, Special Collections, University Archives Division (MSCUA), University of Washington Libraries, for permission to reproduce the photograph *Serpentine Glacier,* by Edward S. Curtis; and to Susan Otto, Manager, Photography Collections, Milwaukee Public Museum, for permission to reproduce the photograph *Spirit of the West,* by Sumner Matteson.

I owe a special debt of gratitude to Catherine Beston Barnes for graciously granting me permission to reproduce previously unpublished passages and the image of the title page from the original manuscript of Henry Beston's *Outermost House*.

For assistance in many forms I thank the staffs of the New Hampshire

Audubon Society and the State Library of New Hampshire, both in Concord; the Brown Memorial Library, in Bradford, New Hampshire; the Berkshire Athenaeum, in Pittsfield, Massachusetts; several libraries at Dartmouth College; the Colorado Historical Society; and the Denver Public Library.

I cannot mention all the times when friends, colleagues, and new acquaintances have generously given support and advice on this project, sometimes joining me, literally or figuratively, in my quests. I should, however, mention at least a few of these people, including Ethan Carr, Francelia Mason Clark, Grady Clay, Dan Donelin, Meg Fearnley, Bernd Foerster, Pete Foster, Elizabeth Happy, Sarah Hartwell, Laura Linke, Mike Mc Cormack, Dawn Mahoney, Elizabeth Meyer, Bryan Poovey, Joshua D. Shaw, Betty Steele, John R. Stilgoe, Mary Stoll, Brian A. Sullivan, Judith Tankard, Barbara Walton, Donna M. E. Ware, Nelson Whittier, and Hugh Wilburn.

For the inspiration of their work and some brief but memorable exchanges of words in Vermont I thank David Lowenthal, Susan Flader, and Curt Meine. A debt to Arline Eckbo and the late Garrett Eckbo, perhaps less evident in these pages than elsewhere, is implicit in whatever I have written and may yet write about the San Francisco Bay Area and its landscape architecture.

For reading portions of this book in draft form and offering astute comments, essential corrections, and genial encouragement I thank Phoebe Cutler, Robin Karson, Christopher Vernon, and Donna M. E. Ware. To the anonymous reviewers of the original book proposal and the entire final draft I am grateful as well. The insights they offered and the interconnections they pointed out were fascinating. Perhaps they will detect in the final product some traces of their own critiques, heeded and acted upon. Whatever shortcomings and flaws remain are, naturally, of my own doing.

The editors at the University of Virginia Press, Boyd Zenner and Ellen Satrom in particular, have been extraordinarily supportive and helpful. Ellen, as managing editor, swiftly responded to my queries and cleared some daunting paths along the way. The gleam of an idea for this book came from a conversation with Boyd. Since then, her support and enthusiasm for the book as it evolved have helped to shape it as only a few legendary editors may have done. What could have been a series of polite exchanges became an adventure shared.

Saved for last are thanks to some people in Massachusetts, Colorado, and elsewhere: the large extended family to which my husband and I owe so much. Their support and love cannot be adequately acknowledged here. I would, however, like to thank my parents for introducing me to a few things relevant to this study: mountains, cameras, and the public library. To my husband, Brian, my thanks for the frontispiece and infinitely more.

My own mind feels more at home with the unsystematic approach
of writers like Montaigne and Goethe, let us say; and especially in
the field of music it seems to me important that we keep open what
William James calls the "irrational doorways . . . through which . . .
the wildness and the pang of life" may be glimpsed.

AARON COPLAND, Music and Imagination

beautiful

Introduction

This story has been told many times, with variations in detail and coloring: A young man with a new job as "recreation engineer" in the U.S. Forest Service spent the summer of 1919 investigating national forests in Colorado, Wyoming, South Dakota, Nebraska, and Minnesota. Around Trappers Lake, a 313-acre remnant of a glacier in the White River National Forest of Colorado, he was supposed to survey the land for a shoreline road, a few hundred summer home sites, and a circular highway. He did as he was told but also informed his supervisor that he was opposed to the scheme. Given the exceptional beauty and serenity of the setting, he would have preferred to keep development away from the lake. In that way, people could come to it as a sanctuary, quietly, on foot. His supervisor, Carl J. Stahl, said little more than "Maybe we've got something here."[1]

A few weeks later, Stahl asked the young recreation engineer, Arthur H. Carhart, if he could meet with the assistant district forester from the Albuquerque office, Aldo Leopold. The two met on December 6, 1919, in the Denver office. And, as Carhart later recalled, Stahl sat in as a "third man."[2] After many hours of conversation, Carhart and Leopold found that their views on the value of wilderness were remarkably similar. Leopold, the elder by a few years and much higher up in the Forest Service hierarchy, asked Carhart to write a memorandum of their meeting. In doing so, Carhart produced a key statement in the history of wilderness preservation. "Time will come when these scenic spots, where nature has been allowed to remain unmarred, will be some of the most highly prized scenic features of the country," he wrote, "and unless the Forest Service has thoroughly exerted all influences possible to preserve these areas, severe criticism will some day be meted out by the collective owners of this territory, the public. . . . The question of how best to do this is perhaps the real question, rather than shall it be done."[3]

Years later, Carhart recognized the importance of his meeting with Leopold. Noting that no one person could take credit for the idea of wilderness recreation as "justifiable human use," he did single out Leopold, "whose genius and clear-sightedness gave shape, form, and direction to the wilderness idea."[4] Carhart also credited his superior, Stahl, and two sportsmen, William McFadden and Paul Rainey, who had sat up until midnight with Carhart in a tent by Trappers Lake, arguing against the house lots, cars, and motorboats that would accompany development. Having learned from all these people, Carhart later took some credit as a pioneer in recognizing that one of the most valuable forest products was the re-creation of the spirit, something he had only begun to understand at Trappers Lake, in the summer of 1919.[5]

In the decades since the Wilderness Act was passed, in 1964, the search for pioneers in the movement to preserve wilderness has intensified. In the 1970s and 1980s a controversy arose over whether Carhart deserved credit as the "father of the wilderness concept," thereby overshadowing the larger vision of Leopold (whose proposal, of 1922, to preserve the 500,000-acre wilderness in the Gila National Forest, in New Mexico, was finally approved in 1924). In time Leopold's biographer, Curt Meine, gracefully defused the controversy by concluding that, although Carhart and Leopold were not the first to raise concerns about wilderness, their meeting on December 6, 1919, "gave birth to a new endeavor within the Forest Service: to act on those concerns before the wilderness was gone."[6]

The timing was critical. Time, place, the distance from civilization, the maturity of that civilization, our own interests and needs—these are critical to the way we perceive wilderness. Some people do not perceive wilderness at all, apparently. They live in and know intimately places that others call "wilderness." To recognize wilderness, it seems, one has to come from somewhere else. "If it were not for Washington and New York," wrote the naturalist and political scientist Louis Halle in the mid-1940s, "I would take the wilderness for granted." Born in New York City, Halle thought of those cities as walls, without which he had no window on the wilderness.[7]

It so happened that two native Iowans—Carhart, a landscape architect, and Leopold, a forester—came together in Denver in 1919, at a time when their relatively new professions already represented opposing views of wilderness. To the landscape architect, wilderness was a source of beauty, a sequence of scenes to enjoy at leisure, an environment in which one could heal the mind and soul, having shed the burdens and stresses of urban living. That is what Frederick Law Olmsted had found in the Yosemite Valley of California in the 1860s, and that is what his successors took on faith or found out for themselves. But to the forester, particularly one who had lived and studied in Europe, wilderness was a source of timber, without which civilization could not exist. From this perspective, wilderness was less valuable for what it was than for what it could become—a well-managed, periodically logged forest.

From both perspectives—wilderness as sanctuary and wilderness as raw material—the devastation of American forests, through wasteful logging practices, the setting of fires to clear land, and the resulting erosion of soil, flooding, and silting up of streams, all seemed a kind of madness. Or was it blindness in the name of progress? Bernhard Fernow, head of the Division of Forestry in the U.S. Department of Agriculture from 1886 to 1898, had seen it all before in the pages of history. Born in Prussia in 1851 and trained in a forest academy there, he knew about

Fernow

Prussian

wasteful slashing and burning in the forests of Germany. But that had occurred hundreds of years earlier. By the twelfth century, regulations for logging and grazing had begun to bring some order to the forests of his native land. Now, in the nineteenth century, at a pace greatly accelerated by modern technology, the United States was simply moving through the stages that Europeans had already moved through more slowly.[8]

Fernow was a skillful leader in the development of American forestry, not only in government but also in academia. He established the nation's first school of forestry in an academic institution, at Cornell University, in 1898. He also edited three influential journals: *The Forester,* in 1897; the *Forestry Quarterly,* from 1902 to 1916; and its successor, the *Journal of Forestry,* from 1917 until just before he died, in 1923. In addition, Fernow was a leading advocate for setting aside forest lands from private acquisition—several years before the Forest Reserve Act was signed in 1891.[9] Still, it appears that Fernow did not wield the unique sort of influence that his younger colleague, Gifford Pinchot, held over aspiring foresters. And for all his calm assurance, no doubt drawn from technical mastery of his field, Fernow could be irritating in print. He suggested, for instance, that the inauguration of Arbor Day, in 1872, by the State Board of Agriculture in Nebraska, might have a "retarding influence" on the practical forestry movement; for it might mislead people into thinking that forestry was merely a question of planting trees. What was worse, Fernow noted, Arbor Day brought into the discussion of forestry "poetry and emotions, which have clouded the hard-headed practical issues and delayed the earnest attention of practical business men."[10]

It was Gifford Pinchot's great achievement to take this fundamentally utilitarian profession, forestry, make it inspiring to his followers, give a new meaning and dignity to public service in the federal government, and at the same time not lose sight of the private entrepreneur's goal of profit. This was a balancing act, an art requiring fine skills of diplomacy. But a certain ruggedness was no hindrance, either. Out in the field Pinchot was a "man's man" who could "outride and outshoot any ranger on the force," according to one of his successors as head of the U.S. Forest

Service, William B. Greeley. After one trip with Pinchot, marking timber and climbing mountains to locate fire lookouts, Greeley remembered things that his boss had found thrilling: a glimpse of snow-covered peaks, a well-thinned stand of young timber, a single, stately sugar pine.[11]

Born in Simsbury, Connecticut, in 1865, educated at Yale, and trained in European schools of forestry, Pinchot could be equally at home in the city or the countryside. Then, too, inheriting a sense of noblesse oblige, he remained committed to a high standard of public well-being. "The greatest good of the greatest number for the longest time" was a maxim he shared with his fellow crusaders for forestry.[12] But when Pinchot came face to face with a poet whose natural habitat was not merely country-side but wilderness—the Scottish-born poet in prose John Muir—con-flicts between utility and aesthetic, spiritual sensibilities could, in time, stand out in sharp relief.

Pinchot and Muir first came together in the 1890s, in wild lands east and west and at Pinchot's father's home in New York. Adventurous, opti-mistic, deeply concerned about the fate of American forests, the two men of different generations naturally formed a bond. And yet, as Pin-chot's biographer Char Miller explains, their relationship was compli-cated by differences as well as affinities.[13] Interestingly, Pinchot's pub-lished recollections tend to focus on the affinities. Once at the Grand Canyon, he and Muir parted from the others in their party to spend a day and an unanticipated night on the rim. They made beds of cedar boughs and talked until midnight, while a campfire kept them from freezing. The next day they had to apologize to the others for the anxi-ety their disappearance had caused.[14]

That was in the fall of 1896, during the excursion of the seven-mem-ber National Forestry Commission, which had been formed by the Na-tional Academy of Sciences to advise the Department of the Interior on how best to move beyond the broad provisions of the Forest Reserve Act of 1891. Already presidents Cleveland and Harrison had proclaimed sev-enteen forest reservations, totaling some 17.5 million acres. But there was no established policy, no legislation or provision, for administering these reserves. Meanwhile, as waste, theft, arson, and other illegal practices on the reserves continued, the losses to the federal government were estimated at some $37 million. The commissioners, all eminent men of science, knew the gravity of the situation and assumed their responsibilities with modest funds for expenses and no pay. Pinchot, the youngest member, served as secretary. And Chairman Charles Sprague Sargent persuaded Muir to join as an ex officio member. Known for writings imbued with poetic feeling for wild living things, Muir was apparently expected to report on the commission's findings, lending his imagination and fervor to stories that could stir the public.[15]

As it happened, Muir wrote three long, detailed articles about the Forestry Commission's cause.[16] Anyone who anticipated entertaining stories, dour Scottish humor, and the occasional lift into higher realms of reverence and awe in the presence of God's wondrous creations would not have been disappointed. Yet these were *hybrid* pieces that considered aesthetics and spiritual well-being along with the benefits of tourism, the "greatest good for the greatest number," and the rational administration of forests. The second article, "The American Forests," in the *Atlantic Monthly* of August 1897, begins with a sweeping glance over the American continent in search of "God's forestry fresh from heaven," then slips into long quotations and paraphrases from Gifford Pinchot's "Government Forestry Abroad" and Edward A. Bowers's "Present Condition of the Forests on the Public Lands," both of 1891.[17] Muir ends the article in his own distinctive voice, noting that "any fool can destroy trees," while only Uncle Sam can save trees from fools. But the whole is grounded in solid facts, figures, and details of European legislation and acts of Congress—the kind of information routinely gathered by "practical" men such as Pinchot and the former inspector of the Public Land Service, Bowers.

Muir's three articles of 1897 and 1898 provided good public relations for a sterling cause. In fact, two of them were later reprinted in his endearing, partly autobiographical work, *Our National Parks* (1901). Yet the poet in Muir must have been somewhat disappointed by the inconsistent tone of "The American Forests." Perhaps in the struggle to help preserve wild landscapes from imminent destruction, Muir was willing

6

to draw heavily from the research of Pinchot and Bowers, even though their language and their framing of the issues were not akin to his own. For that matter, Pinchot, too, had had to glean information from others, both in Europe and at home. On one trip to the Calaveras Grove in California, in the hot, dry summer of 1899, Pinchot accompanied Muir and C. Hart Merriam, head of the U.S. Biological Survey. Years later, he recalled the ubiquitous dust and the delightful conversations. "They had camped and adventured all over the West from Alaska to Mexico," he wrote of Muir and Merriam. "They had seen what they looked at; and they were full of facts I needed in my business."[18]

This sort of exchange is really the point of looking for overlaps among people differently educated, with different sensibilities and aims, yet with a common cause. Muir could have remained in California, tending his father-in-law's orchards in Martinez, watching his own two lovely daughters develop, and making excursions now and again, alone, into his beloved Sierra or among the glaciers in Alaska. But if he was to help preserve the beauty and majesty of the whole North American continent, he had to understand and then articulate in his own words, if possible, something of the pragmatic, utilitarian, and even commercial interests of people unlike himself.

With good reason, Muir and Pinchot are often viewed as opposites in the conflicts between preservation of wild landscapes and conservation (or "wise use") of natural resources. Muir's aesthetic and spiritual values can be set against Pinchot's utilitarian purposes, and a good case can be made for either side. Consider the conflict over the damming of the Hetch Hetchy Valley in Yosemite National Park (discussed in chapter 6). This was perhaps the best-known situation in which Muir and Pinchot took opposite sides. Some observers have assumed that after President Wilson's final decision on Hetch Hetchy in December 1913, bitter feelings remained between the two adversaries. Yet soon afterward Pinchot quoted his friend Muir with approval. Writing about the personal qualities that every good forester must have, Pinchot repeated the advice that Muir used to give young men: "Take time to get rich." And he explained, with evident sympathy, "[Muir's] idea of getting rich is to fill his mind and spirit full with observations of the nature he so deeply loves and so well understands; so that in his mind it is not money which makes riches, but life in the open and the seeing eye."[19]

***

That was something landscape architects wanted to cultivate—the seeing eye. But at the end of the nineteenth century, none of them could convey their perceptions with anything like Muir's passion and verbal agility. By 1895, Olmsted was retired from practice and a long writing life. Two years later his articulate young partner, Charles Eliot, died at age thirty-seven. The younger Frederick Law Olmsted was still learning about his profession, not yet writing about it. H. W. S. Cleveland, a colleague of Olmsted in the Midwest, lived only until 1900.[20] Later in the new century, new voices would emerge from Jens Jensen and O. C. Simonds in the Midwest, Arthur Carhart in Denver, Frank Waugh and Warren Manning in Massachusetts, Beatrix Farrand in New York City, and others. Meanwhile one man—a scientist and a southerner— was writing about forests and the visual qualities of landscape in a way that could have led young foresters and landscape architects toward a common ground, where science and art, sociology and ecology came together.

Nathaniel Southgate Shaler, geologist, geographer, published poet, and exceedingly popular professor, was one of those prolific nineteenth-century figures—George Perkins Marsh and Frederick Law Olmsted come to mind—for whom a single title seems inadequate. Like these two, Shaler was fascinated by the larger questions of civilization and culture in a rapidly industrializing, urbanizing, modernizing nation; at stake were the bounty of the earth and its beauty, recognizable in both wild and cultivated states. Like Marsh in particular, Shaler was deeply troubled by the waste of natural resources, especially forests, in both the Old World and the New. But unlike Olmsted and Marsh, Shaler was a trained scientist, once a favorite student of the naturalist Louis Agassiz at Harvard. In time, Shaler sided with Agassiz's intellectual foe, Charles Darwin, in the controversies over theories of evolution. But more significant for our purposes was Shaler's role as a mediator, straddling two perspectives identified by his biographer David Livingstone—"the aesthetic and the pragmatic."[21]

Born in Newport, Kentucky, in 1841, Shaler was nearly two generations younger than the Vermont farmer, legislator, and foreign minister George Perkins Marsh, whose now classic environmental study, *Man and Nature* (1864), Shaler considered a "great masterpiece."[22] Marsh, however, came to his conservationist views of natural resources not through his own scientific research but by many routes retraced by his biographer David Lowenthal—notably by wide reading and travels, keen observation, contacts with other scholars and statesmen, and an "intuitive grasp of natural and historical processes."[23] Shaler developed kindred views from his scientific studies and professional work. In the 1870s he directed the Kentucky Geological Survey, and from 1884 to 1900 he was head of the Atlantic Coast Division of the U.S. Geological Survey. He also taught paleontology and geology at Harvard as a full professor for nearly forty years. Both Marsh and Shaler reached wide audiences with their arguments for conservation, but Shaler's stance was that of a scientist and educator.

Writing of forest destruction in *Scribner*'s magazine in 1887, Shaler pointed out that soils—"the harvest of the ages"—were virtually irreplaceable, yet often were eroded when forests were destroyed. He also predicted the substitution of solar energy for coal, which he believed would disappear from the earth by the year 3000.[24] This was a mere millennial moment, for Shaler's story of forest destruction was intertwined with the history of the earth and the evolution of human perceptions. The forest began as a cradle: a human habitat and source of food. As human societies evolved, forests became obstacles to agriculture; and so they were destroyed, by axe and fire. More recently, forests had come to be valued for maintaining climate, timber supply, soil, and watersheds. Conservation was thus urgently needed, yet Shaler's tone was calm. He appealed to reason and a sense of fairness in handing down, unimpaired, the inheritance of the forests for generations to come.

Shaler was equally calm in discussing wilderness, landscape beauty, and the human spirit. In 1898, writing in the *Atlantic* on landscape and

Shaler

culture, he assumed that the humanized landscape, a place where some traces of human presence persisted, was universally more interesting than wilderness, even to a well-trained eye. A geologist or a geographer, who understood the elemental forces that shaped the land, might recognize in the natural world a "spirit like our own" and feel the currents of the life of nature "even as we do those of our own bodies," Shaler wrote. And yet for most people he recommended a sequence of places in which to develop the art of seeing the landscape: first, common landscapes, close to home or in the midst of a city; then a rural landscape, humanized by tilled fields yet expressive of nature; finally, primitive lands, where scientific knowledge and spiritual quests could deepen one's appreciation. The important thing was to find time for contemplation—either alone or otherwise withdrawn from people and from the distractions and duties of everyday life.[25]

In his last book, *Man and the Earth* (1905), Shaler still upheld these views of wild and humanized landscapes. "Only the more expanded souls can rejoice in the untrodden deserts, the pathless woods, or the mountains that have no trace of culture," he wrote. Trusting that the national parks and forests would preserve a great deal of wilderness in the United States, Shaler assumed, too, that certain remote and inhospitable areas would also be left intact—the Arctic, the western deserts, and the higher mountains. But, as many primeval forests, streams, and waterfalls were in imminent danger of destruction, he counted on landscape architects to shift their focus of concern from gardens to the larger landscape and to "those aspects of the earth which are of value to the spirit of man."[26]

If Shaler was overly optimistic, he did point the way beyond polarized debates over wise use and preservation, science and spiritual values; it was a way of seeing that involved not only aesthetic perception but also a complex harmony of human beings and natural forces. Anticipating the day when the earth would be entirely domesticated, no longer free, Shaler pointed to the beauty of England, Holland, and Egypt, which lacked "that quality of the primal which the wilderness alone can give, but in place of that single note of the deeps we have the great harmony of man's life."[27] Shaler's *Man and the Earth* is permeated with this vision of harmony, which is still a human-centered vision, but one sufficiently enlarged to take in innumerable associations of nonhuman creatures. Chapter 10 gives a glimpse of Shaler's incipient ecological vision, including his thoughts on what we now call "endangered species."

As dean of the Lawrence Scientific School at Harvard from 1891 until his death in 1906, Shaler was able to institutionalize his environmental values, which were basically social values as well. Toward the education of foresters, the way had already been paved elsewhere—for instance, at the forestry school begun by Bernhard Fernow at Cornell in 1898; and at the Yale School of Forestry, established in 1900 with funds from the family of Gifford Pinchot.[28] Then in 1902–3 Shaler devised Harvard's program of studies in forestry, with the help of Gifford Pinchot, who had succeeded Fernow as chief of the Division of Forestry in the U.S. Department of Agriculture.[29] Some years earlier, Shaler had hoped to start a similar program in landscape architecture, to be directed by his former student and Olmsted's young partner, Charles Eliot. After Eliot's death, in 1897, that role fell to Frederick Law Olmsted Jr., who set up Harvard's new degree program in landscape architecture in 1900–1901.[30]

After teaching for a while at Harvard, the younger Olmsted went on to develop a wide-ranging practice in landscape architecture and planning. Years later, as a Council member of the Wilderness Society and as a small landowner, Olmsted would express some views on wilderness and half-wild places that are considered in chapter 6. While his new program in landscape architecture was just getting under way at Harvard, however, the writings of Charles Eliot, brought out in 1902 by his father, Charles W. Eliot, president of Harvard, became the students' bible of landscape architecture.[31]

Charles Eliot secured for Boston and other New England towns many parks, riverways, shorelines, and reservations of relatively wild landscapes. As a partner of Olmsted, Olmsted, and Eliot, a member of the Council of the Appalachian Mountain Club, and in other capacities, Eliot garnered support for creating the Trustees of Public Reservations in Massachusetts—the first statewide preservation and conservation organization in the United States and the precursor of the National Trust of Great

Britain.[32] A skillful, persuasive writer, he also wrote many of his firm's park reports, and his letters and articles appeared frequently in *Garden and Forest* and local newspapers. Among these writings are more than mere traces of two mentors, the senior Olmsted and Nathaniel S. Shaler, but a new voice emerges in Eliot's assertive, sometimes sharp manner.

"The scenery of the earth was made for man, not man for scenery," declared Eliot in a review of Charles Platt's *Italian Gardens* (1894). Civilized landscapes are necessarily artificial, he went on. They may be beautiful or ugly, but to condemn them for not resembling wild nature was futile. Here Eliot restated his now-familiar principle, applicable to an Italian villa or an American country road: "Fitness for purpose is the safe foundation of the art of arranging land and landscape for the use and enjoyment of men." Whether a natural landscape be transformed (and destroyed) or somehow preserved, Eliot would first ask: Was the resulting landscape fit for its purpose?[33]

While traveling in Western Europe and along the Atlantic seaboard, camping and sailing off the coast of Maine, and living at his parents' summer home on Mount Desert Island, Eliot came to know landscapes tinged with varying degrees of wildness. His writings on the "wild and untamable" coast of Maine reveal his appreciation of the land's rugged, natural beauty and his horror of all attempts to make of these raw materials an English garden or a Newport lawn.[34] But what strikes us today is his focus on "scenery" and "man"; rarely does he mention smells, sounds, habitats, or food for wildlife, or even the song of a bird. In 1896 Eliot did describe the duties of a new kind of woodsman, a "landscape forester," who would be familiar with the fauna and flora of the woods and work under the supervision of a landscape architect.[35] But the implication remained: the person with intimate knowledge of local plants and wildlife would be a subordinate, his (not yet "her") services subcontracted by a landscape architect.

Here was one hint of the professionalism and specialization that were coming to both landscape architecture and forestry. By the 1890s, tensions were already developing between those bent on developing a profession, with its own body of expertise, and some of their elders, who were generalists with a wide spectrum of interests and skills—men such as Olmsted, once a farmer, journalist, park superintendent, and organizer of the U.S. Sanitary Commission, or like Charles Sprague Sargent, director of the Arnold Arboretum, who had begun with an amateur's interest in landscape gardening and later developed both a scientist's understanding of trees and an artist's feeling for landscape design. Pinchot was frustrated by his fellow forestry commissioner Sargent, who refused to consider forests from what Pinchot considered "the forester's point of view." And this was somewhat embarrassing—for Pinchot admitted that he owed much to Sargent (and to Olmsted) for entrée into his professional work. Still, as the first American-born trained forester, Pinchot took it upon himself to define the purpose of forestry—"to make the forest produce the largest possible amount of whatever crop or service will be most useful, and keep on producing it for generation after generation of men and trees."[36]

Unlike Pinchot, Eliot seems to have had little cause to question the wisdom of *his* elders, Olmsted and Shaler. Eliot did, however, question the work of one author whom Olmsted was counting on as a defender of his young, often misunderstood profession.[37] This was the art and architecture critic Mariana Griswold Van Rensselaer, a graceful, urbane writer who was Eliot's senior by eight years. Born in New York in 1851, she had come of age in Europe, while living with her family in Dresden, Germany, and visiting art galleries, parks, and gardens on the Continent. She wrote about architecture and landscape design—a biography of H. H. Richardson, a profile of Olmsted, and many other articles— largely from firsthand experience, then, and from an informed, but initially not a scholarly or professional, interest in fine buildings and landscapes.[38]

Eliot shared Van Rensselaer's interest in art and the aesthetic qualities of landscape, yet he had misgivings about her book *Art Out-of-Doors* (1893), which revealed no grasp of the breadth and depth of landscape architecture. Rather than discuss the art of landscape as if it were "much like house-furnishing," Eliot would have emphasized the foundations of his art, "rationality, purpose, fitness." He would have shown how the art of landscape dealt with factories and railroad yards as well as with gardens and shrubbery. "The essentially virile and practical nature of the art and profession is ignored, together with most of its greater and more democratic problems," he chided. Yet the style and tone of the book he found "exceedingly good."[39]

Overlooking the hint that women did not belong in the field of landscape architecture—Van Rensselaer could brush that one aside—we can agree that *Art Out-of-Doors* left out many of the social and environmental concerns that Olmsted and Eliot addressed as professionals. Van Rensselaer admitted as much in a preface that amiably warned readers of her book's limitations and focus on art. Accessible, readable, and reprinted with new material in 1925, the book probably reinforced the popular misconception that a landscape architect was some kind of "beauty doctor," the tag Carhart couldn't shake off while working in the Forest Service in the early 1920s. But a fledgling profession needs all kinds of coverage, popular, scholarly, and professional. Then, too, several more comprehensive books by professional landscape architects in the early 1900s could begin to fill the gaps that Van Rensselaer left behind. Like Shaler, whom she read with interest in the mainstream magazines, she herself served as a durable bridge between professionals and the general public.

"On an ocean-beaten shore, we may feel the power of the sea in the overhanging cliffs even when there are no waves," Shaler noted in the *Atlantic Monthly* in 1898.[40] This may be an unconscious echo of Van Rensselaer's observation in *Garden and Forest,* in 1888: "A splendid sky and the breath of a tearing wind tell us of the splendid sea, even when it lies out of sight."[41] Whatever the possible links between these observations, they represent a plane on which an art critic and a scientist can arrive as equals. Their minds may be stored with different kinds of understanding, yet some of their aims can be similar: to experience and later to convey a deeper feeling for landscape that goes beyond knowing.

One could argue, along with Bernhard Fernow, that feelings and emotions would only cloud the important professional issues to be addressed, from forest devastation and soil erosion to the loss of natural beauty, _graves_

habitats, and species. But one of his successors thought otherwise. In the early 1930s the former chief forester Henry S. Graves took stock of what had become of forestry since the 1890s, when his older college friend Pinchot had recruited him. Along with a coauthor, Graves wrote, "The profession is older and the call of romance in a pioneer undertaking is not so alluring as it was in earlier years."[42] By 1925, having spent ten years as the nation's chief forester and thirteen years as dean of the Yale School of Forestry, Graves had already seen (and inevitably fostered) a great deal of specialization within his field. He would not deny the continuing need for new knowledge, yet he did point to other needs as well: for vision, creative ability, faith, courage, and the enrichment of one's intellectual and spiritual life. Though his students could no longer be "pioneers," as in the old days, they need not become mere technicians, bent on solving a set of given problems. They should find out for themselves what the current problems really were and be prepared to face the unknown. But how? Graves had a number of suggestions. Let the years of formal education be broad and rich in quality. Let students do some independent, thoughtful work. Allow time for studies in literature, history, and other humanistic pursuits. Give students an intellectual background for their lifework.[43]

humanistic pursuits w/in forestry

***

Although _Forest and Garden_ has been written with some detachment, in order to present the people, the issues, the gardens, and the landscapes of a certain period as fairly as possible, I would like to declare one bias. I side with Graves, not Fernow. To detect problems as yet unrecognized or undefined, we may need help from people stirred by powerful emotions and heightened sensibilities, the Robert Frosts, the Willa Cathers, the Ansel Adamses, the Rachel Carsons, and the Loren Eiseleys of our time. Meanwhile, this study reaches only halfway into the twentieth century, to a time when feelings and emotions could still permeate an eminently clear-headed, "reasonable" book like Aldo Leopold's _Sand County Almanac_ (1949).

Within the frame of that half century, some of the chapters below are centered on a few decades at most. Some in part 1, focused on a region, hover about the early twentieth century. Some in part 2, pursuing an idea or an issue, cannot neatly be contained by the half-century frame. The result is not so much a traditional historical narrative as a composite of stories built up in layers, like watercolors on paper, somewhat transparent yet ultimately able to blend in the mind's eye. Each chapter is meant to stand on its own; yet if all are read in sequence, certain trends and ideas will become more apparent: a growing awareness of conflict, for instance, between natural processes and the processes of civilization in the modern Western world; trends toward the professionalization of a body of knowledge, values, and purposes, and toward specialization within a profession; a growing appreciation for small remnants of once-wild lands, as farms lose their wide, wilder margins and as cities become vast metropolitan areas; at the same time, a growing desire to preserve vast tracts of wilderness for the well-being of nonhuman creatures as well as of humans; and an increasing sense that boundaries between ways of knowing and ways of being need to be overcome—that neither deep, poetic feeling for "nature" nor sophisticated, specialized knowledge of natural processes will alone be sufficient in the years ahead.

Some of these ideas have emerged from small clues in unlikely places. One would not normally turn to Aldo Leopold for a definition of art, for instance. Yet in 1942, speaking at the Seventh North American Wildlife Conference in Washington, D.C., Leopold pointed to things that every liberally educated person should understand about the world; and he emphasized not "wildlife" but the landscape as a whole. "Land ecology is putting the sciences and arts together for the purpose of understanding our environment," he observed. "What are the sciences? Only categories for thinking. . . . What is art? Only the drama of the land's workings. . . . Who is the land? We are, but no less the meanest flower that blows. Land ecology discards at the outset the fallacious notion that the wild community is one thing, the human community another."[44] I came across these words of Leopold late in the process of research and writing. Now it appears that no one has expressed more economically what *Forest and Garden* attempts to bring forward, among its fragments of wisdom from the past.

key ways of knowing and ways of being need to blend for the future

praxis

key figure: Aldo Leopold

Much earlier in the process, I had come across *The Great New Wilderness Debate* (1998), edited by J. Baird Callicott and Michael P. Nelson.[45] This work includes essays by some of our best-known writers on wilderness— Thoreau, Muir, Theodore Roosevelt, Aldo Leopold, Robert Marshall, Roderick Nash, William Cronon, Gary Snyder, and others—along with writings that challenge the canonical works from many perspectives, eastern and western, male and female, Native American and other-American. I read on, fascinated, yet I sensed that *Forest and Garden,* my work in progress, could not contribute much to this debate, except perhaps indirectly. William Cronon's essay "The Trouble with Wilderness" (1995), reprinted in this collection, had already alerted me to some differences between wilderness and wildness.[46] Now one thing seemed clear: One could hardly discuss wilderness without mentioning some stark contrasts and polarized concepts. But in wildness, a quality independent of size or scale or specific terrain, one could recognize vitality, a life force, a feeling of something elemental that need not be canceled out or extinguished by the presence of opposites. The violet could still burst through a crack in the pavement.

That exemplar of irrepressible life—a violet—appears in Louis Halle's *Spring in Washington* (1947), a record of one man's quest for health, sanity, freedom, and wildness within a great city. Only recently I came across the ecologist Daniel B. Botkin's *No Man's Garden* (2001), a kindred work in some ways. Showing how Thoreau, despite ambivalence, managed to reconcile civilization and nature, science and spirit, Botkin offers some intriguing alternatives to dichotomies and either/or debates.[47]

Some debates about wilderness will continue, of course, for the political, ecological, economic, and social issues at stake are vitally important. Meanwhile, *Forest and Garden* follows traces of wildness that persist against the odds. As modernization and urbanization continue, these traces should become more valuable, perhaps as clues for contemporary planners and designers. As globalization becomes a fact of life, perhaps regional qualities or traits will be appreciated more than ever.

But why consider five regions, not ten? Why a few landscape architects and foresters here and there, not fifty? As Thoreau would put it: to simplify. And why begin in the desert? To clear the air of preconceptions. If deserts are often dismissed as wastelands, here we begin with two individuals, John C. Van Dyke and Mary Austin, who found there a world of beauty, harsh, austere, yet wondrously stirring with life.[48] Neither foresters nor landscape architects, Van Dyke and Austin begin a story that, from here on, is dominated by no single profession or point of view. Rather, it is moved along by another echo of Thoreau: "In wildness is the preservation of the world." From time to time we simply ask for a bit more precision: What kind of wildness? To what extent can the wild and the artificial coexist? And how have other people overcome the old dichotomies—man vs. nature, city vs. country, reason vs. emotion—in their efforts to come to terms with a modernizing world?

"wildness" = violet in the sidewalk

PART ONE

Across the
Continent

Desert

Land of Little Rain,
Great Beauty

John C. Van Dyke freely admitted that the desert was not livable or lovable, like the meadows of his native New Jersey. It was not pretty or picturesque, but "stern, harsh, and at first repellent." No sacred poet had ever sung its praises. In *Nature for Its Own Sake* (1898), Van Dyke himself had made only passing reference to the world's deserts, mainly those in Africa. "Nothing but barren waste below and burning heat above," he had remarked.[1] Nonetheless, in the summer of 1899 he set out to explore the deserts of the American Southwest, seeking health but also something more.[2]

Van Dyke, professor of art history at Rutgers College (now University) and also head of the Sage Library at the New Brunswick Theological Seminary, liked to move from scenes of a highly cultivated, civilized life to wilder terrain shaped mainly by the forces of nature. The contrast between the two extremes he found refreshing. Yet it seems that the southwestern deserts were something of a revelation to him. On horseback and on foot, with only a dog for a companion, he made his way through the Pacific Coast Range, the San Bernardino Ranges, and the old

Silence and Desolation *was the title of this photograph, used as the frontispiece in John C. Van Dyke's* The Desert *(1915). The site remains unknown; the book has become a classic meditation on the beauty and mystery of arid lands. (Photographer unknown.)*

Salton Basin (now the Imperial Valley) into Arizona and across the border into Mexico. Some old-timers told him he was crazy. But he kept on with his explorations of basins and ranges, ancient habitations, clouds and skies, fleeting illusions, unforgettable colors and light. Coming away a lover of the desert, he returned again and again. What he found and felt and feared he set down in the book by which he is probably best known today, *The Desert* (1901).

Apart from the more striking qualities of the arid Southwest—immensity, solitude, silence, sublimity—Van Dyke was particularly intrigued by its wildness and mystery, qualities of nature then under siege by the forces of civilization. And it is not surprising that an art historian should take up the cause of nature, the source of all art. But nature was more than that; for Van Dyke, she was Nature, always feminine, full of beauty and wonder, cruel or benign, ultimately unfathomable. "Man," the personification of humankind and its civilizing pursuits, Van Dyke identified as the enemy. Once these familiar battle lines were drawn, he could then address certain issues that were important to him, including clean, dry air; unfenced, unplowed expanses of grasses and wildflowers; unmined mountains; and the infinitely varied color and light that were continually transforming the desert lands and clouds.

Against the promoter's vision of a million acres of desert made fertile, Van Dyke argued, "To turn this desert into an agricultural tract would be to increase humidity, and that would be practically to nullify the finest air on the continent." He did not explain what scholars later discovered—that he suffered from respiratory ailments.[3] But even without this bit of medical history we can appreciate Van Dyke's arguments in light of what has since become of our western deserts under irrigation and suburbanization. "And why are not good air and climate as essential to human well-being as good beef and good bread?" Van Dyke asked. Aware of then recent efforts to preserve forests for the sake of timber supply and watershed protection, he wished those measures had been put in place forty years earlier. "But how is the water supply, from an economic and hygienic stand-point, any more important than the air supply?" he persisted.[4]

Van Dyke knew that the desert air was not entirely pure. It contained particles of dust that broke up and colored the light, especially at dawn and dusk, when the sun's rays penetrated the earth's atmosphere at low angles and streamed across the landscape, and at the height of summer, when the heat and winds were intense. The desert air could appear as a colored haze, rose-pink or golden or lilac-blue. And yet the air seemed thin, rarefied, scentless, clear. "You breathe it without feeling it," he noted, before posing a few scientific explanations for the interactions of air, light, and color.

Assuming that the intensity of absolutely pure, direct sunlight would be unbearable for any length of time, Van Dyke explained the degrees of intensity in sunlight by the combinations of dust, soot, smoke, salt, and water vapor that make up the atmospheric veil in different parts of the world. On rainy or foggy days in England and Holland, the light would be whitish or milky white and visibility limited. On a sunny day among the high plateaus of Wyoming, the air relatively free of dust and vapor made a mountain seventy miles away seem much closer, sharply etched against the sky. On a sunny day in the desert, dust in the air would "parry the sunshaft, break and color the light, increase the density of the envelope." In the upper reaches of the dust-laden atmosphere, the relatively weak blue rays of sunlight would be stopped and held in the upper air, while the stronger red and yellow rays would not be stopped until they were much nearer the earth's surface. Hence the deep-blue skies and the warm tones of color characteristic of the desert—an effect independent of the local color in each rock, plant, or landmass.[5]

However imprecise these explanations may seem today, Van Dyke's more lyrical descriptions of desert light, air, and color remain persuasive and satisfying. He wrote of sunbeams "weaving skeins of color across the sands," the blue-tinted buttes appearing to drift upon the sky, the mirage of water in the wavering heat, and the hints of opal, turquoise, lapis lazuli, silver, burnished brass, and fiery red at different times of the day or evening. Van Dyke's prose may induce a dream state in some readers, but he can also jar us back to reality with issues of health that concern all life on earth. "Grasses, trees, shrubs, growing grain, they, too, may need good air as well as human lungs. The deserts are not worthless wastes. You cannot crop all creation with wheat and alfalfa," he insisted. "The deserts should never be reclaimed. They are the breathing-spaces of the west and should be preserved forever."[6]

These and other statements about landscape preservation punctuate but never dominate Van Dyke's writings on the desert. Perhaps someday he will be recognized as more than a connoisseur of aesthetic qualities in different kinds of landscape and warrant a paragraph or two in the history of environmentalism. In any event, he should be better known for certain perceptions about wildness that still seem fresh today.

In *The Desert* Van Dyke rarely wrote of wilderness. Without defining the term, he seems to have meant by "wilderness" an apparently confusing, inhospitable place where human beings don't quite belong. Already in his day, as the forces of civilization continued to overcome wild Nature, places that he would consider wilderness were disappearing from the face of the earth. They could still be found in the desert, one of the earth's last great inhospitable places. Yet Van Dyke knew that human beings had long ago found ways to live in the deserts of the American Southwest. And he was sufficiently curious about—or perplexed, or haunted—by the traces of their ancient habitations to devote his first chapter to the mystery of how those unknown, vanished people once lived.

Alerted by such scholars as Peter Wild, who have for some time pursued the tracks of Van Dyke, we might consider this desert lover's tales a composite of fact and fiction. "Van Dyke was a wily man and a wily writer," warns Wild.[7] Seemingly without craft at all, Van Dyke lures us into his desert book with clues that might be sprinkled through a mystery novel. In the chill of a morning, before sunrise, he leaves the adobe ranch house where he is staying, having learned nothing about the isolated range of unnamed desert mountains way off in the distance—his destination for the day. Riding for several hours toward their base, he spots some wildlife: wrens, linnets, finches, rabbits, squirrels, an old gray wolf. But the mystery begins to take shape only when he is ascending one of the peaks, on foot, over boulders and splintered rock. The trail, now running along a diagonal, seems too deliberately and intelligently formed to be the work of a mule deer, one of whose hoofprints Van Dyke has detected in petrified rock overrun with silica.

The clues accumulate. A horseshoe-shaped enclosure of stone, about waist high: a sentinel box to guard the trail? A parapet of loose stone: the ruins of a fortified camp? On the mountain's flat summit, a mound: a burial place? A hole in a rock and perhaps a rude pestle: for grinding maize? Who built this primitive encampment? When did the people arrive? From where and why? This entire scene could be an invention, a mirage fleshed out with plausible detail or simply a narrative device. Whatever its origins, it allows Van Dyke to plant seeds of curiosity and wonder in the reader's mind, while he speculates like an anthropologist about whether the vanished people who camped here found plenty of game and a fairly easy life or whether, despite the harsh conditions of life, they loved the open country, the sunlight, the view, the sunsets, and the moments when cloud and sky, mountain and mesa all dissolved into a pink mist.

"Mystery—a mystery as luminous and yet as impenetrable as its own mirage—seemed always hanging over that low-lying waste," Van Dyke sighs. And he mingles speculations about how those vanished people might have felt about this vast, arid country with his own convictions about how they must have felt, having experienced the solitude, the silence, and the desolation that "every" desert wanderer eventually falls in love with. The vanished people were content to love the land without knowing precisely why, Van Dyke decides, before considering the possible influence of those heroic Spanish missionaries who lived and died without concern for earthly rewards. In Van Dyke's time, the Spirit that had burned in the padres' hearts lived on; for he had seen crosses made of wood or fiber hanging on the walls of houses in every Indian and Mexican village he came upon. "The dwellers beside the desert have cherished what the inhabitants of the fertile plains have thrown away," Van Dyke asserts. They lived a simple life, close to the earth, "beside the desert they loved, and (let us believe it!) nearer to the God they worshipped."[8]

Van Dyke's attention to the aesthetic qualities of light, color, air, and atmospheric transformations in the desert is so acute and so pervasive that his opening remarks about vanished people and animals, religion and spirit, the simple life and civilization may be overshadowed. But if his wanderings in the deserts of the American Southwest were in fact a revelation to him, several clues lie in this opening chapter about spiritual values and organic life—human, animal, vegetable—that mingle in a terrain commonly dismissed as "waste." Only three years earlier, in 1898, Van Dyke had prefaced the first of his studies of natural appearances with the warning that in discussing Nature he would make no reference to animal life of any kind. He would not consider Man an essential factor in Nature. Rather, he would discuss "lights, skies, clouds, waters, lands, foliage—the great elements that reveal form and color in landscape, the component parts of the earth-beauty about us."[9] But somewhere in the deserts of the American Southwest he recognized a much more complex picture of Nature, in which human activity, the local flora and fauna, spiritual and emotional connection to a place, and transforming forces, both human and natural, all came together in some kind of harmony—or conflict.

These desert wanderings at the century's end were not Van Dyke's first exposure to wide-open spaces and people living close to the earth. Born in 1856 and reared in what he recalled as a "child's paradise"—a country place near New Brunswick, New Jersey, with gardens, a bit of forest, a stream, and tilled fields nearby—young Van Dyke longed to go west and become a great hunter. His father, at one time or another a lawyer, a judge, a mayor, and a congressman, one day decided to move the family to a homestead in Minnesota, on the banks of the Mississippi. Van Dyke was about twelve at the time, and soon he was old enough to hunt buffalo and antelope with a band of Sioux and impressionable enough to let the first distant glimpse of the blue-and-silver Rocky Mountain skyline burn into his memory.[10] However he may have embellished his stories of adolescent adventures many years later, it seems clear that Van Dyke gave free rein to his romantic and aesthetic impulses early on. Perhaps it was only later, seeking cleaner desert air to breathe in middle age, that he could begin to sympathize with nonhuman creatures.

The upshot must have been sobering, humbling. After he had observed the way coyotes, turkey buzzards, and other creatures adapted to the extremes of desert conditions with remarkable deftness, economy of motion, and endurance, it struck him that their constant struggle had made them admirable, even physically beautiful. "Not in the spots of earth where plenty breeds indolence do we meet with the perfected type," he noted. "It is in the land of adversity, and out of much pain and travail that finally emerges the highest manifestation." In contrast, at a high level of civilization one could find heightened sensitivities for sound, form, and color (Van Dyke's own sensitivities, for instance); but he wondered if these might also be signs of some kind of physical degeneration or "racial decay." Not that he would give up his fascination with nuances of light, color, and air. But the desert had tested him, as it tested other living beings, through heat, thirst, and hunger. Never again could he indulge in the "magnificent complacency" of viewing Man as one of Nature's favorites.[11]

On one peak in Southern California—apparently the mountain of San Jacinto—Van Dyke looked east toward the desert and west toward the Pacific Ocean; and he speculated that glaciers might once have carved out the mountain stream beds below. Now, before their waters could reach the eastern base of the mountain, they would be drunk up by desert sands and disappear. These thoughts led Van Dyke to muse about sand, wind, earthquakes, volcanoes, inland seas, Nature's plans, Man's interventions, and the ceaseless buffeting as one force or another tried to reclaim some territory. Thinking of the life and death of individuals and species, he assumed that in the fullness of time all would pass away. "Is then this great expanse of sand and rock the beginning of the end?" he mused. "Is that the way our globe shall perish?" As dusk fell, lights faded, and lilac-blue mists drifted across the valleys below, he had no answer. He could only assert once again the beauty of what he had seen in the wilderness and insist that these things had been "good to look upon whether they be life or death." He ended by yielding to mystery, "that haunting sense of the unknown."[12]

In yielding, however, Van Dyke went against the progressive spirit of his time. His friend Andrew Carnegie and other titans of industry, along with scientists, engineers, and homesteaders, were united in a common cause to control Nature by discovering, manipulating, subduing, or otherwise wresting from the raw materials of wilderness the finished products of civilization. As a connoisseur of painting and a Rembrandt scholar, Van Dyke was not about to renounce civilization and all its trappings. To a great extent, he was integrated with his civilized contemporaries, and he appreciated, even shared, their yearnings for mastery. Yet he also held back, somewhat aloof. If he never quite resolved the tensions between wilderness and civilization, yielding and mastering, he left us no excuse for complacency. Perhaps the enduring appeal of his studies in natural appearances, of which *The Desert* may be his masterwork, lies in the ways we are drawn in, captivated, and led to dream, but also shown how aesthetic and environmental concerns are intertwined. John Muir accomplished this feat for American landscapes of surpassing beauty and nearly universal appeal. Van Dyke did this for the unpromising desert.

***

"Man is not himself only. . . . He is all that he sees; all that flows to him from a thousand sources, half noted, or noted not at all except by some sense that lies too deep for naming. He is the land, the lift of its mountain lines, the reach of its valleys. . . ."[13] Mary Austin was speaking for herself as well as for humankind, using the word "Man," despite her strong feminist convictions. It was a conventional use of the word that reader and writer shared at that time, the 1920s. And Austin was not bent on upsetting all conventions of good writing. Like one of the desert creatures that she once detected along a mesa trail—a flat, horned, toadlike animal that could barely be distinguished from the ground it occupied—Austin's language can be so unobtrusive that it disappears while the subject of her story claims all our attention. Then, like the horned creature that scurried across the trail, Austin will suddenly make us aware of her presence. In one story in her *Land of Little Rain* (1903), "The Scavengers," she describes cattle dying by starvation, the fear in their eyes, the calls of the buzzards, and the coyote that looks up to see where the carrion crows are gathering before he will emerge from his lair. One scavenger, the Clark's crow, Austin finds "very clean and handsome." The details of this story are vivid but not grizzly, and the tone is objective to the very end: "There is no scavenger that eats tin cans, and no wild thing leaves a like disfigurement on the forest floor."[14]

And so Austin reminds us that civilized people of an industrial society could learn something about hygiene from the carrion crows, just as they could learn from the dwellers in the pueblo of Las Uvas, where houses are made of the earth (adobe), meals are all made with chile, religion is plain, and souls are sometimes too complex for an outsider's understanding. "Come away, you who are obsessed with your own importance in the scheme of things, and have got nothing you did not sweat for," Austin writes, "come away by the brown valleys and full-bosomed hills to the even-breathing days, to the kindliness, earthiness, ease of El Pueblo de Las Uvas."[15]

This was not the first time a middle-class Anglo-American had exhorted readers to come to the American Southwest and experience another way of life, less stressful and perhaps more conducive to good health than any they could find east of the Mississippi. In *Our Italy* (1891) Charles Dudley Warner made a few detours from his main subject, the Los Angeles region and its delightful habitability, to describe the Laguna Pueblo and the Grand Canyon. In venturing beyond the more densely settled parts of Southern California, the Massachusetts-born Warner, a contributing editor of *Harper's Monthly,* appreciated some of the qualities of the desert that appealed to John C. Van Dyke—the sunshine, the waves of color, the vastness and sense of freedom, the "air like wine to the senses." But unlike Van Dyke, Warner also took pleasure in the vision of a desert transformed by irrigation into "fields of fruitfulness."[16]

Then, too, unlike Austin, Warner seemed satisfied by merely a passing acquaintance with the Native Americans. At the Laguna Pueblo, in New Mexico, he "came to know them well," the whole community, in the span of an hour.[17] All told, Austin spent about half a lifetime in contact with native people of the Southwest. She admired them, learned from them, and worked to advance their interests, yet could not claim to know them well. Rather, she acquiesced when the Paiute basket maker withdrew into the privacy of her blanket. Austin came to these people perhaps for a poultice on her wounded hand or a piece of pottery they might sell. She came away intrigued by their unfamiliar ways, of living not off the land but on it and telling time not by hours and months but by the time of the white butterflies and the time of the young quail running in the chaparral. Eventually she would shuttle back and forth between different ways of living and ways of knowing, those of her European forebears and those of the people native to the southwestern mesas and canyons and desert sands. "The secret of learning the mesa life is to sit still, to sit still and to keep on sitting still," she noted, in one of many attempts to explain a people by the land that was part of their very being.[18]

The land was also part of *her* being: the aspiring town of Carlinville, Illinois, where she was born in 1868; the ground beyond her family's orchard and beneath the walnut tree, where, at age five or six, she discovered God and wholeness, feeling at one with the bee and the wild foxglove; and her first glimpse of the desert at age nineteen, on a train journey through Utah and Nevada, as she sensed "something brooding and aloof, charged with a dire indifference," not frightening but intriguing.[19] On that train were also Austin's widowed mother and younger brother, the three of them bound for San Francisco, where a ship would take them south to Santa Barbara. After visits with extended family in Los Angeles and San Diego, they crossed the California desert by wagon train and horseback and reached their promised homestead in the San Joaquin Valley—but not before Austin herself was hit hard by a desire to stop and spend some time alone by the dry creeks (arroyos) that reminded her of the Greek god Pan, some "beauty-in-the-wild, yearning to be made human." For years afterward she longed to return, to give herself up to those mysterious arroyos. Then came marriage, motherhood, and eventually a breaking of family ties, but no return to that particular beauty-in-the-wild.

Van Dyke and Austin were both drawn to the mysteries of desert life, whether prehistoric, marked by shells and shards along the desiccated shores of vanished inland seas; or still viable, conserving energy and holding out against drought and wind. The two writers reveled in the beauty of the desert's fleeting visual appearances and also sought scientific explanations for these phenomena. But in Van Dyke's most intense studies of landscape beauty in the desert, traces of humans fell outside the frame. Austin came to know the desert landscape as a vast, sweeping continuum in which humans and other creatures, beauty and utility, all had a place. She was fascinated by rhythms and patterns—in the landscape, in language, in a Paiute basket, and among the mingled threads of Native American, Mexican, and Spanish culture in the American Southwest. In middle age, her reputation as a writer assured, she would be equally at home (and not at home) in New York, London, Rome. By the time she settled in Santa Fe, her sensibilities had been developed from many sources—college courses in biology and botany, contacts with H. G. Wells and the Fabian socialists in London, talks with John Muir and Ansel Adams in the Southwest, and the wisdom of the Shoshone medicine man Winnenap, who had lived for years among an alien tribe, having been wrenched from his native painted hills.

In her autobiography Austin recalls telling her father, a Civil War veteran and well-read lawyer, that she would someday write "all kinds" of books.[20] Having slipped into relative obscurity after her death in 1934, she is now a respected literary figure, perhaps best known as a nature writer and as a feminist writer of novels and essays. But what she had to say about land, about wilderness, half-wild places, and webs of associations among the many life forms in her midst is still occasionally obscured by her tendency to slip into a mystical, otherworldly tone of voice. As the literary critic Carl Van Doren noted, Austin "mastered herself by generous surrender to the earth and sky," then returned, eyes cleared, to the world the rest of us muddle through. Hence her Sphinx-like, prophetic stance. "Her books were wells driven into America to bring up water for her countrymen, though they might not have realized their thirst," Van Doren added.[21]

Yet in Austin's lifetime, Americans increasingly felt a thirst for wide-open, unspoiled places—shorelines, national parks and forests, the far West, even the frigid North. Her friend Jack London wrote a tale about a gentle dog from the benign Santa Clara Valley, a crossbred St. Bernard and Scottish shepherd dog that was brutally thrust into sled-dog bondage in Alaska; and that best-selling tale, *The Call of the Wild* (1903), remains in print today. One collection of London's writings includes an appreciation by Carl Sandburg, who wrote in 1906, "The more civilized we become the deeper is the fear that back in barbarism is something of the beauty and joy of life we have not brought along with us. We all feel these artificialities that so easily cramp and fret our lives."[22] Austin, too, understood that fear, those artificialities. Still, of the stars in a desert sky she wrote, "Wheeling to their stations in the sky, they make the poor world-fret of no account. Of no account you who lie out there watching. . . ."[23] One thing that separated Austin from Jack London and other friends of hers in Carmel and Santa Fe was her tendency to shift abruptly from apparent sympathy to coolness; to write from the point of view of the stars, not of the rest of us out here watching.

In *Land of Journey's Ending* (1924), among studies of people, plants, and varied forms of cultural expression coming out of the American Southwest, Austin devotes a few pages to the Grand Canyon, which had recently been designated a national park.[24] She writes of the "noiseless dance of island towers," the "cliffs burning red from within," and rivers of clouds that turn into a shepherdless flock, then into ships with glittering sails. These are brief, spirited impressions of a natural wonder that defies summing up. But if her probing mind is absent at the Grand Canyon, it will be found in less spectacular places, among her studies of desert vegetation—the saguaro, the palo verde, the ocotillo, the miles of golden poppies after spring rains, and the forests made up of widely scattered pine or mesquite, each specimen surviving in its own domain of bare earth.

Here, in desert landscapes that often remain nameless, Austin takes the measure of human time, season by season, but also of earth time, marked by the adaptations that each plant has made, "from its primordial home in the sea shallows, to the farthest, driest land." Scientists may flinch at her allusions to a shrub's "intelligence underground" and the "soul of the creosote," sitting and waiting. But what would they make of her Vegetative Spirit, making experiments "on its way up from the sea-borders to the driest of dry lands"? From that point of view—the view of the primordial earth in evolution—the great saguaro, *Carnegiea gigantea*, is the most successful experiment of all; and Austin salutes it "in the name of the exhaustless Powers of Life."[25]

By the time these words appeared, in 1924, the deserts of the Southwest had become known for more than scorching heat and dry air, in part because of fairly comfortable, well-publicized travel by rail; destinations such as the Grand Canyon; and such magnetic characters as Mabel Dodge Luhan and her Native American husband, Tony Luján, at Taos, Mary Austin and the poet Witter Bynner in Santa Fe, and their friends Georgia O'Keefe, Paul Strand, and D. H. Lawrence. In 1929 the young couple Ansel and Virginia Adams came to stay with Mary Austin in Santa Fe, and out of that visit came a portfolio of Adams's superb photographs, *Taos Pueblo* (1930), with a text by Austin. "Tap-rooted, the charm of Taos should endure for another hundred years, even against the modern American obsession for destructive change," wrote Austin.[26] All change is of course destructive of something. What mattered to Austin was the degree of change and its consequences.

As a struggling homesteader in California, first in the San Joaquin Valley and later with her husband in the Owens Valley, Austin had a practical interest in the change from inhospitable, desertlike quarter sections to livable, productive farmland through irrigation. What she protested was a certain scale of change—so large and so pervasive that the interests of small homesteaders like her family were ignored. The complex story of how the water from the Owens River was drawn away from the rural communities of Inyo County, California, to the Los Angeles metropolis, over 200 miles away, has been told elsewhere.[27] Here we should be aware that in some of her fiction and essays and through her participation in the second Colorado River Conference, in Denver in 1927, Austin recommended development of the diverse, geographically varied area of the Colorado River basin into an economically viable part of the country with its own strong regional culture. What she opposed was the "phenomenal material expansion" of Southern California (that is, of Los Angeles) through standardization and vast enterprise at the expense of diverse smaller communities in other counties and states.[28]

These views of the ways in which civilization might reasonably come into contact with wilderness and change it do not appear in Austin's early works, particularly her best-known *Land of Little Rain*, where traces of modern American civilization are few and either slight or slowly deteriorating. And so a professional designer or planner, perhaps newly arrived in the Southwest, might not at first find in Austin's works much of practical value. In *California: The Land of the Sun* (1914), for instance, Austin gives as much attention to the Spanish lady Doña Ina and her imperious quirks as to her old Spanish garden in the New World.[29] But that is just the point: Austin does not try to separate the human from the nonhuman in the landscape. Man is the land, she insists. He is all that he sees.

In Austin's view, then, Man in America is not what one might gather from a study of Sinclair Lewis's prize-winning novels *Main Street* (1920) and *Babbitt* (1922)—that is, Man as a rootless, conventional product of boosterism and the machine age.[30] Rather, Man in America is regional, too variable for national stereotypes. He is the land, and the land is always particular, part of a locality and a region: "By land, I mean all those things common to a given region," she explains, "the flow of prevailing winds, the succession of vegetal cover, the legend of ancient life; and the scene, above everything the magnificently shaped and colored scene."[31]

* * *

Soon after the completion of El Tovar Hotel, on the South Rim of the Grand Canyon, a new guidebook appeared, George Wharton James's *Grand Canyon of Arizona* (1910). An English-born writer and sometime Methodist minister transplanted to the American West, James had already written one book on the Grand Canyon, having wandered up and down its trails in the 1890s, when travel and accommodations were fairly rough. Like Charles Dudley Warner, Harriet Monroe, Gifford Pinchot, John Muir, John Burroughs, John C. Van Dyke, and other late-nineteenth-century visitors, James would most likely have endured a long journey to get there: first by rail to Flagstaff or Ash Fork, Arizona, thence by stagecoach, relay after relay for some sixty-five miles, to a primitive camp or a log-cabin hotel on the Canyon's south rim. Complaints about the heat, dust, and dangers of the journey were routine—although the popular lecturer John L. Stoddard found the journey by stagecoach delightful one September day. Still, Stoddard would have agreed with James: for people not particularly robust, at the canyon itself there would have to be some sort of "commodious, well-kept inn" commanding a splendid view to attract tourists.[32]

El Tovar Hotel, begun in 1903 by the Santa Fe Railway and furnished and operated by the Fred Harvey Company, more than satisfied these expectations; and by 1910 at least two trains a day, with Pullman sleepers, chair cars, and coaches, brought patrons to the hotel via the new railway line from Williams. In James's guidebook, photographs of El Tovar's ample interiors reveal sturdy Mission-style furniture, heads of deer, elk, moose, mountain sheep, and buffalo on the rough wooden walls, Navajo rugs on the smooth wooden floors, and rustic sandstone fireplaces. Exterior shots show pines casting pools of shade on the sand at midday, the long, low-pitched roof of the entrance porch on the east, and a hint of the views west toward the canyon. And, as James explains, among the rocking chairs on the porch of the hotel are some small tables with "a push-button handy for ordering light refreshments."[33]

Service on demand, effortless, at the edge of the Grand Canyon! John C. Van Dyke, an occasional guest at El Tovar, does not mention those little push buttons in his Grand Canyon book of 1920. Yet they symbolize what he is trying to wean his civilized readers away from—what John Muir alluded to in 1902, writing of the tourist and the many workers who make "everything easy, padding plush about him, grading roads for him, boring tunnels, moving hills out of his way."[34] Here Muir may have lightly nudged a few readers; but his main interest was to charm them into a frame of mind and spirit more receptive to the Grand Canyon's wonders. In *The Desert* (1901) and *The Grand Canyon of the Colorado* (1920), Van Dyke was of two minds. He wanted to charm readers, but he also wanted to give them a jolt or two. In *The Grand Canyon* he promised both song and sermon, then noted that "the song outsoars the sermon."[35]

Van Dyke sang of the Grand Canyon's ineffable beauty and mystery, of the canyon as Nature, the great goddess, serene, radiant, ultimately harmonious unto herself. His sermons were few but sobering. Yes, civilization had come to the canyon, but its native dwellers were now tamed, impoverished, and stricken by disease. "The old order has changed, giving place to a new that is no improvement so far as the Indian is concerned," he noted. Adversity was the natural condition in which desert birds, beasts, and plants had been reared; and, accepting adversity, they had become part of their environment, reflecting Nature's patience and serenity. "Are we as harmonious in our artificial environment? Are we?" The Grand Canyon cannot be plowed or plotted, Van Dyke observed.

Poets and painters inevitably fail at capturing its essence. So be it, he implied. Let some things remain beyond our reach.[36]

In the end, having tried to make sense of the Grand Canyon's geological, social, and natural histories, Van Dyke thought the canyon should remain aloof, the great goddess Nature cloaked in mystery—just as he had urged that vast areas of the desert remain unirrigated lest the clean, dry air be destroyed forever. If pressed, he would probably have sided with preservationists of the Muir camp against conservationists of the Pinchot camp. And yet the Grand Canyon Van Dyke described is layered with evidence of human industry on a small scale—patches of gardens, fragments of forts, pictographs, dwellings such as wickiups and hogans— some deserted, some in use at that time. "Even Indians require living space, with some measure of ground to cultivate and some flow of water for irrigation," he noted. "They cannot subsist on the view."[37] Nor would a person with respiratory problems expect to thrive on polluted air in a damp environment. For Van Dyke, then, the desert was much more than a magnificent picture, moving and changing before his eyes. It was an environment to be valued and cared for.

***

With a few more glimpses of the desert, we move beyond issues of human health to consider the health of the land.

Aldo Leopold's ties to the arid lands of the Southwest began in 1909 in Albuquerque, New Mexico, at the headquarters of District 3, U.S. Forest Service, where he was a new recruit, fresh from the Yale School of Forestry. By June 1915 he was investigating conditions for recreation at the Grand Canyon, then a national monument. But not until May 1917 did he spend a full week below the rim of the canyon, this time among a group that included the landscape architecture professor Frank A. Waugh, a Forest Service consultant for recreation. With the help of Leopold and his colleagues, Waugh devised a plan for a new village on the south rim; but that plan was shelved after the Grand Canyon was transferred to the National Park Service in 1919. Nevertheless, out of those experiences came mutual respect between Leopold the forester and Waugh the landscape architect.[38] Then, too, the contrast between the somewhat cluttered and commercialized rim and the wild lands below was memorable. As Curt Meine concluded from Leopold's letters describing that Grand Canyon trip, "Once below the layer of human development, . . . the power of the wilderness overcame him."[39] Though there were no mountain sheep, the flora was rich, the company congenial, the weather perfect.

Nearly two decades passed between that Grand Canyon experience and Leopold's pack trip to the Chihuahua Sierra of Mexico, in September 1936. In the interval, Leopold rose fairly rapidly through the ranks of the Forest Service. With a lateral move in 1924, he returned to the region of his childhood—not to Iowa, where he was born, but to Madison, Wisconsin. There he remained in the Forest Service for four more years, as assistant director of the U.S. Forest Products Laboratory. The four years of work that followed, however—an extensive survey of game throughout the Midwest for the Sporting Arms and Ammunition Manufacturers' Institute—were much closer to his evolving professional and personal interests. Then, during one of the bleakest years of the Depression, 1933, he brought out his landmark book, *Game Management,* and became the University of Wisconsin's professor of game management—the first in the nation to be so named.[40]

During those intervening years between two wilderness experiences, in the Grand Canyon and in the Chihuahua Sierra, Leopold's received notions of forestry had not only evolved; when put to one critical test, they had somehow failed. In the late summer and fall of 1935 he had spent three months investigating the fastidiously neat, productive German forests, which had long been held up as a model. But he had come away saddened by their lack of wildness. In an undated speech written for a German audience, he noted that the impulse to save wild remnants was probably the forerunner of the "more important and complex task of mixing a degree of wildness with utility."[41]

Then in September 1936 Leopold confronted the Chihuahua Sierra of Mexico, where intense conflicts between the Apaches and the Mexicans had long discouraged grazing and development of the mountainous terrain. Leopold was struck by all the natural beauty there, a "picture of ecological health," which at the time he traced to stable soils, lack of grazing, the presence of mountain lions and wolves, and occasional natural fires that left watersheds intact, with live oaks on the hills and trout in the streams beneath the cottonwoods and sycamores.[42]

Ten years later Leopold wrote of the Chihuahua Sierra, "It was here that I first clearly realized that land is an organism, that all my life I had seen only sick land, whereas here was a biota still in perfect aboriginal health. The term 'unspoiled wilderness' took on a new meaning."[43] As Susan Flader has pointed out, the trip to the Chihuahua Sierra in 1936 made Leopold realize that predators not only played a role in maintaining the health of an ecosystem, they "let him see what health was."[44] Yet on that pack trip Leopold had also come across hundreds of loose-masonry dams, apparently constructed long ago by native people; and the 200-year-old pines growing behind the dams gave a clue to the dams' antiquity. Since these small dams appeared around the edges of high, dry mesas as well as in the bottoms of canyons, Leopold deduced that their purpose must have been to create "little fields or food patches" by impounding soil to be irrigated by even a brief rainfall.[45]

Since Leopold's time, one implication of those small dams seems to have gone unnoticed: the "healthiest" land he ever saw contained evidence of human industry—on a small scale. True, the dams he found were abandoned. But when? And what was the health of the land when those dams were serving the needs of native people? Could this be one starting point for considering Leopold's complex task of "mixing wildness with utility"?

This is not to suggest that all wild places ought to be accessible for all kinds of utilitarian purposes. Leopold, a founding member of the Wilderness Society in 1935, would never have come to that conclusion. And yet his experience in the Chihuahua Sierra, followed by reflections on that experience toward the end of his life, suggests that at one moment in time, human industry of limited scope may not have posed a threat to the healthiest land that Leopold ever saw.

Van Dyke, too, came across evidence of human industry in the arid lands of the Southwest, even in and around the Grand Canyon. He seems to have taken more than a passing interest in mounds, forts, pictographs, Indian dwellings, and the Indian way of life; and yet the eloquence of his writing on the purely aesthetic qualities of the desert seems to have cast his other concerns, sociological and environmental, into deep shadow. As a result, he can be conveniently labeled an aesthete—particularly in our age of specialization—while Leopold is just as conveniently labeled a conservationist, a forester, or an expert in wildlife management. In this regard, Mary Austin was fortunate: having slipped into obscurity for a time, she could be rediscovered as the complex, exceedingly articulate woman she was, attentive to people, plants, and the land in a way that defies the familiar categories of art and science.

Van Dyke, Austin, and Leopold will reappear in the pages below as their lives and interests overlap with those of people in different regions of the country. Meanwhile, one common theme or tension in their work and thought will surface now and again: the relations between aesthetic and scientific perceptions, whether harmonious, mutually supportive, strained, or at odds.

For example, in my own copy of Van Dyke's *Desert* (the reprint of 1915) there is an unsigned inscription in handwriting expressive of a more leisurely age than ours:

> The author has been criticized by the ultra-scientists because perforce he describes a blue cactus-blossom. Parrish of Leland Stanford, the recognized botanist of the Pacific Coast, declares that such never existed and, seeing no farther than the end of his nose, declares that Van Dyke has seen *nothing* accurately. However we who know and love the Desert get many hours of happiness from him and know that he is accurate and has a poetic conception and genuine sentiment for its wonders.

Whoever wrote these words was no "ultra-scientist," apparently, but a person with some interest in both scientific accuracy and poetry.

Now consider Leopold's views on the state of the profession of wildlife management in 1940: "We are not scientists," he asserted. "We disqualify ourselves at the outset by professing loyalty to and affection for a thing: wildlife. A scientist in the old sense may have no loyalties except to abstractions, no affections except for his own kind." Leopold went on to admit his doubts that science could take credit for "better tools, comforts, and securities" and at the same time deny responsibility for "bigger and better erosions, denudations, and pollutions." If science had to be held accountable for the bad along with the good, then perhaps people in the young profession of wildlife management, people who must at least deal with science, could do something to correct the situation, Leopold suggested. As mediators or moderators, they might help revise the definitions and objectives of science. Otherwise, he warned, "our job is predestined to failure."[46]

These concerns about science, shared by others, will recur in chapters below. Not that Leopold would or could dispense with the scientific method or the tools of applied science. In fact, in 1940 he was calling for more scientific research, not less; but he urged that more research be directed toward long-term interests, including subjects that might have no apparent economic value, such as wildflowers. Then, too, disturbed by continuing abuses of land and the environment, he was already looking beyond the conventional boundaries of science for some way to change the public's notions of what land was for. Convinced that the great dramas of ecology and evolution were worthy subjects for the fine arts, he suggested that the "senseless barrier between science and art" might someday disappear. Meanwhile, he was encouraged by the British ecologist Fraser Darling and the American naturalist Donald Culross Peattie; for in their scientific writings he found literary quality, with poetic expression and at least a hint of wonder and respect for "workmanship in nature."[47]

TWO

Prairie & Plains

Myth, Symbol,
Cultural Independence

Wildflowers on the unbroken prairie, waving in the wind and mingling among the taller prairie grasses beneath a clear blue sky on the far frontier—a century ago, a finer symbol of freedom and abundance could hardly be found for artists and writers of the Middle West. But one correspondent to *Garden and Forest* magazine in 1897 was not looking for a symbol. Writing from Pineville, Missouri, Lora S. La Mance simply told of her delight in the native flora, some of it unfamiliar, some as common as goldenrod and Turk's cap lily (*Lilium superbum*). Some local woodland flowers—violets, anemones, gentians, dicentras—could be transplanted to a garden; but flowers from the prairie might look a bit weedy, she noted, when taken from their native habitat. This was incidental, if useful, advice for fellow gardeners with "hard, formal borders" to fill. La Mance's main point was the beauty of the wild: "Wherever the sod is yet unturned, or the verdure unchecked by close grazing, it is like a rainbow-hued flower garden in which one may wander and gather at will and yet leave a world of bloom behind."[1]

Four decades later, the Danish-born landscape architect Jens Jensen would evoke a similar vision of the unbroken prairie flowering in abundance. But La Mance was writing of the present; Jensen was reflecting on the past, the mid-1880s. "When I first set foot on Illinois soil," he wrote, "the buffalo still roamed the western prairies, and the Indian still dared assume his rights against the white man." By the late 1930s, Jensen could point to only a few remains of primitive vegetation not yet turned under by the plow. The last stand of the prairie flowers, he observed, was along the railroad rights-of-way.[2]

Looking for more traces of wildness on the prairies and plains in the early twentieth century, we find fewer accounts of the present than stories like Jensen's—memories of an invigorating past, sometimes tinged with regret for the people, animals, and plants that had somehow suffered in the wake of the farming, grazing, and human settlements that had spread across the continent. In time, wildness became so rare that one often had to probe memory—or history—to find it.

The historian Frederick Jackson Turner was particularly attentive to wide-open spaces. Born and reared in a frontier town, Portage, Wisconsin, in 1861, he envisioned the Midwest and the West as "free spaces" before their discovery and occupation by people of European ancestry during the westward movement. "We are the first generation of Americans who can look back upon that era as a historic movement now coming to its end," Turner wrote in 1914. Previous generations, he reasoned, had been so caught up in the movement that its significance eluded them. They could not conceive that land and natural resources were limited. Nor could they see that "their most fundamental traits, their institutions, even their ideals were shaped by this interaction between the wilderness and themselves."[3]

Turner is best known today for an earlier statement of this thesis, derived from information in a government report. In 1890 the superintendent of the census in Washington observed that the line of the frontier in America could no longer be detected; the unsettled lands were now dotted with isolated human settlements. Three years later, addressing his fellow historians at the 1893 World's Columbian Exposition in Chicago, Turner recognized in that bit of census information the end of America's great westward movement. And he went on exploring the implications of his controversial thesis for years: "The existence of an area of free land, its continuous recession, and the advance of American settlement westward, explain American development."[4]

Unpersuaded, some historians demanded clearer definitions of terms.[5] Others might reject the idea of a definable "American character," which Turner traced to qualities needed on the frontier—acuteness, inquisitiveness, individualism, the grasp of material things, the buoyancy and exuberance born of freedom, and more. Perhaps some preferred not to contemplate an America shorn of its frontier and its freedoms. In any event, Turner's historical vision, in its focus on land, geological formations, and geographical variations, is still intriguing; and it will be reconsidered in chapter 7. But many Americans might have remained oblivious of the insights of an academic historian such as Turner were it not for such people as Emerson Hough, a popular novelist and journalist as well as a sportsman, wildlife conservationist, and advocate for wilderness.

Hough made history read like a great adventure story, with short sentences, a plot of sorts, and many exclamation points. In 1918 Yale University Press published Hough's *Passing of the Frontier: A Chronicle of the Old West,* after he had already made his reputation with novels of adventure and romance, such as *The Way of a Man* (1907), which Pathé made into a silent movie. Born in Newton, Iowa, in 1857 and educated at Iowa State University, Hough eventually made his way through many parts of the old Wild West. It happened that he was at Yellowstone National Park in February 1894, when a poacher of one of the park's few remaining bison was caught after a dangerous chase on skis. (Both the pursuers and the pursued were armed.) Quickly writing up the story for *Forest and Stream* magazine, Hough aroused public concern for the park's endangered wildlife. Three months later, in May 1894, Congress passed an act protecting the birds and animals of Yellowstone.[6]

Hough may have known of Turner's frontier thesis, perhaps through Turner's articles in the *Atlantic Monthly.* If so, he animated and amplified that thesis with vivid accounts of the land and the people, the devastation left by grazing sheep, the exhausted soils left by bonanza wheat farms, and the drain of homesteaders from the United States into Canada between 1900 and 1913. "The frontier! There is no word in the English language more stirring, more intimate, or more beloved," Hough sighed. "It means all that America ever meant. It means the old hope of a real personal liberty, and yet a real human advance in character and achievement. . . ." He concluded, "We had a frontier once. It was our most priceless possession. . . . It was there we showed our fighting edge, our unconquerable resolution, our undying faith. . . . We shall do ill indeed if we forget and abandon its strong lessons, its great hopes, its splendid human dreams."[7]

Hough's *Passing of the Frontier* was written while the United States was embroiled in Europe's Great War; hence the grand rhetoric that sometimes overwhelms the sense of a real physical place and its living beings. To get a keener sense of what his native Middle West meant to Hough, we can turn to his more personal writings, such as "The Plains and Prairies" of 1912, where he remembers the prairie as a youthful world and himself as a boy standing in a primeval sea of grass shimmering in tones of silver and undulating in a continuous wave.[8]

Hough cherished his prairies and plains—the ones in memory, before the plow, when the waters of little streams ran clear, shaded by forests of oak, hickory, and walnut trees along the banks; when prairie nights were warm on the higher ground and chilly in the swales; when both prairie land and prairie grasses lay in undulations, and among the grasses grew wild phlox, tall sweet Williams, violets, and prairie roses; when sunflowers knew their place—west of the Missouri River, not east of it. Admittedly, Hough was guilty of that familiar wish to build a wall and keep out newcomers (in his case, European immigrants); he longed to preserve the land's youth, beauty, and freshness, which he knew had nearly vanished from the prairies and plains by 1912. Still, his vision was not misanthropic. "If ever there is to be a brotherhood of man," he wrote, "it will be born in a quiet river valley, in some level land." Leaders would depend on that land as a source of wealth and wisdom, of national poise and gravity, calmness, sanity. If some of the best chapters of American history had already been written on the prairies and plains, more were still to come, Hough predicted. "Their landscapes were large, calm, sufficient; and their landscapes wrote themselves on human souls, as landscapes always do."[9]

There may be no reason to assume that Willa Cather knew of this piece by Emerson Hough on the plains and prairies, published in *Country Life in America* on October 1, 1912. By then it had been a year since Cather had left her position as an overworked editor in the New York offices of *McClure's Magazine,* and the long-evolving manuscript of her forthcoming novel, *O Pioneers!,* was just about completed.[10] Had she read Hough's piece, she might have been reassured by his affection for the wide-open spaces that she, too, had learned to love. But the lesson had not been easy. For a girl of nine, whose childhood had been nurtured in the tranquil, long-cultivated Shenandoah Valley of Virginia, her family's move to a farming community on the Nebraska divide in 1883 was a shock. Years later Cather recalled, "I would not know how much a child's life is bound up in the woods and hills and meadows around it, if I had not been jerked away from all these and thrown out into a country as bare as a piece of sheet iron."[11]

It was a long journey from Cather's early experience of dislocation on the windswept Nebraska divide to her mature appreciation of both wildness and cultivation there, but a few of her stories give clues to her evolving sense of how wildness in a landscape can affect people, even unconsciously. And these stories, in turn, reveal her affinities with the landscape architect Jensen as well as with the novelist/journalist Hough.

In "The Enchanted Bluff" (1909) Cather doesn't mention wildness as such. But the bluff-bordered river that winds through cultivated land is something willful, unmanageable, attracting unfamiliar birds now and again. True, the water is brown and sluggish, "like any other of the half-dozen streams that water the Nebraska corn lands." But springtime floods continually stir up the silt and reshape the contours of land and stream bed, eventually yielding something fresh: an island, like a "little new bit of world, beautifully ridged with ripple marks," something that even the free-spirited Sandtown boys take care not to spoil when they swim out to it and rest on its sands. One of the boys hates the idea of leaving to teach school on a distant windy plain covered with windmills, cornfields, and pastures, where there is no river, nothing "wilful" in the land. Meanwhile, the boys build a fire on the island, set up camp, try to spot constellations in the darkening sky, and wonder about the old Spanish explorers and the enchanted bluff that someone's uncle once saw down in New Mexico. Their imaginations kindled, all the boys dream of going there someday. Then twenty years pass. None of the boys, now grown men, has ever gone there. Selling stocks and bonds or minding the store or an early death has prevented such a trip. But one, at least, has told his son about the enchanted bluff down in New Mexico, and the son keeps that dream alive.[12]

In 1921 Jens Jensen, too, wrote of bluffs worth dreaming about. But they were not in New Mexico. They could be found here and there on the prairies and plains of the Midwest, overhanging the streams and rivers. Densely wooded, mysterious, these bluffs were like worlds unto themselves, with microclimates that made them sanctuaries for birds and plants native to other regions. In an otherwise cultivated and productive land of corn or wheat, these bluffs and their watercourses were the last remains of the primeval, Jensen noted; they were food for the soul, the places where artists were born and poets sought inspiration. "All of our history has been written in these woody bluffs and the flowing streams below," he wrote. "They represent the only book of history that we have." And so Jensen urged that the wooded bluffs and their watercourses be preserved, perhaps as public land, so that they could be easily accessible and work on the imaginations of all the people, young and old. Then someday, when every inch of tillable soil was under cultivation, when villages had become towns and towns cities, there would remain these "ribbons of primitive America" spreading through the fertile farmlands. In essence, this was Jensen's vision of the "Mid-America of tomorrow," first presented in a study, *Proposed Park Areas in the State of Illinois* (1921), which was written by a group that he founded, the Friends of Our Native Landscape.[13]

In subject matter and mood Cather's " Enchanted Bluff" and Jensen's argument for preserving bluff-lined rivers are roughly comparable. But in Jensen's argument, with its faintly Utopian ending, there is no room for sluggish brown water and unrealized dreams. His vision is unblemished, idealized—to compete with the enticements of the enemy, which Jensen identified as "the Dollar, the God of our Age."[14] Cather, too, was wary of that enemy and its enticements in a developing, modernizing America. But she was writing fiction, where messy things like contradictions, tensions, and ambivalence not only were tolerated, they were the stuff out of which an even more penetrating vision just might emerge, whether that vision be artistic or social or environmental or a blend of them all.

Consider the main goal of Cather's pioneering farmers—to subdue the earth and make it yield at least the bare necessities of life. In *O Pioneers!* (1913) and *My Ántonia* (1918), the heroines are women with great physical strength, imagination, and endurance. In hard times they could go out and plow the earth, plant the seed, bring in the harvest, or run a business, as well as keep order and some degree of refinement in the home and the garden. In each novel there is also a sensitive, sympathetic young man who cherishes the traces of wildness he finds along the creeks and draws and among the wild ducks and the coreopsis, the sunflowers and the miles of copper-red grass. These sensitive young men go away for years, then return with misgivings about the new agricultural improvements. "This is all very splendid in its way," Carl says to Alexandra, the heroine of *O Pioneers!* "but there was something about this country when it was a wild old beast that has haunted me all these years."[15] Though the land now offers milk and honey, Carl thinks of an old German song and wonders where his beloved land has gone.

Carl's thoughts are like foils to the many human dramas that play out in *O Pioneers!* At times they seem to merge with the voice of the narrator: "But the great fact was the land itself, which seemed to overwhelm the little beginnings of human society that struggled in its sombre wastes." As an adolescent, Carl cannot articulate this idea, but clearly he feels it. Mingled with his bitterness—an expectation of defeat that enhances Alexandra's eventual triumphs as a successful farmer—is Carl's precocious sense that wild land is worth something in its own right; "that the

Among shocks of wheat in the Red River Valley of Minnesota a woman stands as if lost in reverie. This image, sometimes titled Spirit of the West, *recalls a few novels by Willa Cather and some passages of Carl Sandburg's poem "Prairie." (Photograph by Sumner Matteson, 1904. Courtesy of Milwaukee Public Museum.)*

land wanted to be let alone, to preserve its own fierce strength, its peculiar, savage kind of beauty, its uninterrupted mournfulness." If this is really a novel about land—or about people's relations to the land—in the end Cather suspends the ambivalence about wildness and cultivation by turning to issues of inheritance. "The land belongs to the future," Alexandra says to Carl. "We come and go, but the land is always here. And the people who love it and understand it are the people who own it—for a little while."[16]

Cather's own values can be detected in both the strong, imaginative farm women and the sensitive young men who come and go—as Cather came and went, to study at the University of Nebraska in Lincoln, to edit

a magazine in Pittsburgh (and later teach there), to edit a more prominent magazine in New York, to visit fellow writers in and around Boston,
and to travel to Europe for pleasure and on business. Then, too, in the
spring of 1912, before finishing *O Pioneers!* Cather made her first trip to
the Southwest and confronted wildness of a different order: "a whole
new landscape—not only a physical landscape, but a landscape of the
mind" that encompassed ancient cliff dwellings, contemporary Indian
villages, the Grand Canyon, and the Rio Grande.[17] Immediately afterward, between the two extremes of desert and New York City, she fitted
in a trip to her old home in Nebraska at harvest time, when the landscape that had once seemed bleak and raw now appeared benign, manageable.[18]

My Ántonia, written during the First World War, picks up the familiar theme of wild land versus land that is tamed, conquered, ordered,
productive. Some of the tensions, along with some of the incidents, of
Cather's earlier stories reappear with fresh details. The land is still a major
player. "There was nothing but land," Jim recalls of his first glimpse of
Nebraska, "not a country at all, but the material out of which countries
are made." A bluff-lined creek is both an impediment to farming and a
place where cottonwoods and ashes grow wild, their leaves glittering like
silver and gold as in a fairy tale. A road runs here and there, "like a wild
thing." Adolescent country girls on a bridge peer down at Jim "like curious deer." And happiness, in childhood, is the state of being "something
that lay under the sun and felt it, like the pumpkins," the state of being
"dissolved into something complete and great."[19]

And so wildness is still something positive, linked with youth, joy, freedom. Wildness is the source of freshness; wild places are the stimulants
for dreams and curiosity. The waters in the main current of the bluff-
lined river are still muddy; but one of its minor streams, cut off by a long
sand bar, runs "perfectly clear." Opposite qualities and characters are thus
balanced, suggesting a truce or some kind of accommodation. The story
of the immigrant Ántonia is like a rutted, convoluted path toward a
remarkable degree of order, productivity, and refinement. When Jim suggests that she should never have left the country for the town, Ántonia

disagrees; despite some setbacks and betrayals, it was in the town that she learned to cook, to keep house, and, in time, to bring up her own children so as not to be like wild rabbits. And yet wildness remains in her landscape: the road that used to "run like a wild thing," the road that had brought her and Jim to Nebraska in their childhood, has not yet been totally obliterated by the plow. A stretch of it remains in a pasture and traces remain in the draws, where wheel ruts had filled up with rainwater for too many years to heal. A road of destiny, unpredictable, that wild road remained in fragments, traceable still in memory and imagination.

Among the great passages in *My Ántonia* is the scene by the bluffs in summer, which culminates in a sunset: a red disk poised on the horizon and in front of it the black silhouette of a plow. Another passage centers on Ántonia's grape arbor, with its seats and table, set in the middle of the orchard, which is protected from wind and snow by a triple enclosure of wire fence, thorny locusts, and mulberry hedge. "There was the deepest peace in that orchard," Jim recalls. A third passage, central to all these things, reveals Jim at his desk by a window that looks out onto the prairie. Propped open is a Latin text, the great poem in celebration of agriculture, *The Georgics.* And among the lines in translation that linger in Jim's mind is Virgil's ambitious yet humble desire: "for I shall be the first, if I live, to bring the Muse into my country."[20]

In the novel Cather explains that "my country" does not refer to Rome but to something more familiar: Virgil's own little countryside. That was Cather's desire as well, to make a work of art out of *her* countryside, the Nebraska divide and its region of plains and prairies. Whether she was the first to do this is not our concern. She did so, memorably, in words. And there were others in her midwestern region who wanted to do the same—with living trees and shrubs, stone and wood, even with the flowers they found running wild through the tall grass.

***

Ossian Cole Simonds, born in 1855, earned a degree in civil engineering in 1878 from the University of Michigan. Frank Lloyd Wright, born in 1867, worked part-time for a civil engineer in 1886 while studying at the University of Wisconsin. Jens Jensen, born in 1860, studied at an agricultural school in Tune, near Copenhagen, in 1880. By the early 1900s, Simonds, Wright, and Jensen were all colleagues in Chicago and members of a prominent men's club, the Cliff Dwellers. Wright and Jensen kept offices in Steinway Hall and collaborated on a few projects—not always agreeing, but maintaining a mutual respect. By then Simonds (who had studied architecture as well as engineering) and Jensen were practicing as landscape architects; occasionally they provided landscape designs for the progressive young architects—Wright, Walter Burley Griffin, Marion Mahony (Griffin), George Grant Elmslie, William Gray Purcell, and others, all of whom looked to Louis Sullivan as their mentor.[21]

It was the Progressive Era, a time of "new cities and new people," as Carl Sandburg announced in his poem "Prairie" (1918). He spoke for a generation of American-born sons of European immigrants, some no doubt with pasts like his own: childhood in a prairie town, a little schooling, a string of odd jobs in the wheat fields, on the railroads, in a carpenter's shop and a hotel kitchen, then a lucky break and a rise from obscurity by willpower and imagination. For these young men the past was "a bucket of ashes." The world held "only an ocean of tomorrows, a sky of tomorrows." But not all of Sandburg's contrasts between past and future were so stark. In the poem "Prairie" he wrote of sod house doors and skyscrapers, wild ducks and a Fourth of July picnic, the songs of mockingbirds hidden in their eggs and dreams of another sunrise, as well as memories and dust. Weighing a bit heavier in the balance, however, was the future: the new-turned sod and tomorrow.[22]

Poets such as Sandburg, Harriet Monroe, and Vachel Lindsay, and social reformers and theorists such as Jane Addams and Thorstein Veblen, all mingled with sculptors and painters, architects and landscape architects, city fathers and society matrons, at a time and place now recalled as the "Chicago Renaissance." And out of these associations came the occasional commission for a designer or political backing for a crusade to preserve some precious landscape or other. One biographer of Jensen, Robert Grese, has reconstructed many of the overlapping circles of Jensen's friends and clients, noting that the wife of Julius Rosenwald, the founder of Sears, Roebuck, was a charter member and the first vice president of the Friends of Our Native Landscape. This group, dedicated to the conservation and preservation of landscapes, was founded by Jensen in 1913. A few years earlier, in 1908, Jensen had offered a name, the Prairie Club, for another group, set up to manage "Saturday Afternoon Walking Trips" to such places as the dunes along the shores of Lake Michigan, south of Chicago and eastward, in Indiana.[23]

The story of how Jensen tried to help preserve these dunes from encroaching industry and urban settlement has been told before, in impressive detail.[24] Working with Henry C. Cowles, an ecologist and University of Chicago professor; Stephen T. Mather, director of the National Park Service; and Carl Sandburg, among others, Jensen and the Friends of Our Native Landscape helped lay the foundations for a series of preservation efforts at the federal, state, and local levels. In time the Indiana Dunes State Park (opened in 1926) and later the Indiana Dunes National Lakeshore would coexist with sand mining, steel mills, and an industrial harbor. But here our main interest is in the early days, before the end of the First World War, when, on days of pageants and festivals, traces of the Old World and the New, of ancient Greek and Native American cultures, were brought together—if somewhat incongruously—to enhance the still evolving spirit of the place. The dunes were then a sort of unofficial public park, an "everybody's land," as J. Ronald Engel described it. Accessible by the South Shore railroad and already threatened by the mining of sand, the draining of marshes, and the careless picking of rare wildflowers, the Indiana Dunes were still a natural and national treasure.[25]

Today, as we learn of those joyous excursions to the dunes, rainstorms notwithstanding; as we gaze upon the old photographs of ladies in broad-brimmed hats and long, dark skirts trudging up the windswept dunes along with the men and the children; and as we linger over the snapshots of smiling, barefoot young girls (city dwellers, presumably) draped in vaguely Grecian veils dancing by the shore of Lake Michigan in a pageant or a masque, some of the incongruity slips away. It does, after all, seem like an evocation of Sandburg's "new cities and new people," for whom tightly gridded streets, prim front lawns, and boxlike dwellings would never be sufficient for a full life.

Perhaps it was inevitable that once the design work of the younger Chicago architects and landscape architects became known and published, someone would come along and proclaim it a new cultural phenomenon. "What a revolution they represent!" Wilhelm Miller wrote in 1912, referring to the designers who mingled at the Cliff Dwellers. Until recently, Miller noted, the lonely, overworked pioneers had feared and hated the prairie, its blizzards and its summer droughts and fires, its wolves, its monotony. But now, he wrote, designers were intrigued by the prairie. They repeated its horizontal lines of land, crops, woods, and sky in their buildings. They also found horizontal lines in the branching structure of native hawthorns and crabapples, which they planted to frame a vista. In Miller's view, these designers were artists, who delighted in the flatness of the prairie and shunned exotic trees and flowers; for they preferred the prairie's wilder plants.[26]

In 1915 Miller showed how homeowners, too, could express their love of the land and evoke the "prairie spirit" in landscape gardening. They could plant trees, shrubs, and flowers native to the prairies. For inspiration they could visit Graceland Cemetery, near Chicago, designed by O. C. Simonds. They could walk along the "prairie river" that Jensen designed in Chicago's Humboldt Park. Along the bluffs above Lake Michigan in Lake Forest, Illinois, they might see what the landscape architect Warren Manning had achieved at the Cyrus McCormick place. They could read Henry C. Cowles's ecological study, *The Plant Societies of Chicago and Vicinity* (1901). Then they could follow three principles (conservation, restoration, repetition) and three steps (to idealize a farm view with a frame of trees, to conventionalize the prairie by planting flat-topped flowers, and to symbolize it by planting prairie roses).[27]

Miller, who had earned a doctorate under the horticulturist Liberty Hyde Bailey at Cornell University, was a journalist and educator driven by a then familiar ambition—to achieve cultural independence. At the University of Illinois in Urbana from 1912 to 1916, he continued to press

ACROSS THE CONTINENT

prairie gardens

for a truly American style of gardening, free of European traditions. Recently he had gone to see for himself why English gardens were so highly esteemed. Beyond the advantages of England's climate, beneath its mellowed old surfaces he had recognized a serenity and luxuriance that he believed American gardens could also achieve. The key was *American* plants. William Robinson's concept of wild gardening, introduced to England in 1870, had offered a clue. And in the spring of 1909 Miller had been delighted by Robinson's water gardens at Gravetye, in Sussex, where land and water mingled without clear separation. Thereafter Miller urged, "Let every country use chiefly its own native trees, shrubs, vines and other permanent material, and let the style of gardening grow naturally out of necessity, the soil and the new conditions."[28]

Miller's crusade was understandable, and Jensen apparently allowed his work to be shown as exemplars of the "Prairie spirit," along with work by O. C. Simonds and Frank Lloyd Wright. But Simonds and Wright were reluctant to be linked with Miller's crusade. Each had misgivings about labels and styles and said as much to Miller in private correspondence.[29] Wright was adamant about this in print as well.

In 1908 Wright acknowledged that a "New School of the Middle West" might emerge someday. "The prairie has a beauty of its own," he noted, a quality that could be accentuated by sloping roofs, low proportions, quiet skylines, suppressed chimneys, sheltering overhangs, and walls that reached out and enclosed gardens. But rather than focus on surface appearances, Wright sought a root principle, the organic—an understanding of nature's ways developed from a close study of nature's works, in root, stem, branch, leaf, and flower, in natural color, natural materials, natural textures. The machine, the tool of his civilization, was to be used honestly in the kind of work it could accomplish well. The result should be an architecture increasingly more simple, expressive, plastic (or sculptural), fluent, coherent, and organic.[30]

By 1914 Wright was disturbed by the premature success of the so-called Prairie School of architecture. In response, he exhorted readers to get beyond surface appearances and try to understand the nature of a building, which should be as true to its purpose as is any tree or flower.

Don't emulate the letter of the law, for "the letter killeth," he insisted. Attend to its spirit. "*Style* is a byproduct of the process and comes of the man or the mind in the process," he wrote. To take up a ready-made style was ultimately never to reach a style. And so—back to square one, to nature, the source of all art and design.[31]

Nature could mean different things to different people. In 1914 in Chicago it could mean the land of one's childhood, the environs of a farm or a small town. And it happened that Simonds, Wright, and Jensen could all look back to life on a family farm. Near his father's farm just outside of Grand Rapids, Michigan, Simonds used to enjoy the bluffs, birds and other wildlife, nuts, fruits, and a great variety of colors, textures, sounds, and fragrances throughout the year. In his professional life, Simonds drew upon his rural upbringing, using native plants unself-consciously and selecting hawthorns not necessarily for their branching structure but because their branches had thorns to protect the adder's-tongues, blood-roots, trilliums, hepaticas, and anemones that grew beneath them.[32]

In 1920 Simonds advised that the farmer's woodlot should contain a wide variety of hardy trees, not merely a single species; and the reason he gave was not ecological or economic but social. The lives of a farmer's sons and daughters would be richer, he believed, as they got to know the birds, animals, and wildflowers in a woodlot that resembled a natural forest of great charm and beauty. The purpose of farms was much more than to supply food for the cities, he asserted. It was to supply people for the cities: healthy, hardy, stable people, rugged in character yet sensitive to natural beauty. Simonds then touched on an idea that lies close to the heart of Virgil's *Georgics:* "The beauty of the farm, the farm which is the foundation of our prosperity and most of our happiness, leads to that love of country which is true patriotism."[33]

Frank Lloyd Wright's home at Taliesin, set in the valley of his mother's immigrant parents near Spring Green, Wisconsin, has been so often burned, rebuilt, altered, and transformed, then analyzed and interpreted with such sophistication that it may now be difficult to imagine the whole environment as Wright first experienced it—naively, as a child. Scholars and others note discrepancies between Wright's recollections in his *Auto-*

wright

biography and the verifiable facts.³⁴ Nevertheless, the prelude of the *Auto-biography* remains endearing and believable. Uncle John's footsteps in the snow made a long, straight, purposeful line up the slope. Nine-year-old Frank's footsteps ran here and there, back and forth across that line, embroidering it "like some free, engaging vine." Uncle John's lesson for the day was biblical, "Straight is the Way." Young Frank's lesson for a lifetime was bound up in the armful of dried weeds that he had scurried to gather on that morning walk. They were clusters of bronze marks and seed pods against the white of new-fallen snow. They were patterns of blue shadows on white. They were tall and brilliant, turning golden in the sun. In his arms they were his treasure. But proud Uncle John didn't see them. He left out something, "something that made all the difference to the boy."³⁵ What was it? Spontaneity, play, freedom, beauty—or wildness?

Wright was fond of weeds and wildflowers. At his grandparents' farm on Sunday mornings he would bring masses of them to the pulpit in the chapel. In his parents' home in Madison, Wisconsin, were vases of dried leaves. In his attic bedroom were clusters of pod-topped weeds. In his collaborative work, *The House Beautiful* (1898), twelve photogravures of weeds and wildflowers precede the text.³⁶ How did Wright make the transition from weed and wildflower to the elegant linear abstractions that frame the text of *The House Beautiful*? And why? It is as mysterious as a myth or a parable; and Wright, the son, grandson, and nephew of ministers and preachers, knew the power of myths and parables to get at truths that lie too deep for rational explanation.

Nature, freedom, democracy: Wright could symbolize these ideas with flowing spaces defined by stone, brick, wood, and stained glass. Jensen symbolized these ideas as well, with more expansive flowing spaces out-of-doors and with materials less refined and abstracted from their wild state. That degree of abstraction was one difference between the two; Wright resisted the kind of realistic imitation of nature that he noticed in Jensen's landscapes. But in Jensen himself Wright found a "loveable soul" as well as beliefs and values worth debating in the course of a long, sometimes stormy friendship.³⁷

Wright could speak and write so righteously that his grown son John affectionately called him a "modern Isaiah." And Wright apparently acquiesced.[38] The epithet refers to a passage in his *Autobiography* where Wright told of his rebellion against the prophet Isaiah. Along with all the other grandchildren of the Welsh patriarch and preacher Richard Lloyd Jones, young Frank had been compelled to memorize chapter 40 of the book of Isaiah, where faded flowers and withered grass were belittled while the word of God was exalted. But the boy knew that withered grass kept the cows alive all winter, that some flowers died so that others might "live more abundantly." This thought led the boy—or perhaps the mature autobiographer—to suggest that grass and flowers might themselves be the word of God.[39]

Here Wright came about as close as he would ever come to Jensen. "In the work of nature, man feels the Creator's mysterious power," wrote Jensen in *Siftings* (1939). "In all its various moods, during all seasons of the year, [Nature] brings to us the message of the infinite." The idea is not new; Emerson and Tennyson, among others, had expressed it before. But the nature they referred to may not have been quite so wild as the nature Jensen had in mind. "Deep down in the primitive there lies the secret of the significance of life and of the infinite," he continued. "It is a hidden, creative force." And as his words call to mind the mentors he had found in America—not only Emerson but Thoreau, John Muir, John Burroughs—it is as if the aging Jensen and his prized remnants of a primordial nature were stubborn survivors in a Depression-haunted yet relentlessly modernizing world. Then, too, Jensen's time frame was infinitely long. At the end of *Siftings* he noted, "We are today living in a machine age. What is to follow no one knows, but there is one thing sure: nature will survive."[40]

Jensen also had a trace of the harsh Old Testament prophet. It surfaced in the 1920s and 1930s, when he denounced materialism (the dollar as God) and the tendency of machines to "crush every bit of our God-given freedom to be ourselves."[41] But Jensen's more characteristic tone was benign, otherworldly. Some Americans considered him aristocratic as well. His improbable rise from Chicago street sweeper to civic leader and landscape architect, friend of Fords and Rosenwalds, can in part be explained by the comfortable social position of his family back in the Old Country. Still, as his biographers Robert Grese and Leonard Eaton have shown, the strands of influence from Jensen's birth, rural upbringing, folk and agricultural schooling, German military service, and travel were so interwoven that it is not clear precisely why Jensen chose to emigrate.[42]

In *Siftings* Jensen reveals that he loved the land of his birth—the province of Slesvig, in South Jutland, still part of Denmark in 1860. The bluffs over the sea, the dunes, the farm staked out on a windswept point by a pioneer great grandfather, the wildlife in the hedgerows, the first flowers in spring, summer concerts and campfires in the forest, the bog with the footmarks of his ancestors: to leave all this was, he recalled, "like being torn up by the roots."[43] But there were incentives to move on. Since 1864, Jensen's homeland had been under German rule. And in that socially stratified country, Jensen's well-placed father would not accept a young woman of humble origins—Anne Marie Hansen—as a daughter-in-law. For these and perhaps other reasons, Jens Jensen, the eldest son, and his fiancée, Miss Hansen, left in 1884 for America.

Once settled in Chicago, Jensen had more journeys ahead: upward from menial labor to a profession; outward to the prairies, forests, river bluffs, and dunes; and inward to those reservoirs of memory and imagination out of which he tried to make sense of a new country. Jensen did this by means of symbols and myths, as did others during the Chicago Renaissance, with their works of art proclaiming their freedom from criteria set down in New York and Boston, London and Paris.

Had Jensen's landscape designs more closely resembled those of his mainstream colleagues on the eastern seaboard—that is, had they been more eclectic, responding to whatever Italian, English, French, Spanish, neocolonial, or modern style the adjacent buildings aspired to—there might be more terraces, garden structures, and allées of trees with which to reconstruct his intentions today. But that sort of garden did not interest Jensen. And when he worked with Wright, there was no question of who was responsible for the built work; it was Wright. Jensen cared much more for individual plants, which, "like human beings, have their own individuality," as he put it.[44]

How Jensen came to emphasize native plants and avoid exotics will be considered in chapter 8.[45] Here we need to realize that in his imagination, plants really were like people. He was fond of plants he called "pioneers"—hawthorns and crabapples that seemed to have wandered from the forest to the prairie, then invited their neighbors to join them. He admired plants that had to struggle to survive—a wood lily on a rock ledge facing the northwest winds, a prairie rose pushing red berries up through the snow—both expressing freedom and "the urge to be."[46] He loved the prairie, a great symbol of freedom, and the prairie river, symbol of flux and flow and thoughts that know no bounds. From Danish forests he recalled the campfires, symbol of fellowship, place of storytelling and song. And he tried to recreate or symbolize these phenomena in parks and gardens that remained much the same in character, whether private or public. In many of them lay his stone council ring, promise of fellowship around the campfire at its core.

One surprise in Jensen's work and thought is the contrast between his efforts to preserve wild landscapes and his reluctance to preserve gardens shaped by human beings. "Art must be a guide," leading toward higher, spiritual goals, he wrote in 1939. But as a work of art, the garden need not be preserved after its maker has gone. Let those who come afterward solve their own problems; otherwise art will decay, he cautioned. "Let the garden disappear in the bosom of nature of which it is a part . . . . The maker's spirit would then live as long as the plants he planted would grow and scatter seed.[47]

***

While Jens Jensen, nearly eighty, was setting down these thoughts about garden making and posterity, a younger man was reconstructing the past, where human history merged with the history of the land. That land was black loam with "a million years of wealth in it," Donald Culross Peattie explained. It lay in the state shaped like an arrowhead—Illinois—where Peattie himself was born in 1898. That was too late for him to see what he later read about: the miles of grasses, mingling with bird's-foot violets, shooting stars, blue-eyed grass, horsetail, and other wildflowers. The surface of the virgin prairie had once been "a soft fragrant cheek turned to the sun." Now all he knew of it at firsthand was a thin remnant on the edge of a bit of high ground he called a "prairie grove," with welcome shade, drier soil, and birds' songs heard from deep within the grove.[48]

Peattie's *Prairie Grove* (1938), a beautifully written story-within-a-story, introduces certain ideas about native soils and plants that were derived from ecologists' fairly recent findings. Having studied under the plant ecologist Henry C. Cowles at the University of Chicago, then at Harvard, Peattie spent three years in the U.S. Department of Agriculture as a botanist dealing with the introduction of foreign plants and seeds. He had the scientific background to write with some confidence about the land and its flora and fauna.[49] Then, too, he had grown up in the country south of Chicago, among the dunes by Lake Michigan, in a big old house that sheltered three generations, including his parents, both of them readers and writers. An avid reader, Peattie brought to his many writings on natural history an unusual sensitivity to language and a sense of place. And yet *A Prairie Grove* stands out from his other works. Aldo Leopold, for one, welcomed this "ecological novel" as a sign that scientific writing could have literary value.[50]

What unites Peattie's stories of the prairie and of the various people who left their marks on it is a recurring perception that "root touched root." Sometimes this is a literal description of the way the flora of the unbroken prairie was able to guard the soil's fertility and survive through an infinite web of cooperation underground: "They locked grips, hugged earth as only the truly native can." But "root touched root" also applies to a biota: the bison, elk, rodents, prairie chickens, lark sparrows, rattlers, prairie grasses, flowers, roots, and earth. It is an "empire of locked roots," a kingdom where the only serious threat is the pioneer who arrives with axe, plow, wheel, and a new combination of animals and plants, all domesticated. At one time the pioneers, too, represented root linking with root, through settlement and intermarriage. But running through all these efforts to set down roots is the tension of civilization warring against wilderness.

Like Willa Cather, Peattie was ambivalent about the change from unbroken prairie to fields of corn and apple orchards. "It had to be—the shrinking of the slough, the tilling and the fencing, the shuddering bang of the freight cars, the shriek of the mill," he writes. But he knows that something vanished along with the buffalo, elk, prairie chicken, and sandhill crane—"something that was ample and native and dark, like the first loam and the slough water." He imagines a moment of balance sometime in the mid–nineteenth century, a point of tension between the sown and the unsown lands, where "man's will met with roots' will" and human order met with primeval wildness, both beauties "nourished by impartial earth." Yet his parting words about the now populated and bountiful land are faintly elegiac: "Still sometimes when in fall or spring the wind turns, coming from a fresh place, we smell wilderness on it, and this is heartbreak and delight."[51]

The naturalist Edwin Way Teale tells a more lighthearted story of his childhood on the borderlands between the prairie and the sand dunes by the shores of Lake Michigan. In *Dune Boy* (1943) Teale, born in 1899, recalls the sand dunes of northern Indiana as a remnant of wilderness that he could gaze upon whenever he climbed the mossy roof of his grandparents' farmhouse. On those long summer holidays away from his home in Joliet, Illinois, the dunes stirred his boyhood imagination as they shone in the summer sunlight. In time that landscape changed, yet any feelings of regret or ambivalence are absent in the retelling.[52]

Some deeper, darker feelings surfaced two years later in *The Lost Woods* (1945), where Teale recalled the forest where he and his grandfather went one winter to fell trees and cut firewood. As his mind wandered from his tasks, young Teale sensed the life of the woods suspended, as if enchanted, while he stood in what seemed like a "charmed circle." Once he and his grandfather left, he imagined, the woodland life would go on as before; and that aura of secrecy and wildness left him intensely curious about the woods and its creatures. But years later Teale was unable to find that enchanted place. Perhaps the forest had been felled to clear a field for plowing. Now it would remain his "Lost Woods of childhood."[53]

The popularity of Peattie's and Teale's books at mid-century suggests that more than a few readers may have known a lost woods or some other childhood haunt that had been obliterated by axe, plow, or dredging machine. When Aldo Leopold came to assemble his reminiscences and essays in what became known as *A Sand County Almanac* (1949), he could have appealed to similar feelings of loss with his own memories of childhood. Clearly he respected Peattie's efforts to dramatize the tensions between civilization and once-wild lands, drawing upon the findings of science as well as profound human emotions. And no nostalgia blunted Peattie's environmental message. In any case, Leopold's early years, along with his boyhood haunts lost to development or cultivation, cannot be pieced together from reflections in *A Sand County Almanac*.

A boyhood friend of Leopold, however, has left a memoir of their wanderings among the bluffs and ravines, woods and streams of Burlington, Iowa. In the early 1900s, when they were both in the first two years of high school, young Edwin A. Hunger had a paper route that brought him early in the morning to Leopold's neighborhood on the bluffs over the Mississippi. Around five o'clock one morning he happened to notice young Leopold scanning the trees with field glasses, looking for birds. The two became friends; and Leopold, by far the more knowledgeable about birds and other wildlife, casually became his friend's teacher.[54]

As Leopold introduced Hunger to the Lone Tree Hunting Club, across the river in Illinois, the birds they spotted opened a whole new world of interest for Hunger: red-eyed vireos, crested flycatchers, warblers, orioles, scarlet tanagers, and water thrushes. With a single-barrel shotgun Leopold might shoot an English sparrow—those birds killed other birds, Hunger wrote—but mainly the two boys hunted with field glasses or the naked eye. They also took risks, swimming among the huge rafts of logs that were tied up at the base of North Hill bluff. But over time the boys grew apart. Leopold went east to the Lawrenceville School, in New Jersey. Hunger eventually went east to college. Years passed. On a visit back home, Hunger returned to their old haunts and regretted the loss of Ransom Hollow, a small ravine with a brook not far from the Leopolds' home. A row of houses now stood there, and the ravine was filled in with dirt. Hunger remembered the flock of evening grosbeaks that Leopold had pointed out to him there. That was the first big discovery, and there were many more. "What a wonderful little bird sanctuary this ravine would have made," Hunger reflected.[55]

again focuses on people

THREE

Forested Mountains

Sierra Nevada, Rockies, Appalachian Trail

"He has only half expressed himself in his books—the real Muir is only half there." So wrote John Burroughs, a reliable witness, despite the differences in their preferred habitats, wild and half-wild. In New York City, at the Grand Canyon, in Alaska, Burroughs and Muir had come together, shared a few adventures, and exchanged a few good-natured taunts at a time when each was a seasoned author, widely admired for his profound insights into the world of living beings and natural processes. Yet Burroughs insisted, "No one could thoroughly know John Muir, or feel his power, or have any idea of the rank, cantankerous, and withal lovable Scot that he was, until he met him."[1]

Today, long after Muir's death in 1914, we remain intrigued by the man from Dunbar, Scotland, who went home to the Sierra Nevada—the man who climbed its peaks, studied its glacial remains, cherished its wildflowers, found kinship with its wild creatures, and claimed no greater ambition than to get others, as well, to see and feel all those glorious reflections of the Creator. Burroughs, Mary Austin, Gifford Pinchot, and others recalled Muir telling long, sparkling stories of his adventures in the wilderness.[2] But his innermost thoughts seem to have been reserved for a few close friends, to whom he sent letters sometimes charged with the energies that he sensed flowing around and through him even as he wrote. In contrast, many of his essays and books are genial, informative, enthusiastic, persuasive, humorous, ironic, with traces of controlled anger over some environmental abuse or other; but the voice is often more public, less intimate.[3]

Consider Muir's essay "Wild Wool," which appeared in 1875, soon after his descent into the San Francisco Bay Area. After roaming high up in the Sierra Nevada for some six years, he happened to find convincing evidence that the wool of wild mountain sheep was far superior to that of a domesticated flock. And, like Thoreau, whose works he had begun to read, Muir preferred the piquant wild apple over the softened, pulpy orchard apple that had long been cultivated for human use. In a seemingly offhand way he noted that Nature might even be viewed from a standpoint other than human use; that wild wool was made for sheep, not man; that Nature had her own uses for wild apples. He concluded, "A little pure wildness is the one great present want, both of men and sheep."[4] Here, with a few pokes at the unexamined beliefs of his contemporaries, Muir stayed within certain bounds. As Frederick Turner has pointed out, "Wild Wool" reveals Muir speaking as a man of civilization.[5]

So what about that man of the wilderness, less guarded and more expressive about what thrilled him in a Yosemite meadow or on the highest spire of Cathedral Peak? What could the general public know of him—that is, while Muir was alive and before the letters and private journals were entrusted to archives? In 1911 the elderly Muir brought out an edited version of some journals he had written as a young man—*My First Summer in the Sierra*. In that summer of 1869, aged thirty-one, Muir was employed to keep track of a shepherd and a flock of 2,050 sheep. And as the flock ate their way from California's hot, dry Central Valley up into the greener pastures of what is now Yosemite National Park, Muir would saunter off in search of the region's flora and fauna, if not of stray sheep. Evidently the seventy-two-year-old Muir looked back on his experiences of that summer as something worth sharing with the public. But, as Michael Cohen has shown, Muir drew from other summers in the Sierra as well; his drafts reveal not only editing but also reshaping and some new writing. The resulting book then "telescoped" Muir's experiences of several summers.[6]

The book also did something more. With its overlay of different voices, youthful and elderly, it allowed Muir, the man of civilization, to say things about wildness and freedom that the public might otherwise find undignified, unscientific, impractical, or inconsistent. The sheep could be described as "hoofed locusts," grazing on precious seedlings and wildflowers and ultimately ruining the land. But lambs could also cry out to their mothers in tones "wonderfully human"; and at night, in the light of fires started to ward off "freebooting" bears, the eyes of thousands of sheep could glow "like a glorious bed of diamonds." Then, too, as the young Muir found his own hunger for bread and need for sleep increasingly annoying, he often wished he could live like the Indians, mainly on pine nuts, leaves, and berries; or like the junipers beside the shore of Lake Tenaya, living "on sunshine and snow" for a thousand years. But was it the elderly Muir who added that lakes up in the mountains do eventually die, as they are filled in with detritus carried along by streams and avalanches, rain and wind?

In the first week of June during that first summer in the Sierra, the young Muir sensed a transformation within himself, a "conversion" and rebirth. "We are now in the mountains and they are in us, kindling enthusiasm, making every nerve quiver, filling every pore and cell of us," he wrote, struck by the sensation of being inseparably a part of nature. Soon he declared that month of June "the greatest of all the months of my life, the most truly, divinely free, boundless like eternity, immortal." Later, in July, gazing down on the valley from the North Dome at Yosemite, Muir thought his sketches would never communicate to others what he felt. "No pain here, no dull empty hours, no fear of the past, no fear of the future . . . the whole body seems to feel beauty when exposed to it as it feels the camp-fire or sunshine, entering not by the eyes alone, but equally through all one's flesh like radiant heat, making

Mirror Lake, with Mount Watkins in the distance, is one of the best-known scenes in Yosemite National Park. On mornings when the waters are calm, reflections may be nearly flawless. One challenge for John Muir and others, however, was to get visitors to appreciate more than scenery in the national parks.

a passionate ecstatic pleasure-glow not explainable." Thus aroused before that display of God's power, Muir was eager to toil for eternity "to learn any lesson in the divine manuscript."[7]

The intensity and irony of these passages are heightened by some awareness of Muir's past: the corporal punishment inflicted at school in Dunbar whenever he failed to memorize a given passage from the Bible; the enforced labor on two Wisconsin homesteads in succession, helping his father by breaking up sod for the plow and breaking through rock to find water; the leveled forests and exhausted soils left in the wake of the Muirs and other unenlightened homesteaders of their day; the escape from his father's literal reading of the Bible and narrow view of life into a world of mechanical inventions, scientific inquiry, classical learning, and sympathetic mentors at the University of Wisconsin; and the recurring sense of being unfitted for what the rest of the world considered work. Hence, in the Sierra, Muir's frequent mention of sauntering, drifting, intermingling, the dissolving of all sense of time and separations between things, and the yearning to remain there for eternity. "Up here all the world's prizes seem nothing," Muir declared. By the end of summer, the memory of things artificial, even the most carefully leveled pleasure grounds, seemed coarse, while all meadows shaped by glaciers were beautiful. And all was flowing: the streams, the snow, the air, the volcanic rocks, the flocks of animals, "while the stars go streaming through space pulsed on and on forever like blood globules in Nature's warm heart."[8]

These were thoughts that Muir could not easily communicate to a congressional committee, a cabinet secretary, or perhaps even the readers of the *Century* or the *Atlantic Monthly.* And so when he came down from the High Sierra eventually to defend the environment he cherished, his language and arguments gradually changed. Only years later would he leave a published record of what he had once felt in the High Sierra, blending the thoughts of the young Muir and the elderly Muir. In *My First Summer in the Sierra* he also left a few insights gained sometime between 1869 and 1911: Mountains are fountains, "beginning places" where streams start on their journeys to the sea (and where Muir himself found a new life). Mountains are the place where longing ceases; "we go home into the mountain's heart." Everything is connected to everything else in the universe. "More and more . . . we feel ourselves part of wild Nature, kin to everything." The charms of the Sierra Nevada—a Range of Light—transcend reason; they are as mysterious as life itself.

But those charms could obscure some unpleasant realities. Muir was troubled up there in the Range of Light not only by his need for bread and sleep but by his glimpses of Native Americans. He did admire their ability to subsist on what they could gather or hunt in the mountains. But he recoiled from certain things they ate; and these people did not meet his standards of cleanliness. Aware of the forest fires they had sometimes lit to improve hunting grounds, Muir nevertheless saw Indians as people who walked softly on the land. Whatever traces they left disappeared within a few centuries, whereas white men blasted rock to make roads, stripped the skin off a mountain's face to get its gold, and enslaved wild streams with their dams and channels. "Fortunately for Sierra scenery the gold-bearing slates are mostly restricted to the foothills," he noted.[9] And so in *My First Summer* Muir appears as an ambivalent man of the wilderness encumbered with a few civilized needs, tastes, and perceptions. Then, too, traces of ambivalence remain in the language he later used to protest the destruction of forests.

As we saw earlier, in the late 1890s Muir not only wrote spirited magazine articles to support the Forestry Commission's efforts; he also inserted into his text some writings by Gifford Pinchot and Edward A. Bowers, using not only their words but also their more pragmatic way of framing the issues. The result was a hybrid of utilitarian arguments for conserving the forests' material wealth and Muir's own deep feelings for the forest as a sanctuary, a source of spiritual well-being. The forest as playground was another argument to consider. Around 1869 Muir noticed tourists in Yosemite Valley, looking at the scenery now and again. Years later he would translate his convictions into the language of tourism, extolling the scenic wonders of landscapes that he considered precious mainly for other, almost incommunicable reasons.

In *My First Summer* Muir resolved some of his ambivalence about Native Americans with a few lines of his beloved countryman Robert Burns: "It's coming yet, for a' that, that man to man, the warld o'er, shall brothers be for a' that." But again, he may have had to translate a bit; for how many Americans would understand Burns's use of the Scots vernacular "brithers?"[10] And how many could appreciate Muir's vision of all the works of the Creator as brothers, with "a heart like our own beating in every crystal and cell"? Perhaps some would have to wait until a scientist or a poet could offer a new worldview, some Gaia hypothesis or new way of seeing that could make Muir's vision comprehensible.[11]

In his forties Muir married, helped to rear his two daughters, and took up remunerative work. On his father-in-law's experimental fruit ranch in Martinez, California, he began to raise more popular (and marketable) varieties of pears, grapes, and cherries in great quantities. He also began writing in earnest after prodding from his wife, Louie, and from friends and acquaintances such as Ralph Waldo Emerson, the *Century* magazine editor Robert Underwood Johnson, and the extraordinarily supportive and perceptive Mrs. Jeanne Carr, wife of Muir's former geology professor, Ezra Slocum Carr, at the University of Wisconsin. These educated, civilized people nudged Muir the saunterer into becoming a man of literary and scientific achievements, most notably on the subjects of glaciers and mountains. In turn, Muir helped younger people along their own paths, through his writings, in passing, or as a leader of outings with the Sierra Club, which he and others founded in 1892.[12]

Muir met one kindred spirit not in the Sierra but on the edge of San Francisco. One day in December 1889, at the western end of the new, still half-wild Golden Gate Park, Muir was talking to a group of people on the beach about a handful of plants. When the group dispersed, a young stranger came forward with a plant and a question for the gray-bearded Muir. The stranger was nineteen-year-old Enos Mills, lately arrived from a copper mine in Butte, Montana; but his real, adopted home was among the 14,000-foot peaks of the Rocky Mountains in Colorado. One day he would be known as the "Father of the Rocky Mountain National Park."[13]

***

In the Colorado Rockies timberline hovered at 11,300 feet above sea level. Enos Mills knew that that line was always in flux, however. It was a frontier, the battle line between woods and weather. And, like every frontier, he noted, timberline was aggressive, struggling to advance up the mountain, even as windblown sand, drifting snows, and frigid temperatures worked to push it back down. On the forest's front line were the feisty limber pines and Engelmann spruce, perhaps mingled with Arctic willow or black birch, all dwarfed and twisted by the full force of the elements; yet some lived for hundreds of years.[14]

These wind-sculpted, bannerlike trees high up on the forest's frontier grew more mysterious at night, when partly veiled in moving mist, Mills observed. In the flickering light of a campfire, layers of civilization were lifted as if by magic. Gathered round the fire, people seemed to regain a sense of their primitive selves; they became fire-worshipers in a new, unexplored world. And out of this misty, primeval setting, one thing seems clear: Mills's occasional references to "tree people," trees leading frontier lives, are more than figures of speech. Mills identified with those battered, intrepid trees on the front line. He, too, had struggled against fate and the elements—wind, water, penetrating cold—and had prevailed. His essay "Trees at Timberline" ends on a note of triumph, then, with some intimation of "universal kinship."[15] For him as for John Muir, kinship extended infinitely beyond webs of human relations, although each man arrived at this realization by his own path.

Born in 1870 on his parents' farm near Fort Scott, in southeastern Kansas, Mills suffered from a digestive disorder that kept him away from regular schooling and arduous chores. At fourteen, on the advice of the family doctor, he went west, alone, to the invigorating climate and environment of Estes Park, then a small resort community in the Rocky Mountains some forty miles northwest of Denver. On time off from jobs at a lodge and on a ranch, he explored the upland valley, scaled peaks, and became fascinated by the region's trees, wildflowers, bears, beavers, and other wild things. Within a year he had staked a homesteading claim and begun to build a cabin on a lower mountain slope within sight of the 14,255-foot Longs Peak. He first climbed that peak in 1885, guided by Carlyle Lamb, son of the Reverend Elkanah Lamb, a family relation. By 1902, after working summers in the Estes Park area and winters in the copper mines around Butte, Montana, Mills had earned enough to purchase the Reverend Lamb's small ranch resort, Longs Peak House.

Renamed Longs Peak Inn and rebuilt after a fire in 1906, Mills's rustic inn became a gathering place for civic leaders, writers, naturalists, and other people willing to abide by Mills's prohibitions against dancing, cardplaying, pet cats and dogs, and similar preoccupations of the civilized world. In return, Mills, their host and guide, offered them entrée into the wilderness, with nuggets of information about wild things along the way to the summit of Longs Peak, followed by stories of his own adventures and discoveries back at the inn.[16]

As civilization spread from the frontier communities of Denver and Estes Park, Mills welcomed many of its traces—the telephone, more frequent mail service, a growing number of small landholdings, and automobile stage lines (which, he noted, ended the cruelty to horses on the old stage lines). As a sometime ranch hand, miner, and patron of the Butte free public library, Mills was a part of and beneficiary of the advancing civilization. As a guide—a "nature guide"—he was also a mediator between wilderness and civilization. He could earn a living during July and August. For the rest of the year he could explore, write, lecture, and lobby for yet another national park. And so he hovered at the edges of two frontiers—the forest's, at timberline, and civilization's, in the valley.

The chance meeting with John Muir on the edge of San Francisco in 1889 was critical for Mills. "I owe everything to Muir," Mills once told a journalist. "If it hadn't been for him I would have been a mere gipsy."[17] Muir saw that the young man knew many curious things about plants and animals, but that knowledge was fragmented; Mills needed to organized what he had learned of the natural world and to communicate it in writing. And so, with Muir's encouragement, Mills settled into a long process of self-education, scientific and literary.

*A distant view of trees at timberline in Rocky Mountain National Park gives only
a hint of the struggle between living organisms and the forces of wind and
weather at that altitude. Enos Mills knew that that "forest frontier" was not fixed
but ever shifting, like the contested border between two nations.*

After some early rejections, Mills came to write under the same imprint as Muir (and Burroughs), Houghton Mifflin. Mills's affinity for Muir remained strong as well. They had camped together, and each had endured hunger, thirst, frigid temperatures, and solitude to penetrate deeper into the mysteries of the mountains they loved. In his thirties Mills was even paid to do this; as Colorado's official snow inspector in the early 1900s, he spent a few winters crossing and recrossing the continental divide, camping out, subsisting mainly on nuts and raisins, while he gauged snowfalls to predict water supplies for the coming year. The job yielded some superb adventure stories for such magazines as *Country Life in America* and the *Saturday Evening Post.* Mills also came away with insights into the ecology of the whole region.[18]

Married for the first time at age forty-eight, Mills got to know his young daughter, Enda, only as a toddler. He had evaded a solitary death many times in the mountains, enduring hunger, cold, avalanches, and more. But he died after complications from a subway accident in New York City in 1922. He was fifty-two.

That death eerily recalls Mills's "Story of a Thousand-Year Pine," a much-revised, well-crafted tale of a great yellow pine, read in its annual rings. The tree is struck by the logger's axe. When it hits the ground it shatters and is deemed useless by the sawmill man. Ultimately the tree is consumed in a bonfire. Mills offers no sermon; he simply shows us a tree as he would a fellow human being.[19]

A modest man, Mills once explained that his books were simply "forewords" to the book of Nature, which he hoped to get people to read on their own, everywhere; for that book lay open to everyone, in cities as in the Rocky Mountains.[20] When people took up that suggestion, the nature guide's job was done; and Mills wanted to see that job well done, well paid, and well respected. He didn't call it a profession, but surely it was a calling, open to women as well as men. One of his stories concerns a college student who was inept on horseback and his quietly competent guide, a woman. Mills expected a great deal from such women—high standards for men to follow, athletic ability, knowledge of natural history, and creativity. The guides he had in mind not only knew about glaciers and ptarmigans, bears and wild flowers; they could share that knowledge with others, talking about geology and botany, quoting poetry, not in a classroom but out in the field. "A nature guide is an artist," Mills declared, an artist who could stimulate new interests that would grow and develop yet could never be entirely satisfied, for nature's mysteries were inexhaustible.[21]

Mills praised the guiding skills of others, including John Muir and Shep N. Husted, of the Rocky Mountain National Park. But his own vision of the nature guide as artist may have been unique. Having climbed the high peaks of the Rocky Mountains and other peaks in British Columbia and Europe, Mills remained intrigued by the mountain at his own doorstep, Longs Peak. He had climbed it in all kinds of weather throughout the year, day and night, alone and with other people, young and old. Some might ask why he climbed one peak again and again, or why he climbed at all. Mills would reply with an echo of the poet John Keats: "When one climbs a high pinnacle on the vast cathedrals of this world, where Pan is 'forever piping hymns forever new,' one seems to mingle with the universe."[22]

Does it matter that Mills replaced Keats's "songs" with "hymns"? Perhaps Pan, the pagan god of woods and pastures, was rendered a bit less frisky that way. Still, for some readers, that altered line from Keats's "Ode on a Grecian Urn" must have released a surge of associations: the pipes and timbrels, the wild ecstasy, silence and slow time, beauty, truth, and the magic ability of art to keep boughs forever green, maidens forever fair, youths forever longing, and love itself forever young. The poet knows that art can keep alive those earthly things that would otherwise pass away. The mountaineer knows that something equally alive—or eternal, transcendent—awaits him on the summit, beckoning even when out of sight. And what of the poet/mountaineers who can speak about geology and botany?

Today some may be working in the Rocky Mountain National Park, established in 1915, largely thanks to Mills's strenuous efforts. Or they may be found elsewhere in the National Park Service, a government entity that Mills helped to bring into being in 1916.[23] But in his day, if such versatile guides were rare, then tourists with a keen interest in some aspects of the environment had to work a bit harder.

In 1917, for instance, there appeared an account of travels in Glacier National Park, in Montana, written by two members of the American Rockies Alpine Club, Mathilde Edith Holtz and Katharine Isabel Bemis, both of Minneapolis.[24] Having arrived at the Glacier Park Hotel, the two women soon found their guide. He was a half-Blackfoot named Donald, whom they came to recognize as an aristocrat, quiet, serious, cautious, considerate, with the single eccentric habit of referring to the coil of rope hung from his saddle as "stylish." Other than occasionally pointing out a fine view or a grizzly bear, Donald simply, skillfully led the two women on horseback through mist, snow, clouds, and sunshine. Meanwhile, the women served as their own nature guides, identifying wildflowers, birds, and glaciers, quoting Muir and John Ruskin, and noting the passage of seasons as they ascended or descended the trail.

Walter Prichard Eaton's *Skyline Camps* appeared in 1922—the year Enos Mills died. Younger than Mills by eight years, Eaton was an easterner who knew his way around Boston, Cambridge, Manhattan, and Rhode Island's old South County. By choice, however, he lived on a farm in the Berkshires of Massachusetts, wrote for a living, and hiked often, mainly in New England, occasionally in the West. Like Holtz and Bemis, Eaton hired guides at Glacier National Park and gathered his own facts about wildflowers, for the guides had no interest in them. But Eaton was always trying to get beyond facts to the essence or spirit of a place. At a glance he could not "know" a place as he knew the beloved fields around his home. And so at Crater Lake, in Oregon, he craved time—time to row a boat, drift by the shore, climb the pinnacles, explore the forests, seek out wildflowers, and "come to feel that blue jewel as a living presence, to greet it in the morning, to watch its sunset moods."[25]

Holtz, Bemis, and Eaton were informed amateurs who, with some guidance, set out to explore mountain wilderness that had recently become accessible by new trails and unpaved auto roads. And they had certain civilized tastes. After a day on horseback, invigorated, chilled, perhaps terrified once or twice, Holtz and Bemis appreciated a roof over their heads, a crackling fire, a good book, a clean bed. On a pack trip, Eaton could sleep on balsam boughs; but he prized his pneumatic mattress and admitted to seeing his fellow mountaineers back at the hotel newsstand. Unembarrassed, these authors recognized their own needs for both civilized and primeval ways of being. "The longing to traverse those wild and picturesque regions intensifies the longer [one] lives in the centres of civilisation amid the artificial environment of a modern life," noted Holtz and Bemis."[26]

At the Blackfoot reservation east of Glacier National Park, Holtz and Bemis felt privileged to witness some sacred ceremonies. But as they watched through an occasional cloud of dust in the hot July sunshine, their senses registering color, movement, chanting, drumming, smoke, and fire, they seem to have resisted the spell. "The Red man's way is not the White man's way," they noted. "The Red man is slowly passing." And among the details of what they saw and heard was one tentative interpretation. In the medicine man's bundle they thought they detected something universal, the essence of all religions: "only the blind groping of the human soul for something super-human to lean upon, only a cry from the weak to the strong, only the reaching of the finite toward the Great Infinite."[27]

Eaton paid those Native Americans a writer's compliment: if they had in fact named Going-to-the-Sun Mountain, then they were true poets. In *Skyline Camps* he also slipped in a few poems of his own, including a salute to the trees at timberline, those "prophets of the world's advance" who died with their dreams intact.[28] Written in free verse, Eaton's "Timber Line" recalls Enos Mills's thoughts in prose. And that is no coincidence, for Eaton had several of Mills's books, which he prized and "read often." What Eaton found especially appealing in Mills's writing was a vivid sense of place that could come only from intimate knowledge and affection. In 1918, in a tribute to the interpreters of particular places— Muir, Mills, Emerson, Thoreau, Sarah Orne Jewett, Horace Kephart (in the southern Appalachians), Brander Matthews (in Manhattan), and others—Eaton noted that they had in common the urge to interpret

This scene, Blackfeet Indian Camp at Cut Banks, *is found in* Glacier National Park: Its Trails and Treasures, *by Mathilde E. Holtz and Katharine I. Bemis (1917). Among their tales of adventure, the authors touch on natural history and human history—the art, religion, and way of life of the native people. (Photographer unknown.)*

the "soul" of a place.[29] Such a place was often—although not always—home, a humanized, fairly civilized domain.

The opposite impulse also intrigued Eaton—the urge to get away from civilization and climb to the silence of high places, build a fire, camp out, maybe hear a lone coyote's howl, and get to the state of being where "this thing we call Civilization is less than the shadow of a dream."[30] Writing about both kinds of exploration—on home grounds and in faraway wild places—Eaton earned for himself a place among the interpreters he admired. He also helped to locate and secure small sections of the Appalachian Trail, a scheme that his college friend Benton MacKaye set in motion. But that takes us east across the continent and back a few decades in time.

***

On August 4, 1897, in the village of Shirley, Massachusetts, Benton Mac-Kaye and two friends set off on their bicycles for the White Mountains of New Hampshire. Ten days later, leaving Passaconaway House to wade through the Swift River and head north to the highest peaks, MacKaye was at last on the brink of wilderness—a land "undisturbed by civilization in any form," so he was told. The whole journey, exhausting and exhilarating, lasted until early September. And in the journal that Mac-Kaye kept, some details stand out—a sunrise, a sunset, the boots filled with rainwater that leaked through a shanty's roof, the treacherous "blowdowns" of trees and debris along the trail, the hikers scruffy in the eyes of the smartly dressed tourists at the mountain inns.[31] Writing to family and friends, MacKaye dramatized these details. But there was also another drama unfolding, among layers of civilization and wilderness.

That summer of 1897, after his freshman year at Harvard, MacKaye did not yet perceive this drama. Nor, apparently, did one of his fellow hikers, James Sturgis Pray, eight years his senior yet still an undergraduate. Pray, who had had to drop out of college for a few years because of poor health, was preparing to enter the then little-known field of landscape architecture. MacKaye had not yet settled on a career in forestry. Open to new experiences, not yet analytical, MacKaye simply recorded details along the journey, from the long-settled village of Shirley (where he had lived off and on since age nine and where Pray's family had a summer home) through the back roads of rural New Hampshire to the Northeast's highest peaks. He noted a few punctured bicycle tires, rank roads, abandoned houses, deserted villages, the "edifying manufacturing town" of Harrisville, a lumber camp with its own railroad, a farmhouse turned into a hotel, a barn dance to the music of an organ grinder, and Crawford House—an entrée to the Presidential Range—where the men in tuxedos and women in pink and white dresses were horrified to see the hikers devour quadruple portions at dinner. At one point the hikers totaled five, including Pray's father, who had arrived at Crawford House unexpectedly by train.[32]

These details suggest a region in transition, from an agricultural and small-scale industrial economy to one that was beginning to depend on a blend of logging, tourism, and some accommodation of the old and the new, the civilized and the wild. And in this light, MacKaye's seemingly random notes are revealing. In the northern forests, on a sled drawn by four horses, he noted, loggers were bringing down the mountainside three or four logs at a time, each one about fifty feet long; and these men worked in the wilderness, from 6:30 A.M. until 6 P.M., all year long. In a village on Lake Winnipesaukee, Pray persuaded a tailor to sew up the holes in his trousers for the sum of 25 cents. Intent on roughing it and perhaps to save money, the hikers slept in barns, washed up the next morning in a bucket of water, and managed one ride on a ferry up Lake Winnipesaukee after MacKaye sawed wood for the ferrymen. Benton probably *had* to economize, for his brother Percy noted that all the MacKaye boys worked their way through college.[33] Still, this was merely a summer jaunt for the hikers. The ferryman, the tailor, and the logger were eking out a living.

The next scene of the unfolding drama was Jackson Park, along Lake Michigan in Chicago, where Benton MacKaye stood on the afternoon of July 25, 1914. As one of Gifford Pinchot's early recruits, MacKaye had entered the Forest Service in 1905 with a master's degree in forestry from Harvard; later he had taken time off to teach there. Now, based in the Washington, D.C., office of the Forest Service, he was visiting Chicago and searching for the site of a structure at the World's Columbian Exposition in 1893. That structure, the Spectatorium, was the dream of his late father, Steele MacKaye, the well-known actor and playwright. It would have contained a vast spectacle—a kind of Cinerama with real people, real water, and real ships—to dramatize the coming of Christopher Columbus. Steele MacKaye had raised the bulk of the funds needed, but his structure was torn down when it was only half built, the victim of graft and corruption. Then his strenuous efforts to salvage the scheme and escape financial ruin weakened his already strained system. He died in February 1894, leaving his widow and five children, including four-teen-year-old Benton. Just weeks before his death, he had written to Benton, revealing pride in his son and offering some fatherly advice. Life was a battle; it demanded certain qualities, including courage, persever-ance, patience, integrity, and a just and generous consideration of the rights of others.[34]

Now, on that July afternoon in 1914, a mature Benton MacKaye gazed upon the site of the Spectatorium, a weedy vacant lot with an oak tree at one end and a dump at the other. He assumed that a land speculator was keeping that valuable site undeveloped. A few hundred yards away, thou-sands of people in bathing suits crowded the beach. A few miles beyond were the steel mills of South Chicago, where twenty smokestacks poured out black clouds that streamed across the prairie, blocking the sun. And as he looked squarely at the scene in front of him, from foreground bathers to background smoke, MacKaye detected a "silent drama" under way. In this "diagram of play and work and commercialism in America" he recognized a weak attempt to reach Heaven and success in achieving Hell.[35]

Later, when MacKay was back in Washington and out in the nation's forests, his concern for workers—especially loggers—led him to con-ceive of permanent settlements rather than "gypsy" logging camps for seasoned loggers and perhaps some returning veterans of Europe's Great War. But the U.S. Forest Service could not justify these studies in hous-ing and community. In 1918, then, MacKaye was transferred to the U.S. Labor Department, where he became a specialist in "land colonization" and produced such studies as his ambitious *Employment and Natural Resources* (1919). In that document he recommended settlements on ag-ricultural and forest lands, including "farm colonies" linked with urban markets. His superiors, including President Wilson, were interested; but no action was taken.[36]

This detour from the Appalachian Mountains gives a glimpse of the mind of Benton MacKaye. Like many children of celebrated parents, he felt the burden of trying to measure up to his father's (and older brothers') achievements.[37] He could not, like Steele MacKaye, be the first American to play Hamlet in London.[38] But he could appreciate his father's ability to visualize a scene, a drama, then try to do likewise in his own work of forestry and regional planning. If, as Benton believed, Steele MacKaye had viewed the theater as a "focusing lens," or telescope, to give people new perspectives on their lives, so Benton could try something comparable, to "focus the people's vision" on the forces—economic, social, environmental—that were quietly, relentlessly shaping their lives.[39]

MacKaye's research on the role of forests in protecting watersheds, along with lessons learned earlier from his revered geology professors Nathaniel S. Shaler and William Morris Davis, led him to visualize forces in nature—running water, glaciers—as they obeyed the laws of gravity. He could then visualize the forces in modern, industrial, commercial America as one vast glacier—a metropolitan "invasion"—moving relentlessly (and against gravity!) from coastal and riverside cities into the hinterland, overcoming all in its path. To ward off this invasion—or at least keep it at bay—and thereby preserve an indigenous, locally rooted way of life, MacKaye envisioned some counterforce of primeval and indigenous, rural, community-centered America. The natural stronghold of this counterforce would be the most primeval land—in the East, the spine and flanks of the great Appalachian Mountain system, literally and figuratively the source of all the water and wealth of natural resources that flowed eventually down to the great cities along the rivers and by the sea. Force and counterforce, one great glacier balanced against another: that was the big picture, the vision, presented in MacKaye's philosophical work of regional planning, *The New Exploration* (1928).[40]

A key element in that vision was the Appalachian Trail; and MacKaye is widely known as its "father," although some segments of the trail, in the North and the South, had been blazed years earlier.[41] Whether the idea of the Appalachian Trail first dawned on him during his White Mountain sojourn of 1897, in the Green Mountains with his college friend Horace Hildreth in 1900 (ten years before Vermont's Long Trail came into being), or on some other trek, MacKaye could not recall many years later.[42] But whatever sparked the idea, the sudden death of his wife of six years, Jessie Hardy MacKaye, in April 1921, may have been a blow that urged him on. Jessie, or Betty, as she was known to her many friends, was a prominent suffragist and an advisory board member of the Women's Peace Society. She also had a history of devastating nervous breakdowns. MacKaye viewed her apparent suicide by drowning as her release and his unutterable loss. (They had no children.) "Our ideas upon life were identical and we were wonderfully happy together," he wrote to a friend in May.[43] He wrote to many friends that dark spring. Then in October, his plan for the Appalachian Trail was in print.

Published in the *Journal of the American Institute of Architects,* in October 1921, MacKaye's "Appalachian Trail" is an ambitious scheme for a continuous skyline trail between two peaks: Mount Mitchell in North Carolina, the highest east of the Rockies, and Mount Washington in New Hampshire, the highest in the Northeast. The 1921 scheme also encompasses branch trails to Maine, Canada, Georgia, the Great Lakes, and the eastern seaboard, along with the rural settlements—or "community camps"—that MacKaye had proposed while working for the U.S. Labor Department. To visualize this vast sweep of land, MacKaye presents a giant, his head in the clouds, his feet firmly planted on a mountain ridge. This giant sees what humans may not see so clearly: the tensions and "economic scramble" of modern life; smoky, beehive cities; mental disease, "the most terrible, usually, of any disease"; health and recuperation; wild lands as retreats; community camps and shelters; and care of the countryside—"something to be dramatized."[44]

To bring his scheme closer to reality, MacKaye points to segments of the proposed Appalachian Trail that are already in place, created and maintained by the volunteers of the Appalachian Mountain Club, the Green Mountain Club, and other groups. And implicit in MacKaye's scheme is the work of still more volunteers, willing to come together to plan, blaze, clear, and maintain certain trails that would make up portions of the magnificent whole. (The initial idea was for a continuous trail well over a thousand miles long; today it runs through fourteen states and covers some 2,100 miles.)

Early on, MacKaye's scheme attracted the interest and support of many friends and colleagues. Gifford Pinchot wrote that he was "greatly interested." Aldo Leopold, writing of wilderness issues, asked MacKaye about his "sky line trail." Arthur C. Comey, of the New England Trail Conference; Raymond H. Torrey, of the New York–New Jersey Trail Conference; Walter Prichard Eaton, of the Berkshire Trails Association; Allen Chamberlain, of the Appalachian Mountain Club (AMC); and James Sturgis Pray, then chairman of Harvard's school of landscape architec-

When Benton MacKaye introduced his plan for an Appalachian Trail in 1921, he noted that some sections of the trail already existed. This signpost, bearing monograms of the Appalachian Trail and the Appalachian Mountain Club, indicates trails from the Old Jackson Road to the summits of Mount Washington and other peaks in the White Mountains of New Hampshire.

ture and longtime AMC member, were colleagues in the physical planning stages, while Clarence Stein was MacKaye's collaborator on broad strategies. Stein was also a leader in the Regional Planning Association of America (RPAA, established in 1923). Later Lewis Mumford recalled that the Appalachian Trail was a "social bond" among his fellow RPAA members, whose backgrounds and tastes were predominantly urban; and that MacKaye would not let them forget "the geological and biological foundations upon which our entire civilization rests."[45]

Mumford, who helped MacKaye sort out his ideas and express them in writing, knew his friend's strong points—MacKaye's social instincts and the broad base of sciences beneath his castles in the sky. In the early 1920s, the Appalachian Trail (A.T.) was still only one of those phantom castles. But as it gradually came into being through the work of many volunteers and regional leaders, the trail's rationale became more clearly recreational; it was not, as MacKaye originally envisioned, part of a larger plan for camping, housing, forestry, farming, and rural community building. As realized, the A.T. also had more to do with the appreciation of scenery than with scientific inquiry. Perhaps some kind of shift in priorities was inevitable, for once the A.T. was adopted and promoted by regional groups of volunteers, it could never be the child of one man. Rather, it would take on a life of its own, through the efforts of the RPAA, the Appalachian Trail Conference (ATC, established in 1925), and many regional hiking clubs. By 1923 the New York–New Jersey Trail Conference had completed the first new segment of the A.T. Its chairman, William A. Welch, designed the A.T. monogram.[46] Later the Potomac Appalachian Trail Club, founded in 1927 in Washington, D.C., became a center of power and influence under Myron H. Avery, the club's first president. A longtime ATC chairman, Avery is often given credit for reviving the A.T. scheme after a loss of momentum in late 1925.[47]

Meanwhile, as MacKaye gave more time to publicizing the Appalachian Trail, he elaborated on a hint he had tossed out in 1922. Reporting on the A.T.'s progress that year, MacKaye mentioned the idea of a handbook for the student or amateur scientist "in quest of truth as well as skyline," whose interests might lie in geology, botany, ornithology, human geography, or the study of natural resources.[48]

In "Outdoor Culture" (1927) and "Wilderness Ways" (1929), MacKaye considered the broader implications of trails—not only the A.T., the "backbone" of his planning strategy, but also branch trails and ones parallel to the A.T., such as the trail he and others were in the process of clearing, closer to Boston.[49] In these essays MacKaye referred to Mumford, Leopold, Walter Prichard Eaton, and others who shared his environmental values and influenced his thinking. He also conceived of the harmonious civilization as one balanced among primeval wild lands, rural communities, and truly urbane cities. This notion would later influence the thinking of three modernist landscape architects, Garrett Eckbo, Dan Kiley, and James Rose.[50] But another of MacKaye's notions, grounded in the earth and life sciences, was less immediately useful to designers. He wanted to visualize the story hidden in the forest—the "evolution of the primeval home of all living beings," traceable from sometime in the last glacial epoch, to lichens, aquatic plants, and the tallest hardwoods and conifers of the forest. "Here is the ultimate pursuit of the real camper: to unfold the story of evolution on the out-of-doors horizon," he concluded.[51]

From the late 1920s onward, MacKaye's efforts to publicize and shape the Appalachian Trail can be traced to this enduring quest to read the story of the earth. He wanted to read that story (and have others read it) while immersed in the sights, sounds, smells, and aura of the wild, untroubled by the blasts of a car's horn, by Broadway tunes over the radio, or any other trappings of modern industrial society. Unfortunately, that quest led to MacKaye's clash with the ATC chairman, Myron H. Avery.

Avery, the first person to walk the entire Appalachian Trail—in segments, during the 1920s and 1930s—chaired the Appalachian Trail Conference from 1930 through 1952. A skillful organizer based in Washington, D.C., and a tireless worker in the field, Avery insisted that the A.T. be well maintained, well marked, and uninterrupted, "practically endless."[52] In 1935 he and MacKaye had a falling out over the proposed Skyline Drive in Virginia; but their differences ran even deeper. MacKaye asserted that a skyline drive for autos was incompatible with a skyline trail for hikers. Avery was willing to make some accommodations to political realities and Americans' fondness for the automobile. MacKaye insisted that "wilderness, not continuity, is the vital point."[53] Avery countered that the East had no more true wilderness; more important was the need to complete a "connected footway, cleared, and marked, through the wooded, scenic sections of our mountains nearest to the Coast, and stretching the length of the Coast."[54]

By then, of course, the A.T. was no longer one man's dream. It was many people's hard-won reality, nearly completed, imbued with their views and values.[55] Still, MacKaye spoke about the "earth drama" of plant and animal life when he addressed the Seventh Appalachian Trail Conference in June 1935 at Skyland, Virginia, in Shenandoah National Park. He also urged that group to defend the A.T. as a "realm of primeval influence."[56] And he was not alone; among other ATC members, Raymond H. Torrey, Harold C. Anderson, and Harvey Broome backed him.[57] In the mid-1930s they also joined him in supporting a new national organization to defend primeval lands—the Wilderness Society. That society was also the product of several minds and subtly different points of view.[58] Among its founders, MacKaye was perhaps the least tolerant of the sights and sounds of a mechanized civilization—along the A.T. or in any wilderness area.

Often compared with Thoreau, MacKaye is less often recognized as the persevering, introspective son of an outgoing and illustrious father. In "The Appalachian Trail: A Guide to the Study of Nature" (1932), for instance, with maps, charts, sections, panoramas, and text, Benton tried yet again to live up to some approximation of his father's dramatic vision. For Benton MacKaye, forester, regional planner, hiker, and perennial student of earth and life sciences, there was nothing quite like the "primeval drama" of wild lands. And so he outlined an epic of the earth: the birth of a river, the erosion and uplift of land, the genesis of the forest, climatic forest succession, and communities of plant and animal life. The science was fairly elementary, nothing novel, except that for MacKaye it represented the next step in developing the Appalachian Trail: "One more pursuit to get acquainted with scenery: to trace the genesis of primeval life— and know that when the vital spark lights up in you it belongs not to you but to the ages."[59]

FOUR

San Francisco Bay Area

"Nature Controlled by Art"

"We who know California think it the most glorious of lands," wrote the Berkeley poet Charles Keeler in 1907. "The winds of freedom blow across its lofty mountains and expansive plains. There is something untamed and elemental about its wildernesses, and a tender charm about its pastoral valleys."[1] Four years later, a visiting professor of philosophy from Harvard appealed to this same sense of regional pride as he led his Berkeley audience to reflect on their experiences of nature beyond the campus. "When you escape, as you love to do, to your forests and your Sierras, I am sure again that you do not feel you made them, or that they were made for you," asserted George Santayana. "In their non-human beauty and peace they stir the sub-human depths and the super-human possibilities of your own spirit. . . . They allow you, in one happy moment, at once to play and to worship, to take yourselves simply, humbly, for what you are, and to salute the wild, indifferent, noncensorious infinity of nature."[2]

Despite their common themes of freedom and wildness, the poet's and the philosopher's immediate agendas were different. Keeler was indicating the habitats of the birds he was about to introduce to general readers. Santayana was questioning not only an excessively human-centered view of nature but also a pervasive philosophical tradition in the Western world, traces of which we have already seen in Charles Eliot's assumption about landscape—that "the scenery of the earth was made for man, not man for scenery."[3] Eliot's views of landscape would have a long life, particularly among landscape architects on the East Coast. But the San Francisco Bay Area—that land "on the edge of the world," where Santayana momentarily forgot he was in America—seemed to offer a chance for other views of landscape to develop and other philosophical traditions to evolve.[4]

This was a place and time when no professional turf had yet been staked out by landscape architects and foresters. In fact, their professions were still barely recognized in most regions of America; in the San Francisco Bay Area, the first professional degree programs in those fields would not be established until 1913, at the University of California at Berkeley.[5] It seems appropriate, then, to consider Bay Area landscapes of the early twentieth century from a range of perspectives, not necessarily professional ones.

Here we will look at landscapes first as habitats for birds and humans, later as scenery and psychological conditioning at San Francisco's Panama-Pacific International Exposition of 1915. The glimpse of habitats will seem a bit freer, more open to the elements, less weighed down by ideas and abstractions. In contrast, the exposition carried a great deal of cultural baggage. It was meant primarily to celebrate the completion of the Panama Canal. It also signaled San Francisco's recovery from the devastating earthquake and fire of 1906. And although destined to disappear, like all previous expositions, this temporary display of architecture and the allied arts was intended to claim for San Francisco a more permanent role among the great cities of the world—as the "Paris of America," perhaps, or as the culmination of the "westward march of civilization." The war in Europe, triggered by the assassination of Austria-Hungary's Archduke Franz Ferdinand in Sarajevo on June 28, 1914, cast shadows over that westward march. Yet it did not keep individuals, businesses, and governmental organizations from France, Germany, England, Italy, and several other European nations from participating in the Panama-Pacific Exposition. In the end, the war posed yet another layer of meaning for that "phantom kingdom" by the shores of San Francisco Bay.[6]

***

Early one morning in midwinter, when the tide was low along the eastern shore of the bay, Charles Keeler paused to take in the whole panorama before him. At his feet were mudflats, "black, slimy, and oozing from the receding tide." A few miles to the south was the city of Oakland. To the east was sloping ground that rolled and swelled toward the base of the Berkeley Hills. To the northwest across the bay rose Mount Tamalpais and the headlands of Marin County. Across the bay to the west, some seven or eight miles distant and barely visible through the mist, was a long, thin line on the horizon—San Francisco.[7]

For us to imagine that midwinter scene on some unspecified day in the late 1890s, it takes some effort. From the East Bay of our own time we must not only eliminate all the freeways and most of the population, for Oakland, Alameda, and Berkeley together had only about 100,000 people around 1900;[8] we must also take away the bridges across the bay and the Golden Gate, visualize many more ferryboats and vessels under sail, and, of course, extract the fill and structures from countless acres along the shore. Only then can we begin to see what Keeler saw, a vast and variable habitat for sandpipers, curlews, California clapper rails, killdeer plovers, red phalaropes, Pacific black-throated loons, tule wrens, short-eared owls, and other birds, including the gulls that hovered about the distant ferries, darting and swooping for handouts.

At first Keeler's attention is on small things: tiny bubbling fountains that give away the hiding places of clams, and little crabs left in pools as the tide recedes. As dawn gives way to stronger morning light, he notices the white breasts of sandpipers flashing in the sun. Moving always in flocks, the sandpipers are dainty and quick, detecting their meals in the tiny marine life of the mudflats. Less gregarious is the ungainly California clapper rail, lurking in the marsh grass and swamp weeds. The grace-

ACROSS THE CONTINENT

ful red phalaropes, congregating in pools and inlets of the bay, have a habit that delights and mystifies Keeler. "Every now and then, while swimming about, they will stop and whirl around in the water several times, almost as if revolving upon a pivot."[9]

As the hours slip by, the tide begins to turn, then comes lapping back to shore. Other swimming, wading, and soaring birds catch Keeler's attention. He is impressed by their silence. But when they alight on something edible, larger birds such as the gulls will squawk and croak, attracting more of their kind to join in the fray, wings fluttering. "What a host of birds haunt the shores of this great bay," Keeler writes, "each with habits and life of its own, yet how little do the multitudes of men who cross and recross the water know or care about them!"[10] He does not mention "ecotones," a more recent concept of life on the borderlands between ecosystems; yet he recognizes the streaked horned larks and Bryant's sparrows as land birds when he sees them in the salt marshes and bay-shore fields.

There, in places that people commonly think of as wastelands (not yet dignified by the term "wetlands"), Keeler detects some traces of prehistoric life—birds that seem to be relics of evolution, the "march of progress." And he is led to reflect on migration, the birds' mysterious impulse that might be linked with ancestral memories of the last ice age, or perhaps simply with the struggle for existence that birds share with all other forms of life on this earth. Keeler does not go so far as to suggest that humans should pity the birds in their struggle or help them by preserving all their marshy, muddy habitats. His appeal is both broader and more specific: he would like his readers to get to know and love the birds, to develop a sympathy with the "universal life which is throbbing about us," and then try to stop the slaughter of birds by human beings.

When birds perish in a storm, however, Keeler is intrigued. One dark day he goes out to the Cliff House in San Francisco, overlooking the Pacific, and arrives before a winter storm has let up. As waves thunder in and salt spray stings his face, he patrols the beach, looking for the bodies of birds that have just succumbed to the gale. They are not hard to find: the Brandt's cormorant, the western grebe, several kinds of scoter, the

Pacific fulmar petrel (a small relative of the albatross), and other lifeless creatures among the strands of kelp and limp jellyfish. Some would find this work depressing, but for Keeler it is exciting—the clash of the elements and the thrill of discovery, coming across an uncommon bird such as the rhinoceros auklet, which recalls to him some distant geological epoch. At such moments, Keeler the Berkeley poet seems to be overtaken by Keeler the naturalist with an office at the California Academy of Sciences in San Francisco.

Born in Milwaukee in 1871, Keeler grew up in the Wisconsin countryside, source of many fond memories that surface in his writings. In 1887 his family moved to Berkeley, where he attended Berkeley High School and the University of California. Around 1891, apparently on the basis of his wildlife studies and his fieldwork for the U.S. Department of Agriculture, Keeler was named director of the natural history museum of the California Academy of Sciences. In 1893, the year he married, the academy published his monograph *The Evolution of the Colors of North American Land Birds.* A year later his first book of poetry appeared, *A Light through the Storm,* its title taken from a painting of the same title by the Bay Area artist William Keith. These facts indicate Keeler's concurrent interests in both the sciences and the arts, during a time when men were not always obliged to choose between them. Nor did his wife, Louise Mapes Keeler, have to choose one field of endeavor for a lifetime. Having studied entomology at the University of California in Berkeley, she went on to study painting with Keith, and later illustrated some of her husband's books.[11]

Keeler's memoirs of friends such as William Keith, John Muir, and the author/editor Charles Fletcher Lummis would have earned him at least a footnote in history.[12] But he is probably best remembered for his friendship with the brilliant, idiosyncratic, and lovable Bay Area architect Bernard Maybeck, designer of the most widely appreciated structures at the Panama-Pacific International Exposition in 1915. Keeler's contributions are much easier to overlook: poetry that has not stood the test of time; ornithological studies so genial and so accessible to general readers that they may not command the attention of scientists in our time; and a small book, *The Simple Home* (1904), of a fairly broad scope yet addressed mainly to the needs and aspirations of Californians, particularly in the Bay Area. Perhaps Keeler's real significance for our time is still to be uncovered, like a furtive bird to be flushed out of the marshes—or like a gem embedded in one of his poems:

Delve, Science, deeply 'mid thy heaven-sent soul,
And clasp eternally the sacred whole.[13]

Poets may no longer address Science in rhyming couplets. But how many scientists are able to grasp the whole of something and then give it back to the rest of us in a form we can understand? This is what Keeler, at his best, can do. He not only points out curious or mysterious creatures in a familiar environment; he also lets us smell them and hear them, then see connections—between a bird's nest and a human dwelling, for instance. From his "aerie" in the Berkeley Hills, a brown-shingled, steeply gabled home designed by Maybeck, Keeler could look west toward the ferries and gulls and the steamers slipping through the Golden Gate. He could also look about him. In the gardens and secluded canyons of Berkeley and among the live oaks on the hillsides were more habitats of birds, some singing only at dawn and dusk, others during the day or night, offering melodies that Keeler set down in musical form. He found that one tiny bird, the rufous hummer, created the most delicate of nests, "a marvel of a home," perfectly concealed and deftly constructed of thistledown, moss, lichen, bits of bark, and cobwebs. To him, the whole domestic life of this little hummer was proof of "so much of intelligence and passion—so much that we fondly claim as human."[14]

In a book intended to promote the attractions of life in the Bay Area, Keeler pondered the appeal of Berkeley, by 1902 no longer a rural village but a growing town of some 14,000 people. He could not say whether its charm lay in the vine-covered cottages and their masses of flowers, in the splendid views of mountains and bay, or in the people the university was attracting. But he believed that Berkeley's homes were becoming simpler, more artistic.[15] Two years later, in *The Simple Home,* Keeler set out to reinforce that trend, offering guidelines from the point of view of the layman in architecture. A founder of a local Ruskin Club and, with his wife, a maker of furniture for sale, Keeler was very much a part of the Arts and Crafts movement, then on the rise in Britain and America. In houses he hoped to see local materials used in a truthful, straightforward manner, with unpainted surfaces and ornament derived from the forms of animals and plants, not from books of architectural detail. "We must *live* art before we can create it," he insisted, without departing from Arts and Crafts ideals.[16] But he went further, writing of art in the garden.

Ideally, Keeler wrote, the entire home would seem open to the sun and air, hospitable to friends, to the sounds of birds out in the shrubbery, and to sounds of human voices indoors. Ideally the garden would be "nature controlled by art." Yet wild nature would sometimes appear to have the upper hand in this garden—much more so than in gardens by leading Arts and Crafts designers in Britain, such as Gertrude Jekyll and Sir Edwin Lutyens, whose collaborative works can hardly be imagined without some combination of finely crafted walls, walks, staircases, terraces, pools, pergolas, clipped hedges, and exquisitely maintained lawns.[17] Thinking of the small, irregular lots on rough, sloping ground in the Berkeley Hills and mindful, too, of the modest means of most homeowners there, Keeler proposed a compromise between "natural" and formal gardening: "a compromise in which the carefully studied plan is concealed by a touch of careless grace that makes it appear as if nature had unconsciously made bowers and paths and sheltering hedges."[18]

But Keeler's ideal garden could not, in the end, appear truly natural and wild. Given the many microclimates of California—most of them receptive to a vast range of plant species and varieties from the Mediterranean, South Africa, Australia, Japan, China, and elsewhere—he would not deny his readers the chance to mingle exotics among the native shrubs (manzanita, madrone, wild currant, and others) and wildflowers (shooting star, California poppy, and many more). He suggested sequences of exotics that would offer continuous bloom throughout the year. Taking hints from the gardening traditions of Italy and Japan, a California homeowner could then make of the garden a livable place, a habitat, loosely defined by hedges, walls, and trellises and furnished with rustic tables and benches. Such were Keeler's recommendations, reflecting the layman's point of view. In the end, he encouraged people to make the most of their gardens, "studying them as an art,—the extension of architecture into the domain of life and light."[19]

Interestingly, Keeler did not suggest that a homeowner seek out an artist to design the garden. It seems that the homeowner himself or her-

Eucalyptus and other exotics mingle with native species here in the Berkeley Hills, looking south toward Sather Tower, on the University of California campus. The sloping roof of a house by Bernard Maybeck is barely visible in the foreground— a residential area about as wild as Maybeck's friend Charles Keeler could have desired.

self was to take on that role, which would be a pleasure and a work of love in a simple, rustic environment. But the house was another matter, something too complex, too sacred to leave to builders and realtors. Rather, Keeler advised, let those who were to live in a new house engage an artist to sift through their ideas and make of them an artistic whole. He named no artist's names, but *The Simple Home* contained illustrations of Berkeley houses by Ernest Coxhead, A. C. Schweinfurth, and Bernard Maybeck; and the book was dedicated to Maybeck.

***

"Dad has never had the proper reverence for money," observed Wallen Maybeck, on accepting the American Institute of Architects' gold medal for his father in 1951.[20] Nor did the gold medalist Bernard Maybeck have much faith in systems, rules, and what most people called "logic." Having spent four years as a student at the Ecole des Beaux-Arts in Paris in the 1880s, he had been exposed to systematic ways of thinking and working, along with the rational French mind and a range of French architectural theories. Those years of study would be very useful to him for the rest of his long professional life. Yet Maybeck was not a representative product of that school or of any other, for whatever he took in had to be filtered, mysteriously, through his own heart and brain. What he gave back, in the end, would be architecture with some evocation of the life within, something of soul or spirit. As he said to a visiting architect and a colleague or two late in life, "That is the essence of architecture, gentlemen: Spirit."[21]

His biographer Kenneth Cardwell noted that Maybeck's concern for the spiritual and emotional qualities of architecture was balanced by a pragmatic concern for function.[22] To foresee people's movement through volumes of space—to anticipate what they would do and how they would feel—was infinitely more important to Maybeck than that the Corinthian column be so many diameters tall or that Greek ornament be detected on an essentially Roman structure. He was also an inventor of a reversible seat for railway cars, a tinkerer who later experimented with materials and flexible, demountable structures. Here our interest lies with Maybeck the designer of landscapes and buildings as a continuum, working with plants both on his own and with the aid of a friend, the landscape gardener John McLaren.

Born in New York City in 1862 of German-born parents, Maybeck grew up in New York, in an environment where he was encouraged to think for himself and take part in discussions of art, politics, and philosophy. His paternal grandfather was a German master builder and his father a cabinetmaker and woodcarver who had also studied sculpture. Music, drawing, watercolor painting, the writings of German Transcendentalists and of Emerson, their counterpart in America, all formed part of Maybeck's intellectual and spiritual sustenance. Later, as a student in Paris in the 1880s, he chanced to hear voices singing in the Church of Saint-Germain-des-Prés; and suddenly they revealed to him the power of architecture and music combined. Then, too, in the Paris atelier, or design office, of Jules-Louis André, where H. H. Richardson had studied decades earlier, Maybeck learned about the power of architecture and landscape combined.

Years later, then a leading Bay Area architect living in the Berkeley Hills, Maybeck quoted the late professor André in a booklet for the local Hillside Club, around 1906–7: "In laying out a landscape, never take away what there is. Group with it what you add to it. This is the fundamental law of landscape architecture."[23] The booklet continued with an outline of hillside opportunities and cautions, apparently written down by Maybeck's wife, Annie, at his direction. Remarkably concise, the text stated not only what to do and what not to do but why. It began with natural forces working on natural materials: water flowing down from the hills, molding them; hillside trees holding the soil and breaking the wind through the canyons; and irregularities of the ground, calling not for gridded streets but for roads following the contours. There, lots would be irregular, not subject to arbitrary cut and fill but used as is, perhaps by stepping the building masses up the hill. Ideally, with houses built in groups at varying distances from the road, each could retain a view yet remain invisible to the others.

Both privacy and community could be found in this hillside habitat. Berkeley's climate—wet mild winters, relatively cool dry summers, bright or hazy sunshine, periods of dense fog—called for roofs pitched to shed rain, not snow, and for windows to let the sunlight stream in. Materials should be natural, the color of rocks. Building masses should "hug the hill" so as to blend in among the carefully preserved trees—especially those that had survived fires and floods. To achieve "long, restful lines" of vegetation across property lines, neighbors might get together to plan for "big quiet masses" of a single plant species that could spread along banks and terraces. In the end, two professions were one: "Hillside architecture is landscape gardening around a few rooms for use in case of rain—dining porch on the southeast, a play court on the east and an observation porch on the west; room to move and breathe."

Although this Hillside Club booklet was unsigned, Maybeck has long been considered its author and Annie the amanuensis.[24] More recently, scholars have illuminated the wider context for the ideas it contains. Dimitri Shipounoff has traced the origins of the Hillside Club to a group of North Berkeley women who got together in 1898 to try to protect their natural environment from insensitive new development, for houses were already spreading farther beyond the Berkeley campus, over the summer-brown grassy hills and into the thickly wooded canyons. Four years later, in 1902, the women reorganized their club to include men; and Charles Keeler served as the club's president from 1903 through 1905. In passing, Diane Harris has identified Annie Maybeck as one of the club's founding members; but Harris's main concern was to investigate Bernard Maybeck's work in the landscape, documenting where possible the projects on which he formally consulted with his friend John McLaren.[25]

In the early 1900s McLaren was a household name in San Francisco, mainly because of his achievements at Golden Gate Park. Appointed assistant superintendent in 1887, he became the park's fifth and longest-serving superintendent in 1890. The first was the civil engineer William Hammond Hall, who in 1870 had set out to create the park on an unpromising portion of sand dunes and windswept ground, against the advice of Frederick Law Olmsted. During the first few years, Hall made a remarkably good start, but the park then declined during a decade of political and financial instability. Hired at an auspicious moment,

McLaren made the most of his opportunities there. In time, so highly esteemed and widely loved was this Scottish horticulturist that when he reached the mandatory retirement age of seventy, in 1916, the citizens of San Francisco petitioned the city's board of supervisors to change the law. The upshot was that McLaren remained superintendent of the 1,017-acre Golden Gate Park for over half a century, until he died at his home in the park's lodge, in 1943.[26]

Born in 1846, near Stirling Castle in Scotland, McLaren learned about gardening mainly by working at country places near Edinburgh, but also through studies in Edinburgh's Royal Botanical Gardens. After emigrating to America around 1870, he made his way from New York—by ship, by train across the Isthmus of Panama, and again by ship—to San Francisco. He then found work south of the city, in the Peninsula, as a gardener at some of the large country places. Accustomed to opulence in gardens, McLaren nevertheless remained free of pretensions. "He was, first and foremost, a working-man," explains the Golden Gate Park historian Raymond H. Clary, with colorful stories to back up his belief that McLaren "knew and recognized the working-man and gave him credit for his work."[27] It is not surprising, then, to turn to a 1924 edition of McLaren's *Gardening in California* (first published in 1908) and find planting plans for lots as small as 25 feet by 120 feet, along with lots progressively larger, to ten-acre tracts. What is striking is not the range of lot sizes—by then a familiar offering of books on architecture and gardening—but the endearing, expansive spirit between the lines. Clearly McLaren loved to roam freely in "Nature's gardens," then return with fresh ideas to be adapted for the gardens he designed in the city, suburb, and countryside.[28]

Like some late-eighteenth-century British gardening writers—most notably the amateurs Richard Payne Knight and Sir Uvedale Price—McLaren gracefully defers to the models he finds in the wild.[29] "In some of the untouched virgin spots in Nature's garden there are scenes more soft and more beautiful than anything our gardening has yet produced," he writes. Rather than assert his own professional competence to tell us what to look for, however, McLaren invites us to go out on our own, like a painter (or like the eighteenth-century amateur), and seek our own clues for design in natural forests, meadows, and riversides. One might imitate the harmonious ways of Nature first by sketching, then by taking careful measurements of the distance between trees, say, or the width of a grassy bay running through a forest. All these clues could be plotted on a sketch map and later laid out to scale. While this process may seem a bit mechanical, the inspiration behind it is full of life: "There are numerous instances of such spots in our redwood forests and in the Sierras," McLaren observes. "Some of the sweetest landscapes are to be found in these mountain meadows. . . ."[30] There, where others might gaze upward at peaks and waterfalls, McLaren would not miss the riches at his feet: the wildflowers, ferns, and grasses.

Like Keeler, McLaren savors the traces of wild nature in a garden yet does not limit himself to native plants. More than half of McLaren's *Gardening in California* is an annotated catalogue of trees, shrubs, climbers, bulbs, and herbaceous and bedding plants, many of them exotic. Generally he recommends plants that should thrive in a particular setting and fulfill some aesthetic or functional purpose: native hollies (*Heteromeles arbutifolia*) or the exotic olive (*Olea europaea*) for a rocky ridge or hillside; native oaks for long life and a rugged, picturesque character; for scarlet color in the small garden, the exotic *Eucalyptus ficifolia;* for a windbreak, the *Eucalyptus globulus* or the native Monterey cypress and pine; and for accents in ponds and water gardens—the subjects of the most dreamlike black-and-white photographs in his book—a blend of native and exotic water lilies. Water is often the most prominent feature in any landscape, wild or cultivated. But McLaren knows that in summer-dry California, where most grasses naturally turn brown between April and October, the simplest pool or creek or fountain can please the eye and quench one's thirst. His suggestions are often based on such a blend of beauty and utility. On balance, though, they seem weighted toward beauty, the lovely, satisfying scene.

✳✳✳

To paint the Golden Gate and Black Point, the artist chose a spot looking northwest across the bay from the lower slopes of Russian Hill. The slopes are uneven, broken here and there by scrubby gray-green plants, a few buildings, a few shaggy eucalyptus. It may be early summer, for some grass is still green; some has turned golden brown, among patches of burnt ochre and a light burnt sienna—almost salmon. The sky is pale blue, reflected in the deeper blue-green of the bay. In the middle distance are shoreland and shallow waters. On the horizon, all colors pale in atmospheric perspective.

A small reproduction of this painting by Sutton Palmer appears in Mary Austin's book *California: The Land of the Sun* (1914). The image introduces her chapter on the wildlife farther inland and upstream, in the Central Valley. Yet Austin identifies the painting's subject as the site of the future Panama-Pacific Exposition.[31] The painting thus has documentary value, particularly in its delicate coloring and its image of serenity, suggesting a temporary truce between wild nature and human habitation. In contrast, the exposition's official black-and-white photographs depict this site as a dreary place, apparently useless until filled and graded for human occupation. Hence the exposition photographers' focus on men inspecting the "hydraulic fill" and on equipment used to grade the fill for the Machinery Palace.[32]

The Machinery Palace would soon command the exposition's east–west axis, looking westward to the Palace of Fine Arts. In turn, the domain of Fine Arts would look back east, across a buffer of water, land, and vegetation, toward a city of courtyards, domes, and the prominent Machinery Palace. This opposition of machinery and art, of a westward, progressive, future-oriented stance and an eastward, wistful, historically minded stance, was no doubt intended as a symbolic statement. Virtually every piece of sculpture, every mural, every piece of architectural ornament carried a message, to be found somewhere among the exposition's many guidebooks if not inscribed nearby. Not all these messages could be heard in unison; but overall they made up a resounding chorus that proclaimed the westward march of progress, of civilization, of "Primitive Man," "The American Pioneer," "The Pioneer Mother" (with children), "The Adventurous Bowman," "The Fountain of Energy," several versions of "Electricity," and many more human embodiments of the forceful, progressive spirit that had achieved, among other things, the excavation and construction of the Panama Canal.

At that time artists in San Francisco, as elsewhere in the United States and abroad, were sometimes ambivalent about all this material progress, this energetic exploitation of the earth's natural resources, including its people. If many artists involved with the Panama-Pacific Exposition looked back in history for mythological subjects and classical forms rather than to the forms of diesel engines or hydroelectric dams, the words "conservative" and "nostalgic" still do not account for some feelings that may have entered into their work. Consider the piece titled *Earth*, by the San Francisco–born New York sculptor Robert I. Aitken. Is this female form actually "slumbering," as generally reported, or is her upraised arm bent in a feeble attempt to ward off blows? Or consider one of the most popular works at the fair, *The End of the Trail*, by the Minnesota-born New York sculptor James Earle Fraser. Anyone could see that both the Indian and his horse, depicted in agonizing detail, were exhausted. They are no longer "equal" to their task, observed one critic. The Indian is a representative of a "dying race," observed another. Fraser's own interpretation may be lost to history, for he and other visual artists conveyed some messages only implicitly, not primarily in words.[33]

And yet works such as *The Victorious Spirit*, a mural by the San Francisco painter Arthur Mathews, could be read literally. Mathews, the only California artist among the muralists, created for the lunette over the main doorway of the Court of Palms an image of a winged angel defending a nude youth and others from a muscular fellow on horseback who represented "the spirit of materialism." The message is clear, and it may run deep into the city's (and America's) past, with memories of the gold rush and the forty-niners, or of the San Francisco earthquake of April 18, 1906, which left the city hall in ruins, its toppled, poorly laid walls a monument to the $7 million wasted in "notorious graft."[34] Visitors could probe their own memories. The painter and critic Eugen Neuhaus tried to steer them away from literal meanings toward the art's sensuous, aesthetic qualities. Still, the serious visitors pressed on, determined to pierce the mystery of things such as those female figures high up above

Maybeck's colonnade, peering into large boxes. "It is probably the most serious exposition ever known," noted the author of one guidebook.[35]

The exposition's works of art and their messages, along with McKim, Mead, and White's Court of the Universe, Carrère and Hastings's Tower of Jewels, and other spectacles, all formed part of the cultural context for Maybeck's and McLaren's work on the Palace of Fine Arts. Another context was the building site. Did Maybeck and McLaren at first see it as serene and harmonious in its magnificent natural setting, the way Sutton Palmer painted it, or dreary, as in the official photographs? Perhaps the site seemed to lie between these extremes, flawed yet open to possibilities. Willis Polk, the architect originally assigned to the Palace of Fine Arts, was "glum" about the site. As the architectural historian Sally Woodbridge has explained, Polk thought the water-filled bog the worst building site on the exposition grounds.[36] Yet a contemporary of Maybeck asserted that the Palace of Fine Arts had "the finest natural setting on the Exposition grounds." What Polk had resented, Maybeck (then working temporarily in Polk's office) found promising: "a small natural lake and a fine group of Monterey cypress."[37]

To elicit design ideas for the Palace of Fine Arts, Polk held a competition in his office and Maybeck's was declared the finest scheme. The exposition's architectural board agreed. The scheme, a haunting vision of a rotunda rising from a placid lagoon, backed by a semicircular colonnade that stood half in shadow, half revealed in light, drew high praise, especially from Henry Bacon, architect of the exposition's Court of the Four Seasons. (Later Bacon designed the Lincoln Memorial in Washington.) The story of how Maybeck, the architectural draftsman, and McLaren, the exposition's landscape engineer, worked together to create from the shallow bog a dreamlike scene of Roman grandeur tinged with Grecian delicacy (but without clear precedent and notorious for its "incorrect" architectural detail) has often been told. Here we will look more closely at Maybeck's own intentions for the Fine Arts Palace, as set down in his pamphlet *Palace of Fine Arts and Lagoon* (1915).[38]

After Polk publicly credited Maybeck for his scheme and gave him the commission to get it built, Maybeck paid a visit to John Trask, director of the exposition's Division of Fine Arts. Trask requested a "gradual transition" from the excitement of the exposition to the serenity of the art galleries. Maybeck and McLaren then worked out the details for this transition, to be expressed in land forms, water, waterfowl, vegetation, and the temporary structures that were finished in the imitation travertine used throughout the fair. All this Maybeck could have explained in his pamphlet. He could also have told how, if funds had been available, vegetation would have grown high up in the colonnade's boxes, or caskets, as if sprouting from a ruin; and how tall willows would have screened the rotunda on the east. Instead, Maybeck described this work "from the psychological point of view." He had observed that an art gallery was a "sad and serious business," its melancholy relieved by and mingled with the beauty of the works of art. His task, then, was to find the forms of architecture and gardening that would best induce a mood for contemplating the gallery's works of art.

The precedents Maybeck cited are well known: a late-nineteenth-century painting, *Isle of the Dead,* by Arnold Böcklin, which Maybeck and his wife had seen in a Munich art gallery; eighteenth-century engravings of Roman ruins by Piranesi; architectural details from ancient Rome; and other artifacts. Historians have tended to bypass one object at the fair itself, however, which Maybeck thought appropriate as a kind of frontispiece to the exposition's art gallery: a marble sculpture, *The Muse Finding the Head of Orpheus,* placed under an acacia tree near Maybeck's peristyle. This work by the sculptor John Berge led Trask to compose eight lines of verse, ending,

> Man praises man's accomplishment with brazen throat;
> Beauty alone can charm with one low note.[39]

Were Trask and Maybeck thinking of the role of Orpheus in Greek mythology? Or, like Neuhaus, did they see Berge's sculpture mainly as a study in lights and shadows, fixed form and fleeting impressions, all helping to set the mood, or "psychological conditioning," of the scene? In any case, the legend of Orpheus was remarkably apt. Orpheus, the god who tried to bring his wife, Eurydice, back from the dead, and failed, was also Apollo's son, the youth who sang and played the lyre so artfully that "the savage beasts came running to listen and even trees would follow him."[40] In the hands of Orpheus, then, nature was somewhat controlled by art. Berge could have represented Orpheus singing or playing, as victorious as any winged angel or American pioneer. But he chose a somber moment, after Orpheus had been torn to pieces, reputedly by Thracian women who were jealous of his love for Eurydice. Berge's Orpheus lay as a beautiful ruin, then, like Maybeck's vision of the rotunda and colonnade, like some buildings of war-torn Europe, like some of Europe's finest young men on the battlefields.

The organizers of the exposition could have canceled or postponed it when war broke out in Europe in 1914, but they chose not to. Through diplomacy they first persuaded government officials of France, then those of other nations, to participate in this international exposition, after all; for in doing so, they would be reaffirming their high morale and, in a sense, reciprocating for humanitarian aid received during the war.[41]

When Maybeck's scheme for the Palace of Fine Arts was accepted in 1913, he could hardly have known that his scene of ruined classical buildings, reflected in a lagoon where swans glided by in silence, would take on new layers of meaning before the fair closed, toward the end of 1915. But could he have intended some mute commentary on the vanity of human ambitions or a civilization's rise and fall? Was he simply providing a young, fairly raw city with an image of venerable age? Or was he offering a respite from the relentless westward march of civilization? Years later he did suggest that the deteriorating rotunda (which the citizens of San Francisco had not allowed to be torn down) could be entirely surrounded by redwoods, and as the redwoods grew, the rotunda could crumble at about the same speed.[42] Instead, after Maybeck's death in 1957, a wealthy San Franciscan and others had the rotunda and colonnade rebuilt in permanent materials.[43]

Maybeck's willingness to let his and McLaren's lovely evocation of a

The Palace of Fine Arts, with its Rotunda and Peristyle, was one of the most pop-ular attractions of the Panama-Pacific International Exposition of 1915 in San Francisco. Bernard Maybeck and John McLaren managed to make the original temporary structures appear ancient and overgrown. In the 1960s the structures were rebuilt in permanent materials, as shown here.

ruin succumb to natural processes recalls Jens Jensen's similar inclina-tion not to preserve a garden, mentioned in chapter 2. Perhaps Maybeck and Jensen were wary of a certain hubris on the part of civilized human beings. Clearly they welcomed traces of wildness that might mingle with and finally overtake their work. Not long before the Palace of Fine Arts was built, Maybeck had explained to the Chicago architect William Gray Purcell his distrust for "intellectual machinery" and systems of applied logic. "Architecture is the imprint of a greater logic of Man and Nature which no smart brain can take apart and make simpler," Maybeck had insisted.[44] Jensen might not put it that way, but there may be a gleam of truth here that he would appreciate. In any event, he and Maybeck had in common the practice of what we now call landscape architecture. Or rather, Maybeck was an architect who, somewhat like Keeler's land birds at the bay shore, could occupy the edge, or ecotone, between two professions.

McLaren, who spent years planning to supply trees, shrubs, and flowers for the 1915 exposition and who devised its ingenious walls of South African ice plant (*Mesembryanthemum*), earned high praise from many sources. Frank M. Todd, the fair's chronicler, saw McLaren's gardening as "an essential and inseparable part of the Exposition picture." Todd even hinted that perhaps no other feature of "the enchanting scene" gave more pleasure to the people.[45] Maybeck said as much to another writer—that it was the water and the trees that had really delighted the public at the Palace of Fine Arts, not the architecture.[46] In a twisted cypress that McLaren had placed alone against Maybeck's colonnade John D. Barry sensed "the insight and the feeling of an artist."[47] Still, McLaren was regularly praised as a gardener and engineer, not as a landscape architect or artist. No trifle about terms, this issue of professional identity would haunt some designers for many years. But for McLaren and Maybeck it did not seem to be an issue.

Concluding his pamphlet on the Palace of Fine Arts, Maybeck invited readers to think of the exposition as an "expression of future California." He did not specify in what way, exactly. His colleague Jules Guérin, chief of color at the fair, had drawn inspiration from the hues of California's wildflowers, summer-brown hills, golden oranges, and blue sea.[48] Mary Austin, too, responded to those rich hues as well as to the distinctive forms of the land. A member of the fair's Pageantry Commission, she considered the entire fair a kind of "pageant of things": not something final and complete, but a procession, ongoing.[49] Like Austin, Maybeck offered no grand, final statement about the fair. And yet, despite the many contributions from around the nation and the world, he detected in the fair an expression of "the life of the people of California" and trusted that "the future city of California will have the same general feeling, because it will be a California city."[50] What feeling? some might ask. Maybeck did not elaborate. He simply alluded to a humanized landscape that would be distinctive, reflecting the land and the life of the people.

In time a regional tradition of architecture, sensitive to land and landscape, grew from the work of Maybeck and a few colleagues.[51] Diverse in form and setting, the best of that work had in common with Maybeck's work a certain inventiveness, a free spirit, perhaps even a trace of "something untamed and elemental," as Keeler put it, recalling California's wild lands.

ACROSS THE CONTINENT

FIVE

Around New York & Boston

Traces of Wildness, Lost and Found

One of the wildest places that Mariana Griswold Van Rensselaer ever described was not a primeval wilderness. It had a "savage simplicity" not yet altered by the plow, but flocks of sheep had once grazed thereabouts. Now the sheep were gone and there were no trees in sight. Aware that people considered this place "a bit of sandy wilderness isolated in a wilderness of waves," Van Rensselaer looked around more closely. It was September 1888, and she gazed eastward over Nantucket Island, its flat and gently swelling land dotted with ponds but covered mainly by wind-stunted asters, goldenrods, purple Gerardias, and other plants running wild. "Seldom in civilized regions are we swayed by such a sense of breadth, vastness, freedom and the spontaneous action of elemental forces," she wrote.[1]

With these words Van Rensselaer suggested a relation between civilization and wildness—an overlap or coexistence. The region of the Atlantic coast from her native New York to Boston was by then fairly civilized. In fact, the pressures of urban development from those two cities alone would go far to explain the influx of tourists that had been bringing new prosperity to Nantucket's shores since the mid-1870s. Earlier in the century, with the decline of whaling and sheep raising, the island had been steadily losing population. Earlier still, as Van Rensselaer learned from local records, the island had contained uplands, meadows, and woods. But by the end of the eighteenth century, Nantucket's woods had been so depleted that islanders had to import their firewood from the mainland of Cape Cod. Piecing together these observations of past and present, Van Rensselaer predicted that market gardens would one day thrive on the island, given the nature of the soils, adequate manure, and increasing tourism. "But the time to see Nantucket is before this day arrives," she noted—that is, before the vast tracts of wildflowers and low undergrowth of Hudsonia, bearberry, and broom crowberry yielded to the tilled fields of grain and produce that tourism would justify.

Writing about Nantucket, Van Rensselaer did not discuss the emerging art of landscape architecture—or "landscape gardening," the term she preferred. In any case, the island's windswept, fairly flat land offered none of the scenic beauty to which landscape architects usually aspired. But Van Rensselaer, who had a summer place on the mainland not far from Nantucket, on the western shore of Buzzard's Bay, was accustomed to flat and gently rolling land. She liked to ride along narrow, grass-grown roads, their deep, sandy ruts long since formed by vehicles like hers—the local black-hooded one-horse buggy with an unusually wide axle. Her views might be limited by pine groves, and the boughs of deciduous trees might arch over the road. But out in the open, colorful roadside wildflowers could appear as "accents" among the broad effects of nearby salt marshes and vast skies.[2] The conventional scenic beauty of hills and valleys, mountains and wooded ravines was of course absent. For fine scenery, artfully shaped so as to appear almost natural, she would turn to Olmsted and Vaux's work in Central Park, New York; Holm Lea, the suburban country place of Charles Sprague Sargent in Brookline, Massachusetts; or the Arnold Arboretum, Sargent's lifework in nearby Jamaica Plain.

In *Art Out-of-Doors* (1893) Van Rensselaer praised Sargent's country place without mentioning its name. She noted that the owner, a man of artistic vision and wide botanical knowledge, had created a comfortable, convenient, and civilized residence on undulating ground, varied by woods, lawns, shrubberies, and an artificial pond. Although the beauty of the place was "almost altogether artificial," it seemed natural. All was harmonious, composed as if by a landscape painter, with breadth, repose, simplicity, fitness, variety, and unity, while not a single flower with jarring color marred the scene.[3]

Three decades later, Van Rensselaer wrote that Sargent's country place had become even more beautiful over time, with new plantations of mountain laurel along the edge of a woodland. Updating her *Art Out-of-Doors* in 1925, she noted that other landscapes were also changing as more people drove automobiles, new national parks and state forests were established, the numbers and professional stature of landscape architects rose, new schools and programs in landscape architecture appeared, and people had increasingly more leisure time.[4] We know from the many garden and shelter magazines in the 1920s that some leisure time was spent in gardening and the sorts of rural improvements that Van Rensselaer discussed in *Art Out-of-Doors*.[5] But in this case, one person's leisurely pursuit was another's profession; and if anyone at that time could bridge the widening gap between amateurs and professionals in the out-of-doors, it was Mariana Griswold Van Rensselaer, one of the earliest of the very few honorary members of the American Society of Landscape Architects (ASLA, established 1899). Her compact, unillustrated, yet engaging little book turned up year after year on the list of required reading for an introductory course in landscape design at Harvard.[6] And it remained on that list even after the appearance in 1917 of a hefty, well-illustrated textbook written by a professor of landscape architecture at Harvard and the librarian of Harvard's School of Landscape Architecture.

Professor Henry Vincent Hubbard and Theodora Kimball compiled their *Introduction to the Study of Landscape Design* as a comprehensive text for students intent on becoming professional designers; and in this work they noted that Van Rensselaer's book was "written to stimulate a more general appreciation of the landscape art."[7] In 1925 Van Rensselaer returned the favor, citing Hubbard and Kimball's text as "the most important of its kind," without a rival, and useful for both aspiring artists in the out-of-doors and general readers.[8]

Because much of Hubbard and Kimball's text reads like an analytical treatise on taste, style, composition, and materials in landscape design, the rare personal glimpses are refreshing. In one passage, a pack train emerges from the manzanita and deerbrush into a Sequoia grove in the California Sierra. The sun has passed behind a ridge to the west, yet the upper branches of the giant sequoias remain in sunlight. These trees inspire awe.

> . . . you feel a sense at the same time of your own utter insignificance and yet of your being a part of a vast, solemn, ordered, and inevitable scheme. . . . After your camp is set and your supper under way, you sit and smoke and watch the long shadows of the outstanding groups of taller pines stretch across the meadow, and the smoke of your fire make a level film across the open as the first gentle cold drift of evening wind from the snows carries it down the valley.[9]

Could this possibly be a woman's voice? In one biographical sketch, Theodora Kimball (who later married Hubbard, in 1924) was said to find "her chief recreation in outdoor life." But she was drawn to "old English and the New England countrysides."[10] More likely it was Professor Hubbard who wrote of camping in the Sierra. As he told his classmates on the twenty-fifth anniversary of their graduation from Harvard (class of 1897), "For real recreation I have departed to the woods whenever I could get away—two summers in Newfoundland, one in northern Canada, two in the Sierras, and a certain amount of snowshoeing and hiking for shorter trips, in Maine and elsewhere."[11] Notes of Hubbard's outdoor adventures also surfaced in other reports to classmates, as he touched on the merits of travel by canoe versus travel by mule. A member of the Laurel Brook Club (for Boston-area fishing enthusiasts), Hubbard served as the club's president from 1929 to 1940; and one colleague considered him an "unexcelled" fisherman.[12]

Knowing something of how a prominent landscape architect such as Hubbard spent his leisure time gives a new perspective on his professional work—as a professor, as president of the ASLA, and as coauthor of a textbook that remained a kind of bible at least until the 1950s, when the modern movement could no longer be ignored. That text reminds us of the accelerating rates at which wild lands were disappearing by 1917, "before the blind destructive forces of man's enterprise." Now we realize that one of the two authors not only took photographs of scenery in the national parks, used them as plates in the book, and mulled over the consequences of losing all that natural beauty. He also sought out places of less striking beauty, summer after summer, making his way on foot, by canoe, on the back of a horse or a mule, intent on absorbing whatever "unhampered expressions of nature's forces" he could detect in the wild.[13]

In the 1930s, one of Hubbard's sharpest critics was one of his students at Harvard, Garrett Eckbo, then a Young Turk and rising modernist. Reared in the San Francisco Bay Area and accustomed to the artificiality of the terraced and irrigated gardens there and in the drier Los Angeles region, where he had worked, Eckbo was irked by Hubbard's preoccupation with naturalistic design and scenery. He also questioned whether the imitation of nature's expression was really a "higher art" than frankly artificial work. "Why is nature more perfect than man?" Eckbo scribbled in his copy of Hubbard's and Kimball's text.[14] The question could hardly be answered, so far apart were the professor's and the student's sensibilities and experiences in life. Eckbo associated wild landscape with Boy Scout camping trips in Marin County, California—always in the rain, as he recalled. "I was never a nature boy; I was always fascinated by design which could only be expressed by construction," Eckbo explained.[15] To Hubbard, wild landscape was precious; and as a landscape architect he felt a responsibility to preserve it for the recreation and inspiration of future generations.

Clearly, in Hubbard's work the elder Olmsted's influence remained strong. He and Kimball reproduced Olmsted's plans, cited his reports, and upheld his values. But Jack London and Thoreau, as well, may have informed their views on wild nature. "Man is himself only one manifestation of the powers which give form and substance also to animals, to trees, to mountains," Hubbard and Kimball wrote. "It is not remarkable, then, that even modern city-bred men should find something in wild nature which seems to fulfill and complete their being." Perhaps not everyone needed contact with wild nature, however; the two authors assumed that a life spent out-of-doors, not necessarily in the wilderness, would suffice for some. But modern city dwellers did need some relief from an artificial environment. "And such men as have any ability to feel their kinship with the outdoor world must get from nature more than this simple relief from physical oppression," Hubbard and Kimball insisted. "They must have the opportunity of allowing their imagination to lose itself in the infinitely complicated, magnificent, and ordered whole of which they are a part, and the glory of which is their rightful heritage."[16] Olmsted had said as much in his report on Yosemite and Big Tree Grove.[17] Thoreau had intimated as much in an often-misquoted line, ". . . in Wildness is the preservation of the World."[18]

This is not the place to explore what Thoreau meant by "wildness"— the sense of being alive, the state of not being subdued by human beings, and other meanings found in the source of that line, Thoreau's essay "Walking," of 1862. Here our concern is to recognize that Thoreau's idiosyncratic ideas might have informed the work of one second-generation Olmstedian, Hubbard, a partner in the Olmsted Brothers office from the 1920s onward and a mediator between civilization and the wild.

Born in Taunton, Massachusetts, in 1875, Henry Vincent Hubbard entered Harvard in 1893, several years before a professional degree in landscape architecture was offered there. And so, like Charles Eliot, the younger Frederick Law Olmsted, Arthur Shurcliff, James Sturgis Pray, and other aspiring young landscape architects in Boston around that time, Hubbard took special courses at Harvard's Bussey Institution (where agriculture and horticulture were taught) and at Harvard's Lawrence Scientific School (for architecture, civil engineering, and geology). He also spent a year studying architecture at the Massachusetts Institute of Technology before entering the new degree program in landscape architecture at Harvard, begun in 1900–1901. Already well prepared, he received the first degree awarded in that program, the S.B. in Landscape Architecture, in 1901, then entered the Olmsted Brothers office in Brookline.[19]

Organized by the younger Olmsted, with assistance from Shurcliff and the guidance of professors such as the geologist Nathaniel S. Shaler and the architect Herbert Langford Warren, Harvard's program in landscape architecture may have been similar to what students might piece together at any of the major land-grant institutions around the country. What made the program at Harvard a landmark effort was the determination of President Charles W. Eliot, Dean Shaler, and the younger Olmsted to institutionalize and professionalize the field of landscape architecture. For this they needed to establish a professional degree, along with a specialized body of knowledge that could be considered essential for professional practice.

The details of the degree program have been explained elsewhere.[20] Here it is important to realize that the scope of arts and sciences considered essential for a solid foundation in landscape architecture was broad, encompassing fine arts, architecture, aesthetics, and freehand drawing, as well as geology, botany, horticulture, forestry, and civil engineering. Drawing upon statements by the elder Olmsted and his young partner Charles Eliot, both President Eliot and the younger Olmsted considered landscape architecture a fine art embodying important social purposes. In 1911 Eliot, then president emeritus, reassured a gathering of landscape architects in Boston that "all worthy art contributes to the pursuit of happiness, that is, to the pursuit of durable joys and satisfactions; and the profession you practise, gentlemen, is an art, and a fine art."[21] Three years later he outlined the environmental and social purposes of this art:

> The profession of landscape architecture is going to be—indeed, it already is—the most direct professional contributor to the improvement of the human environment in the twentieth century, because it is devoted not only to the improvement of housing and of town and city designing, but also to the creation, preservation, and enlargement of opportunities for

human enjoyment of mountains and valleys, hills and plains, forests and flowers, ponds and watercourses, spring blossoms and autumn tints, and the wild life of birds and other animals in their natural haunts. These are the things that city dwellers need to have opportunities to see and enjoy.[22]

This linking of art, environment, and social purpose, traceable to the writings of John Ruskin and William Morris, was fundamental to the Olmstedian landscape architect's practice. In 1910 Henry Vincent Hubbard asserted that people now recognized a need for beauty in the humanized landscape—not as a luxury but as a "practical necessity."[23] In 1917, asserting the need to preserve both wild lands and naturalistic landscapes as a respite for city dwellers, he and Kimball referred to a paper by the elder Olmsted, "The Justifying Value of a Public Park" (1880), reprinted in 1902. There Olmsted considered how people had used land for recreation over centuries, through their casual access to European gardens, groves, and the woodlands managed by foresters and gamekeepers, at a time when cities were small and outlying lands extensive. By the mid–nineteenth century, with the rapid growth of cities in Europe and America, these ad hoc arrangements had become inadequate. Then the "Genius of Civilization" rose up and called for certain broad open spaces, called "parks." Why? Olmsted paused to suggest the powerful ways in which the scenery of mountains, forests, meadows, and brooks can work on people's sensibilities. He then linked urban growth, habits, and the stresses of urban life with the "self-preserving instinct of civilization" to call for parks.[24]

If in 1880 Olmsted could plausibly link the growth of cities with the need for parks, that need could hardly have lessened during the decades of rapid urban growth that followed. Then, too, his idea of parks as artfully crafted, naturalistic "scenery" rather than as random collections of museums, zoos, aviaries, restaurants, promenades and carriage drives, ball fields, playgrounds, skating rinks, rose gardens, and more, was something that landscape architects still defended in the early twentieth century—particularly whenever a new feature for New York's Central Park was proposed.[25] Landscape architects at that time tended not to question these notions handed down from the elder Olmsted and Charles Eliot. With the coming of the automobile, however, along with the expansion of cities into metropolitan areas and the increasing complexity of urban life, the desire for parks and reservations in a wilder environment, farther from the city, seems to have grown more intense for some people—certainly for Hubbard, who admitted as much in his communications to college classmates. But how much of his desire to heed the call of the wild did this exceedingly reticent man share with his colleagues—those at Harvard and those in the design firm that he maintained from 1906 to 1918, Pray, Hubbard, and White?

Henry P. White, Harvard class of 1899, was the architect whose evocative drawings of gardens and landscapes appear in Hubbard and Kimball's textbook of 1917. We know more about James Sturgis Pray, who would have graduated in 1895 if not for the illness that forced him to leave school. After working for a few years in his father's trading company in Boston and South Africa, Pray returned to Harvard, graduated in 1898, then entered the Olmsted Brothers office. A year earlier, as we have seen, he had hiked in the White Mountains of New Hampshire with young Benton MacKaye. By then, judging by entries in MacKaye's journal, Pray was probably already a member of the Appalachian Mountain Club (AMC, established 1876), which predated the Sierra Club by sixteen years.[26] The AMC's members were easterners who would have been generally sympathetic to Muir and his values—J. C. Olmsted, F. L. Olmsted Jr., and other colleagues of Pray.

In the 1890s Charles Eliot had secured the support of some of his fellow AMC members when he first set out to organize the Trustees of Public Reservations and, later, the Metropolitan Park Commission in Boston. Together these two organizations, with varying powers and jurisdictions, were responsible for acquiring, maintaining, and opening up to the public both historic country places and "wild lands."[27] Young Pray was probably familiar with these organizations and perhaps even acquainted with some of the prominent AMC members who had helped Eliot bring them into being. But it's unlikely that he would join the AMC merely to move in circles of power and influence. Pray was a serious hiker and a conscientious volunteer. In 1902–4, while working at the Olmsted Brothers office and teaching at Harvard, he also took on the demanding role of AMC "councillor for improvements." That role often required him to be in the White Mountains for a month or more during the summers, to inspect existing trails, lay out new trails, and supervise the necessary repairs and clearings. His annual reports to the AMC were succinct and modest, giving other volunteers their due while touching only briefly, objectively, on his own work.[28]

At first glance, there seems to be no connection among Pray's professional and amateur interests: hiking and trail blazing in the White Mountains, teaching and writing about Renaissance and Baroque gardens in Italy, and developing courses in city planning. But there is in fact a connection: Pray was intrigued by networks of communication—trails, paths, roads, avenues—in both wild and civilized places.[29]

Assuming that one important purpose of the Appalachian Mountain Club was to make the scenery of the White Mountains accessible to the public by "well-chosen routes," Pray argued that the club should focus on through trails (analogous to trunk lines of a railroad) and encourage local interest groups to maintain branch trails. He also proposed a system of paths—some broad and graded, some merely rough trails, but all of them reasonably well marked. He would not omit painted blazes or trail markers merely to maintain a sense of remoteness from civilization. As he wrote MacKaye, who was heading for the Presidential Range of the White Mountains in the summer of 1902, men had gone astray and perished up there. Urging MacKaye to hire a local guide, Pray then offered the kind of advice that might not surface in a classroom or in print: ". . . the Great Spirit of the Forest is always close to him who has learned to know and adjust himself to the laws of the Forest."[30]

Were such thoughts ever shared with students? From Pray's course record books we know what he had his students read for an introduction to landscape architecture: the writings of the elder Olmsted, Charles Eliot, and Mrs. Van Rensselaer, along with selections from George Santayana's *Sense of Beauty* (1896), John C. Van Dyke's *Nature for Its Own Sake* (1898), John Muir's *Our National Parks* (1901), Shaler's *Man and the*

Earth (1905), and other works. Pray also recommended Gifford Pinchot's *Primer of Forestry* (1903) and tested students on the terms and practices of forestry.[31] But we may never know if Pray mentioned his own wilderness experiences when he taught. Similarly, we may never know how widely Hubbard's feeling for wild lands was shared. As his colleague Bremer Pond noted, "Any activity or professional work was never allowed to interfere with [Hubbard's] teaching schedule, nor was their existence intimated in any way to his students, although this latter habit was probably due to his extreme reserve as well as to his dislike of talking about what he himself had done."[32]

As professionals, Hubbard and Pray wrote and spoke publicly in ways that were clear, purposeful, socially responsible, but not personally revealing. Whether indoors or out under an open sky, they might pursue what Theodore Roosevelt called "the strenuous life."[33] But as teachers and professionals in the early twentieth century, they did not stray far beyond the fairly wide professional territory staked out by the Olmsteds and Charles Eliot. When circumstances changed—when America's entry into World War I called for new kinds of housing and planning, when postwar landscape architecture students wanted to be planners as well as designers—Pray and Hubbard could still be recognized in the vanguard, as planners and forward-looking educators. What they did not look forward to, however, was modernism in art, architecture, and city planning. Their motivations could be as deeply ingrained as their Puritan ancestry, or idiosyncratic, traceable to temperament and a taste for wild lands.

***

"It is humiliating, but perhaps salutary, to realize that most of us need to have our eyes opened to our daily surroundings," wrote Beatrix Farrand in 1918. "We may think we know every stick and stone of a certain stretch of road or a familiar view, but we are actually quite unobservant. . . . Until a comparatively few years ago we took the whole wild growth of our woodlands for granted."[34] A native New Yorker, born in 1872, Farrand was acknowledging a debt that she and her colleagues owed to the Arnold Arboretum, near Boston. The arboretum's few hundred acres contained a large scientific collection of trees and shrubs, both native and exotic. Laid out with assistance from the elder Olmsted and planted under the supervision of its director, Charles Sprague Sargent, the arboretum was also a work of art, a "museum of trees," she noted. On one unaltered hillside in the arboretum, hemlock and ferns still grew wild. There and elsewhere on the grounds, Farrand had learned how to use plants intelligently and artfully—by learning the plants' natural habits of growth and the "surroundings in which they are happy."

This article of 1918 was a double tribute, to the arboretum and to its director, who, with Mrs. Sargent, had welcomed the young Beatrix to his home in the 1890s so that she could learn about landscape gardening there and at the arboretum.[35] Details of Farrand's life are well known: the European travels with her mother, her aunt Edith Wharton, and others in the extended family; her pioneering status as a woman in a gentleman's field and as a founding member of the ASLA; her designs for elegant gardens—at Dumbarton Oaks, in Washington, D.C.; at The Eyrie, on a bluff above Seal Harbor, Maine; and elsewhere.[36] But what may come as a surprise is Farrand's attention, in 1918, to common plants growing by the roadside and at our doorsteps.

Another native New Yorker, the garden writer and novelist Mabel Osgood Wright, recommended common plants, native and naturalized, for the perennial borders of fairly modest gardens such as her own in Fairfield, Connecticut. Wright told readers how to find those plants "in their haunts" in different seasons, by a stream, in a bog, along the roadside, or by the railroad tracks. Born in 1859, she had known such haunts in southwestern Connecticut since childhood, as summertime alternatives to the brick row house on West 11th Street where she and her family lived in spring, fall, and winter. Her autobiography offers few precise dates; but Tom, who did odd jobs for her family and lived in MacDougal Alley, remembered the tract before West 11th Street was laid out, when it was still part of a farm, with a nearby frog pond and a brook, Minetta Water, that never ran dry.[37]

Wright tells little of her urban front yard, with its tall trees and the wisteria that hung from three-story wrought-iron balconies. Dwelling instead on street cries, markets, childhood games, and her father's books and friends, she gives glimpses of New York in transition from small city to metropolis. One elderly woman used to come down West 11th Street leading her dog cart and calling for "swill," or compostable garbage, to bring back to the squatter farmers who had settled north and west of 42nd Street. Wright recalls a walk down Fifth Avenue with her father, a minister, and the elderly poet and journalist William Cullen Bryant around 1878; looking into Central Park, Bryant predicted that the "spirit of the Park's loveliness" would fade once buildings of eight or possibly ten stories rose up around it on all sides. On another occasion, Wright went by rail with her aunt and uncle to the Bronx, where they dined on frogs' legs at a rustic little Hermitage on the bank of what later became the Bronx River Parkway. By 1930 the elderly Mabel Osgood Wright could appreciate the parkway's beauty and grandeur and its river, curbed, harnessed, and embellished with "just-so" shrubs. Yet she seemed to miss the "wilful, sometimes dancing, sometimes sluggish sleepy stream." She liked to remember its banks sown with the seeds of wildflowers and sweet gum burrs, back in the days when, somehow evading the mounted police, local boys went skinny dipping and caught frogs for the proprietor of the old Hermitage restaurant.[38]

At such moments the carefully reared, very feminine Mabel Osgood Wright has something in common with the somewhat irreverent Charles M. Skinner, who longs to have a home in the unnamed village of his fathers but for the time being must live in a small row house built on coarse fill somewhere in New York. He must also find space for clotheslines, coleus, and pelargoniums in a tin-can-littered backyard, 18 feet by 50. In *Nature in a City Yard* (1897), Skinner may stretch the truth a bit in describing the repulsive neighbor's child who can do no wrong because someone in his family is related to a policeman. Skinner's lists of insects and four-legged creatures inhabiting the backyard represent traces of wildness he could probably live without—and yet he knows that the sky above, the distant fields, and the "striving spirit that animates all things" are what will keep him sane. He keeps on striving, then, for something beyond mere utility—food, a house—as he oscillates between gritty humor and ethereal dreams.[39]

***

To John C. Van Dyke, the question of whether it was more desirable to live in the city or in the country was academic; the fact was, a great many people did live in the city, and more were arriving daily. In *The New New York* (1909) he first approached the nation's largest city from a distance, as if on the deck of a ship heading north through the Upper Bay, at a point where the Brooklyn Bridge had come into view and the skyscrapers of lower Manhattan converged like faraway mountain peaks. From there, seen through a blue mist, New York was as beautiful as Constantinople in its configuration of water and land, and in the way its soaring points (skyscrapers rather than minarets) picked up the light. Yet the resemblance was superficial. Whereas Constantinople appeared enchanting, a dream city, Van Dyke knew that New York was real, its office towers, bridges, tunnels, and subways suited to the needs and purposes of its people. And to New Yorkers who apologized for their lack of Old World cathedrals and campaniles he gave a new criterion of beauty to consider: "a new sublimity that lies in majesty of mass, in aspiring lines against the upper sky, in the brilliancy of color, in the mystery of fields of shadow . . . above all in the suggested power and energy of New York life."[40]

Van Dyke looked upon New York and the desert with the same penetrating gaze. On a hot day in July he studied sunlight on the facade of a skyscraper as he would the light on canyon walls of the Colorado. He detected changes in the city's air, from the cold blue haze of winter to a warm, harmonizing silver-gray atmosphere in early spring, one that seemed to emanate from the rivers, the harbors, the moist ground, the dew. He saw that spring came earlier to the city than to the countryside; even the stems of the maples had a reddish aura about the tips a few days sooner in New York than in his native New Jersey. And the Flatiron Building became a barometer, indicating the degree of humidity in the air by the quantity of its enveloping gray mist.

As in the desert, Van Dyke moved from aesthetic impressions to small, revealing details of the city's land, plants, people, and their assertive individuality. He traced the clear October light to Atlantic Coast sunshine and a prohibition against the burning of soft coal within the city limits. He denounced the poverty and filth of the Lower East Side (without, however, the compassion of the photographer and journalist Jacob Riis, whose work among the tenements he cited).[41] In fact, Van Dyke showed more sympathy for Native Americans of the Southwest than for European immigrants in New York. The more he penetrated the city, the more he was struck by both poverty and the sheer abundance of things. In the opulent, crowded interiors of some houses he sensed a yearning for happiness through possessions, the "nervous energy of business New York," a lack of repose. And all seemed impermanent, even the modest dwellings he considered real homes, within a city of continual building and demolition.

For open spaces Van Dyke turned not only to Central Park—which he compared to an exotic, rare orchid—and Prospect Park, with its higher ground and older trees, but also to the wilder lands of Queens and the Bronx. He liked the primitive, rural quality of Pelham Bay, with its islands, caves, meadows, miles of shoreline, and views of Long Island Sound. And Brooklyn's shore road heading toward Coney Island was memorable. Following that road one moonlit, windy night in summer, he marveled at the glittering waters and the phantom ships with silver sails, all seen in mysterious light and shadow; and he envisioned that road, extended by bridges to Coney Island, as the finest shoreway in the world.[42] But that vision dimmed as he wondered how many parks and open spaces would be paved over as New York kept on growing. There was talk of New York's future port at Montauk Point, when all of Long Island would lie within the city's greater ring. And among the grand aspirations of New Yorkers—for power, money, art, literature, ethical and social ideals—Van Dyke saw no hope of synthesis or reconciliation. As he had noted earlier, at close range New York was full of brash and violent contrasts. To see it whole and recognize its sublimity one needed some perspective, perhaps from a distant spot in the Upper Bay.

Some distance in space and time seems to have sharpened the senses of the literary critic Alfred Kazin as he returned to his origins in Brownsville, Brooklyn, that marginal place of "dead land, neither country nor city," from which the rest of Brooklyn and Greater New York were seen as foreign territory. Born in 1915 of immigrant Jewish parents, Kazin grew up cautious of the local tough guys, infatuated with and nourished by books, and painfully aware of differences. Looking back in 1951, he did not romanticize squalor as he recalled summer evening jaunts to the roaring Atlantic by way of weedy lots, lumberyards, junkyards, marshland, and the refuse dumps and sluice gates of Canarsie. Nor did he mention the wildness of those places. It was on summer evening walks to Highland Park, near Queens, with his fifteen-year-old girlfriend that sixteen-year-old Kazin recognized wildness. The park wasn't like other parks; it was "more like an untended wild growth," neglected, remote, dark, bordered by vast cemeteries—but "interesting." Kazin and his girlfriend would climb up to the reservoir and look west to the skyscrapers of Manhattan, east to the lampposts of Jamaica Avenue. The rest was memory in layers: lying in the grass, the smell of the earth, lights of the distant city, and nearby streetlights "searching out so many new things in me."[43]

While Kazin was learning to walk with a "springy caution" in the mean streets of Brownsville, Lewis Gannett wrote "The Wildness of New York" for the *Century* magazine. Published in July 1925, the essay called attention to barn swallows, phoebes, bats, horse chestnut trees, radishes, petunias, goldenrod, and other living things that native New Yorkers might also notice but perhaps not cherish because of childhood associations, as Gannett did. Born in Rochester, New York, in 1891, Gannett became a journalist and settled his family in a lower Manhattan house that was once a medicine factory, a stone's throw from the Brooklyn Bridge. In this "wildness" piece Gannett showed tolerance for the little boys who tunneled beneath his backyard fence, thereby eroding a corner of his garden and letting his imported soil and single rosebush slip away. Gannett was also fond of his garden's weeds—yarrow, dandelion, veronica, two kinds of cinquefoil, and others—some of them nonnative, he assumed. "We are all immigrants within a fraction more than three centuries at most, and so are these weeds," he noted. As long as he could spot the shy hermit thrush migrating through his garden every spring and fall, as long as he could see real city gardens in the window boxes of tenements as he rode by on the Second Avenue El, New York was not what it had first appeared: a treeless prison.[44]

A month later, in August 1925, the *Century* featured "The Wildness of Boston," by a Boston University professor of English, Dallas Lore Sharp, also known as a nature writer and formerly a minister. Born in Haleyville, New Jersey, in 1870, Sharp grew up among woods, riverbanks, and the shores of Delaware Bay. Yet he lived long enough on Exeter Street in Boston's Back Bay and traveled widely enough to sense that Boston's wildness was unique. It was not so much the crows in a cottonwood tree at the corner of Dartmouth and Marlborough, not the smell of salt cod by the harbor, not the wild ducks along the Riverway, not the phragmites holding their own while other marshland plants had perished when the Muddy River and Fens were cleaned up, but the mind: ". . . the wildest thing in Boston is its mind," Sharp declared. "Boston thinks and feels not wildly, but—naturely, may I say?" To prove his point, he mentioned various people—a businessman, a woman about to preside over some function—whose first thoughts were for a particular bird, not for the business at hand. Then, too, Sharp assumed that any book about nature and wild things written somewhere east of the Connecticut River (except in Rhode Island) represented the mind of Boston. This was perhaps a tolerant, regional view of things. But its urbanity may have been suspect, for Sharp was no longer living in Boston. By 1925 he was living in an old farmhouse in Hingham and commuting by train to Boston University. From an upper window in Hingham, with field glasses he could even read the time on the clock of Boston's Custom House tower.[45]

These last details of Sharp's life in the South Shore town of Hingham are reminders of a growing trend. By the 1920s first- or second-generation city dwellers with some inkling of life closer to forests and fields, streams and shores, were recognizing that a way of life and an intricate web of human values had become frayed and stretched thin by the demands and pace of the city. Some, like Skinner, could not move away from their livelihoods. Some bought abandoned farmhouses for weekends and vacations. Some wanted both city and country, undiluted. One

"The wildest thing in Boston is its mind," wrote Dallas Lore Sharp in 1925, alluding to its citizens' reading habits and interest in birds. This view of Boston Common and the State House appeared in Robert Shackleton's Book of Boston *(1917). (Photographer unknown.)*

publisher, sensing a market, asked two writers to debate the issue of city versus country.

Charles Downing Lay was one likely choice. A New York landscape architect and planner, Lay was also a cofounder and past editor of *Landscape Architecture* magazine. In September 1925 the *North American Review* published "The Freedom of the City," Lay's hardheaded brief for urban living. A year later, Duffield and Company of New York brought out his book of the same title. But some readers may have been perplexed. Was this the same Mr. Lay who in 1924 had told readers of *Country Life* about his small place in Stratford, Connecticut, with a view of Long Island Sound, where he and his family had once raised chickens? Was this the Mr. Lay who wrote that he felt no close identity with nature in the city and considered his modest inherited old place in Stratford "a safe retreat if the city prove unkind"?[46]

It was; and there was nothing unusual in Lay's desires for the intellectual and spiritual nourishment of the city along with the chance to unwind, experiment with plants, welcome migrating birds, and maintain roots in the country. But Lay, born in Newburgh, New York, in 1877, educated at Columbia (in architecture) and at Harvard (S.B. in landscape architecture, 1902), was something of an iconoclast within his profession. He thought small urban parks should not resemble rural scenery but be frankly artificial. Unmoved by primeval wilderness, he also considered a landscape fully, aesthetically satisfying only if it showed signs of human use.[47] He could have absorbed this attitude from the Harvard geologist Nathaniel S. Shaler or from his own father, a painter. In any event, Lay seems to have taken wilderness for granted, like air or sky, while he saw limits to urban growth as irrelevant. Let the city grow to 60 million people, he suggested. Instead of many small garden cities with greenbelts, let there be many urban centers within a vast urban region, with fine theaters, shops, institutions of art and science, jobs, schools, machines for tedious labor, paved roads, and train service to the "wilds." As the city grew, wilderness, with its bears and wolves, would simply be closer at hand, he explained. It was an oddly troubling vision: imaginative, backed by statistics, but cold. In 1924, describing his country garden, Lay had admitted his love for the city. Why, then, in his vision of the city in 1926, was there so little feeling and no trace of love? Was this the professional planner's stance?

Maybe. It may also have signaled one man's acceptance of a more impersonal, modernizing world, full of new tools—automobiles, machines for mass production, rapid transit—and new labor-saving devices that opened up the prospect of more leisure for everyone. Noting that the fare to ride from the far reaches of Brooklyn to the Bronx was only a nickel, Lay assumed that an intellectually and spiritually rich, drudgery-free life would always be more affordable in the city than in the country. And as a planner, he seemed determined to offer a bright future.

Lay's adversary, the man his publisher invited to defend country life, was no professional planner but a former New York drama critic, Walter Prichard Eaton—one of the best drama critics in the country, in the eyes of the playwright Eugene O'Neill.[48] After graduating from Harvard in 1900, Eaton had spent a couple of years in Boston, then eight years in New York, reviewing new plays, writing essays, and in his spare time seeking out bits of wildness that brought back memories of his country boyhood on the fringes of Boston. He had had some success in that search, as his "Wildlife in New York" (1910) revealed. Around the corner from his rented rooms, six flights above Washington Square, he had seen (but not heard) a hermit thrush perched in a half-dead ailanthus tree. One winter day, by the banks of the Bronx River in Bronx Park, he had spotted the unmistakable tracks of a mink in the snow-dusted frozen leaf mold. One day in autumn he had built a fire by the rocks on a grassy mound in the salt marshes near the outlet of the Bronx River. And as his fire burned, he studied the waving marsh grasses as the prevailing winds made them appear to flee before the "advance of civilization." On the front line, so to speak, were tenement houses looming high above the marsh grasses that rustled in the wind, as if fleeing for their lives. "I think I was closer to a sympathy and kinship with wild things and wild places [then] than at almost any other time," he wrote.[49]

But by the time he responded to his friend Lay's *Freedom of the City* with *A Bucolic Attitude* (1926), Eaton was no longer living in New York. Married in 1910, he and his wife had given in to their yearnings to live in the country year round while passing through the Berkshires. At first with a rented house in Stockbridge, Massachusetts, later with an old farmhouse and two hundred acres of their own in Sheffield, the couple put down roots. Writing essays and books, mainly about the natural world, teaching part-time, and taking the train to New York intermittently for business, Eaton managed to earn a living. If his wife also had remunerative work, he did not mention it. In *A Bucolic Attitude* he dwelled mainly on the profound joys and minor irritations of his country life. His work was often intermingled with play, using both hands and mind. He rediscovered the "health of weariness" and the pleasure of a cup of tea after chopping and splitting wood from his own birches to keep warm in winter. He granted New Yorkers their good tapwater, drawn from the Catskills, but cried, "Give me wild water on the run, even if I have to fight it!

ACROSS THE CONTINENT

I like all things better before they are tamed, when they are close to their elemental sources."[50]

In the end, Eaton gave publisher and reader more than they might have expected: a sort of reconciliation of city and country. He recalled the time when a New York minister had offered him the pulpit for an evening service, and Eaton had spoken about "the seeing eye." He had mentioned the row of arc lamps that climbed the slopes of a small unkempt park just outside the church door; a sunset down a side street; tall buildings at twilight, with golden squares in every window. Afterward people in the congregation had come forward with faces glowing as they too recalled bits of unplanned beauty in the city. And that "gospel of the seeing eye" came back to Eaton as he brought his *Bucolic Attitude* to a close. Convinced that "a life without beauty is a life incomplete, unfulfilled," he wrote of the "sensuous loveliness of the world," which more country people might recognize were it not for the blindness that came from too much familiarity. Earlier he had touched on the economic problems of family farms, decaying hill towns, and rural schools run on scraped-together funds, never quite sufficient. And he had offered insights but no precise solutions. He ended this affectionate glimpse of country life, then, by suggesting that "it is not riches, but a richer life, that all of us want, even when we do not know it."[51]

PART TWO

Over Time

SIX

Park Makers &
Forest Managers

Crossing Professional Lines
in the Early Years

"You are weak where I am weak, you are strong where I am strong."[1] The elder Frederick Law Olmsted wrote this to his son and namesake in 1895, when his own mental and physical strengths were waning. He was determined that his son should overcome his own weaknesses, for he knew the young profession of landscape architecture must have exceedingly capable leaders to become a real force in society; and he wanted Frederick Law Olmsted Jr. to become one of those leaders.[2] Ironically, one weakness of both father and son was a lack of mastery of the living materials used in their profession—plants. One common strength was a grasp of complex wholes, an ability to organize and strategize. Another was the ability to clarify ambiguities. Indistinctness in a landscape, brought on by fog or mist or achieved through subtle planting, they could appreciate. But vague assumptions and a lack of sound principles would disturb both father and son.

A case in point was the elder Olmsted's attempt to justify public parks in 1880. He distinguished purposely designed public parks from the domains known as "parks" that European foresters and gamekeepers man-

strength of FLO

aged for monarchs and nobles. He then discussed some vague notions about parks and recreation in the United States. Slowly Olmsted's own argument emerged, hedged with qualifications yet based on what he called "thoroughly reasoned purposes and principles." Urban open spaces, large or small, should be suited to their purposes, economically created and maintained. If certain drawbacks of modern urban life— "nervous irritation," "vital exhaustion," and other ailments—needed some relief, perhaps the influence of beautiful, restful passages of natural scenery in a park was needed. If so, let other activities in the park be subordinated to that single main purpose. Otherwise he could not justify the expense and maintenance of a large urban public park.[3]

The same cast of mind is apparent in the younger Olmsted's distinction between national parks and national forests. In the spring of 1916, when efforts were mounting to establish a national park service, he recognized that the public was already using both the national parks and the national forests as recreation grounds. Yet he opposed any measures to consolidate the administrations of these public lands, for the purposes involved were different. "The National *Forests* are set apart for economic ends, and their use for recreation is a by-product," he wrote in *Landscape Architecture*. "The National *Parks* are set apart primarily in order to preserve to the people for all time the opportunity of a peculiar kind of enjoyment and recreation, not measurable in economic terms and to be obtained only from the remarkable scenery which they contain." That scenery was primeval; and in the normal course of economic development, he reasoned, most of it would disappear. True, in order to make primeval scenery accessible to the public, some development— roads, hotels, campsites—had to occur. Still, like his father, Olmsted would subordinate incidentals to main purposes. Economic returns from the national parks were only by-products, he argued; "and even rapidity and efficiency in making them accessible to the people, although of great importance, are wholly secondary to the one dominant purpose of preserving essential esthetic qualities of their scenery unimpaired as a heritage to the infinite numbers of the generations to come."[4]

This statement is echoed in the bill to create a national park service that President Wilson signed into law on August 25, 1916.[5] And there is no mystery here. Olmsted's contribution to the process, as one of several park service advocates that met in 1915 and early 1916, is well known. The venue was the Washington home of California Congressman William Kent, who with his wife donated the land for Muir Woods National Monument, in Marin County. Among the advocates were Stephen Mather and Horace Albright, who would become the first and second directors of the National Park Service; the sportsman and writer Emerson Hough; the president of the American Civic Association, J. Horace McFarland; the geographer Robert B. Marshall, then the recently appointed general superintendent of the national parks; Robert Sterling Yard, a future founder of both the National Parks Association and the Wilderness Society; and Enos Mills, of the Rocky Mountain National Park. According to Albright, these men had been unable to write a "governing sentence" better than Olmsted's; so it was Olmsted's sometimes conflicting purposes of the national parks that were signed into law: "to conserve the scenery and the natural and historic objects and the wild life therein and to provide for the enjoyment of the same in such manner and by such means as will leave them unimpaired for the enjoyment of future generations."[6]

When the younger Olmsted wrote this, at age forty-five, he had made only brief visits to the national parks and forests. Had his wilderness experience been more prolonged, perhaps he would have drafted a different "governing sentence" for the park service bill. As in his *Landscape Architecture* article, he might have identified a single main purpose of the national parks—to preserve the aesthetic qualities of scenery. He might even have distinguished wilderness from scenery.

In the younger Olmsted's lifetime, wilderness came to be recognized as more than scenery, more than a setting for novels and movies, a myth, or an artificial construct of the European mind. Not easily defined, wilderness remained somewhat opaque to the European or Cartesian mind. Tangled, seemingly without order, it confounded those who demanded clarity. It was uncivilized. Then, too, although the civilized world was then increasingly rationalized, specialized, professionalized, and bureaucratic, not all lines were strictly drawn or all boundaries impassable. Even the profession Olmsted took up was so little known that people could still confuse a landscape architect with a forester.

Born in 1870 on Staten Island, the younger Olmsted grew up in a brownstone row house on West 46th Street in Manhattan and, from 1881 onward, in a rambling clapboarded home/office in Brookline, Massachusetts. As a Harvard undergraduate he took advantage of the college's "elective" system and devised his own program of studies in English, foreign languages, fine arts, mathematics, and the sciences, especially geology. Outside of school, he had the advantages of European travel, summer work on the 1893 Chicago World's Fair, and, in 1894–95, apprentice work in the forests and nursery at Biltmore, George W. Vanderbilt's vast estate in North Carolina. Perhaps equally significant were his journeys by bicycle, canoe, rowboat, and sailboat and his early affiliations with the Boston Athletic Association, the Appalachian Mountain Club, the American Forestry Association, the Massachusetts Forestry Association, and the Society for the Protection of New Hampshire Forests. After graduating from Harvard in 1894, he spent the summer in the Rocky Mountains, serving as a recorder and instrument man for the U.S. Coast and Geodetic Survey on their triangulation of the 39th parallel. Thereafter he often mixed recreation with exploration, "looking at the landscapes of this interesting world, and seeing what people are doing to them and what they do to people," as he put it.[7]

The younger Olmsted joined his father's firm in Brookline in late 1895, the year his father retired. That October Gifford Pinchot was marking poplar trees to be cut on Vanderbilt's land at Big Creek, near Biltmore. Whether the younger Olmsted and Pinchot (who was five years his senior) ever met and had a significant conversation at Biltmore is not clear. Pinchot's memoirs refer only to the elder Olmsted, as "one of the men of the century."[8] In late 1891, after a meeting at Biltmore and an interview in Brookline, the elder Olmsted—a friend of Pinchot's father—recommended this European-trained but inexperienced young forester to manage Biltmore's forests. Vanderbilt hired him on December 6, 1891, and Pinchot's work began in February 1892. A year later, Pinchot described the system he had set up at Biltmore Forest as "the first practical application of forest management in the United States."[9]

Eager to broaden his experience while remaining in charge of Biltmore Forest, Pinchot took on additional work, with Vanderbilt's approval, in 1893. He opened a New York office, put "Consulting Forester" on the door, and began to advise private clients and educators. Traveling upstate, he also explained to New York farmers why the state forest preserves in the Adirondacks should never have been designated "forever wild." That designation, inserted into the state's constitution in 1894 and preserved to this day, remained an affront to Pinchot's concept of forestry. And so, around 1894, he told the New York farmers that "forestry has nothing whatever to do with the planting of roadside trees, that parks and gardens are foreign to its nature, that it has no connection with the decoration of country places, that scenery is altogether outside its province, and that it is no more possible to learn Forestry in an arboretum than to learn surgery in a drug store."[10]

Later, as head of the U.S. Department of Agriculture's Division of Forestry from 1898 and, from 1905 to 1910, head of the new Forest Service, Pinchot would define forestry in positive terms. Meanwhile, as a professor, a partner of Olmsted Brothers, a member of the McMillan Commission and the Fine Arts Commission in Washington, and a leading government planner during World War I, the younger Olmsted would help to define his field as well. And that was not simply an academic exercise. As late as 1899, Secretary of Agriculture James Wilson referred to recent years when landscape work and forestry were "completely confounded." And still the distinction between the two fields was not always made clear, he added.[11]

But to some people the distinction was critical. The American Forestry Association, initially a small conservation-minded group founded in Chicago in 1875, had merged with the American Forestry Congress, begun in Cincinnati in 1882; and the two were incorporated in January 1897 as the American Forestry Association. That year in Louisville, Kentucky, the American Park and Outdoor Art Association (later known as the

American Civic Association) brought together friends of public parks and landscape architecture from around the country. And the American Forestry Association was delighted, for the territorial lines could now be more clearly drawn. "The object of a Forestry Association is an economic one," one writer explained; "that of a Park and Open Art Association an aesthetic one; the only relations in common are that both have to deal with tree growth and both are in existence for a higher civilization."[12]

Once these broad-based associations were established, it would seem reasonable for professionals to set up their own, more clearly focused societies. They did. On January 4, 1899, ten landscape architects, including J. C. Olmsted, O. C. Simonds, Warren H. Manning, and Beatrix Jones (later Farrand), met in New York to organize the American Society of Landscape Architects (ASLA); and these ten, along with the absent F. L. Olmsted Jr., were named the society's "founding members."[13] Not long afterward, on November 30, 1900, seven men met in the Washington office of Chief Forester Gifford Pinchot to consider the idea of forming a new society. Two weeks later, that group, including Pinchot, Henry S. Graves, Overton W. Price, and Ralph S. Hosmer, met again to adopt a committee-drafted constitution for the Society of American Foresters.[14] And so at the dawn of the twentieth century there existed two new professional organizations with certain differences in their outlooks, aside from their leaning toward either utility or aesthetics.

One difference lay between the lines in their statements of purpose. In Pinchot's words, the purpose of the Society of American Foresters was "to further the cause of Forestry in America by fostering a spirit of comradeship among foresters; by creating opportunities for a free interchange of views upon Forestry and allied subjects; and by disseminating a knowledge of the purpose and achievements of Forestry."[15] The ASLA's "Agreement of Association" was more formal in tone: "The Corporation is constituted for the purpose of increasing the efficiency and influence of the profession, and to foster good fellowship among its members, and to promote the public welfare."[16] Clearly, both had an interest in collegiality, but only the foresters seemed to recognize the importance of public relations—that is, using media to make their views and achievements known to the public.

Before they formed their own professional society, foresters had a popular journal devoted to their cause. As we have seen, the magazine that had addressed the interests of both foresters and landscape architects, Sargent's *Garden and Forest,* ceased publication as of December 1897.[17] By coincidence or strategy, the very next month, in January 1898, the American Forestry Association announced its acquisition of the *Forester,* a magazine for the general public begun in 1895. There and in that magazine's successors, *American Forestry, American Forests and Forest Life,* and *American Forests,* foresters, wildlife biologists, ornithologists, and such landscape architects as Arthur H. Carhart would write for a wide audience. Meanwhile, foresters could discuss more technical issues in the *Forestry Quarterly,* founded in 1902 by the Cornell forestry professor Bernhard Fernow. In 1917 the *Quarterly* was merged with the Society of American Foresters' *Proceedings* to form the *Journal of Forestry.* With increasing specialization, these professional and popular publications grew steadily apart in tone and content; yet some leading foresters, including Gifford Pinchot, Henry S. Graves, Robert (Bob) Marshall, and Aldo Leopold, would write for both the popular *American Forests* and the more technical *Journal of Forestry.*[18]

In contrast, landscape architects had no journal of their own until 1910—*Landscape Architecture,* founded, owned, and edited jointly for the first decade by Charles Downing Lay, Henry Vincent Hubbard, and Robert Wheelwright. This magazine was fairly free of jargon and covered some topics of broad interest, yet for years it was not a financial success. Written by and for landscape architects, it was criticized as both too general and too technical, with too many illustrations and too few.[19] To learn more about the field, people might glean something from garden and shelter magazines or special-interest journals such as *Parks and Recreation.* Still, parks, gardens, and horticulture made up only part of the field of landscape architecture.[20]

Another difference between foresters and landscape architects lay in

private/
public forests

their views of government service. Pinchot believed that privately owned and managed forests would never serve the nation's best interests so well as forests owned or at least well regulated by the federal government. As mentioned earlier, he imbued his early recruits to the Forest Service with a sense of mission and esprit de corps, giving them substantial responsibilities and the authority to make decisions on their own out in the field. Ralph Hosmer, who entered the Division of Forestry in 1898, recalled Pinchot's open door at the Department of Agriculture, his simple title, "Forester," the intense loyalty that everyone in the division felt for him, and the common belief in forestry as "a Cause." "One worked with, not for, Gifford Pinchot!" he wrote.[21]

In contrast, landscape architects in the early years gravitated toward private practice. True, in times of war and depression, many of the men served with distinction in the government or the military. J. S. Pray, a planner of military camps and housing during World War I, recalled that period of government service as a time of "wonderful spirit."[22] But once peace and prosperity returned, landscape architects who were not drawn to city or state parks, the National Park Service, or the Forest Service tended to slip back into private practice or academia. In the early years, this trend may have mirrored the lack of jobs for landscape architects in government. Perhaps it also reflected their self-image as artists; they may have felt their work would suffer under the constraints of governmental procedures. Some, such as Thomas Church in California, preferred close contacts with private clients to the impersonal relations and often merely indirect influence of public work.[23] Henry Vincent Hubbard, who had served as a government engineer and planner during World War I, noted in 1941, "When they need advice, [government bureaus] try to seize the adviser and make him a cog in their wheel." In the government, Hubbard implied, he had never felt free to speak openly, without "camouflage."[24] But Hosmer's experience with Pinchot in the early years was different. Anyone's idea might be tested, run through a gauntlet, maybe adopted, he recalled. People felt part of a team, with a personal stake in the game.[25]

These views, however personal or tied to specific situations, provide some context for the ways in which foresters and landscape architects would sometimes meet in the early years—as colleagues or opponents, amicably or warily.

***

With the hindsight of half a century, Gifford Pinchot looked back on his Biltmore experiences with pleasure. "Them was the happy days," he wrote, remembering how he worked in the forest by day, rode a bucking horse at day's end, just for fun, then looked for new fields to conquer.[26]

With more hindsight, we see other things in *Biltmore Forest* (1893), the 49-page pamphlet that Pinchot wrote for the press and for free distribution at the Chicago World's Fair. The frontispiece is a photograph of a "cordwood gang"—eight African American men, some holding wedges or mallets, all standing in full sunlight, contemplating their work among felled trees in a clearing of an undistinguished hardwood forest. Among the other photographs are more workmen, dark-skinned and light-skinned, and more undistinguished forests. Pinchot aimed to make some of these tracts "selection forests"; that is, managed woodlands with trees of different species and ages, from which certain specimens would be periodically selected and cut. Biltmore Forest, south of Asheville in western North Carolina, was "much disturbed by human agency," Pinchot admitted. The previous landowners were small farmers who had cut down the more valuable trees for fuel, fenceposts, or saw logs, then burned some woodlands for pasture and let their cattle roam in the remaining woods. The original condition of much of Biltmore Forest was "deplorable in the extreme," he noted.[27]

As a pioneer forester, then, Pinchot set out not to conquer a virgin wilderness but to repair a damaged landscape. He was perhaps more free to experiment there than in a land of extraordinary beauty. And yet there was an important check to his freedom. Biltmore was a country residence, with gardens, farms, a deer park, and an entrance drive that the elder Olmsted envisioned as a linear arboretum. Olmsted's idea of a splendid arboretum that might have surpassed the botanical riches of Kew, in England, did not win Vanderbilt's support in the long run. But generally Olmsted prevailed; and among Vanderbilt's consultants on the grounds, Olmsted was clearly in charge. On rare occasions when Pinchot's plans conflicted with Olmsted's, Pinchot acquiesced, grateful that he, a young, inexperienced forester, was treated "to some extent as an equal."[28]

Pinchot aimed for three results at Biltmore Forest: profit from wood products, a nearly constant annual yield, and the improved condition of the forest. His pamphlet contains photographs, text, a map of the forest divided into numbered blocks and compartments, a list of native trees, and lists of expenses, receipts, and labor costs. Although Pinchot cared about the general appearance of the forest, he made no claims for its beauty; utility was his primary concern. And his reasoning sounds like a counterpart to the way the elder Olmsted had once justified urban public parks. What ensured the forest's utility was profitable production, Pinchot wrote. "If this were absent, the existence of the Forest would be justified only as it lends beauty and interest to the Estate."[29]

Eight years after the publication of *Biltmore Forest,* an American forester addressed the middle ground between the Olmsteds' domain of landscape beauty and Pinchot's domain of landscape utility. In *Forest Trees and Forest Scenery* (1901) G. Frederick Schwarz looked at trees as expressive, living beings, both as specimens and as elements within a forest. Avoiding technical terms, Schwarz described some great American tree species in their native habitats, then considered how American forests would change as European ideas of practical forestry were gradually adapted for American climates, soils, and specific needs.[30]

The utilitarian aims of forestry underlie Schwarz's discussion from the outset. Yet as he listens for the plaintive song of the thrush or fixes his gaze on some small detail of leaf or branch, some shimmering light or showering effect of foliage in the wind or mist, he conveys impressions of beauty that the forester is presumed to ignore. The sugar maple may be more useful than the red maple, but the red maple is more "agile" in the wind, with an "elastic spring of every part, and a kind of freedom among the many leaves." Schwarz quotes Thoreau on the rustle of withered oak leaves in winter and Muir on the life span of California's Big Trees (*Sequoia gigantea*), along with passages from Wordsworth and

Shakespeare. Having gathered these gems of aesthetic appreciation from the past, Schwarz then suggests new criteria for appreciating our future forests. Now that practical forestry has gained a foothold in America, he explains, forest beauty "stands on the threshold of a new relationship."[31]

Some idea of that relationship could be gleaned from the great managed forests of Europe. But the order and neatness of those forests, the subordination of component parts to a single main purpose, all come at a price. "To an American, if he has seen a little of our wildness, a great charm is wanting in the artificial forests of Europe," Schwarz admits. "It seems, at times, as if the free will and perfect liberty of the air and rain, of the wind, were wanting."[32] Among four types of managed forests, the European "selection forest" would be most like the wilder American forests. The "coppice" would resemble a stump-sprout thicket (which Charles Eliot had considered too dull and tame for public reservations of scenery around Boston).[33] Tended as a crop, perhaps for firewood, the coppice might be hidden among the hills, a "homelike" place of low growth, surrounded by older woods. The "coppice under standards" would resemble an open selection forest interspersed with young thickets. The most artificial type, the "high forest," composed of a single species—typically conifers—would usually be planted in close rows. Within a single section, all trees would be of the same age. The boundaries between sections might be regular or irregular, depending on topography. This high forest would be distinguished by its "noble grandeur." Given good soil and light, its lofty trees would represent the best products of the forest.[34]

For the idea of uniting "forest art" with practical forestry Schwarz credited the German forester and landowner Heinrich von Salisch, who had written about forest aesthetics some twenty years earlier. But Schwarz, too, was an innovator in his own unassuming, quiet way. Born in Baltimore in 1868, he took time to settle upon his lifework, eventually passing up the textile industry and law for forestry, which he studied in Germany (his father's native land) and in France. By 1899 he was working in the Division of Forestry, under Gifford Pinchot. Ralph Hosmer, a fellow forester in the division and later head of the forestry department at Cornell, recalled that he and Schwarz went out in the spring of 1899 to visit farm woodlots in Ohio, Indiana, Kentucky, and Virginia. Two years later, with the appearance of *Forest Trees and Forest Scenery,* Schwarz became (in Hosmer's view) "the first exponent in the United States of forest aesthetics."[35] Schwarz wrote about purely utilitarian issues as well, such as methods of estimating cordwood and the relation of the surrounding forests to the flow of the Rock River in Wisconsin and Illinois. But some of his interests lay elsewhere; by 1904 he had left the (renamed) Bureau of Forestry.

With *Forest Trees and Forest Scenery* Schwarz stepped lightly over a few professional boundaries, blending utility and beauty, poetry and a realistic sense of the inevitable. Some might have balked at Schwarz's notion that the "true" owners of the forests were birds, squirrels, butterflies, and "the large game that inhabits the hidden recesses and adds an element of wildness and strange attraction to these quiet haunts." Others may have wondered at his apparently calm observation that the two great Sequoias, the redwood and the Big Tree, were threatened with extinction. In any event, Schwarz did separate the utilitarian purposes of the national forest reserves (which would be renamed "national forests" in 1907) from the spiritual and aesthetic purposes of national parks. And he seemed confident that the national parks would remain inviolate.[36]

Within a few years, however, Schwarz argued the case for scenic beauty and wildness with more fervor. In 1904 he returned to Harvard (where he had never stayed long enough to earn a degree) and studied aesthetics in relation to forest scenery. He also traveled a great deal, sometimes as a consulting forester. In 1909, when the New York State Forest, Fish, and Game Commission was considering a forest reservation in the highlands of the Hudson, Schwarz called attention to the region's delicate undergrowth of dogwood, mountain laurel, and hornbeam, along with its very old, picturesque trees, all of which might be considered worthless from the practical forester's point of view. Although foresters were doing "splendid work" throughout the United States, applying principles of European forestry as well as they could, Schwarz thought the

blending

forests of the Hudson Highlands deserved special consideration—perhaps even the close cooperation of the landscape architect.[37]

Writing to his classmates many years after he left college, Schwarz downplayed his own achievements and focused instead on a quality of life that he cherished: a life out-of-doors, in a natural environment that could offer health, beauty, and knowledge. "I sometimes think we should aim at elimination, at greater simplicity," he wrote in 1920. "The fundamentals, not necessarily more education, but more rational education, civic responsibility, friendships, more healthful and less hectic lives, an intimacy with Nature (such as is left), etc.—these may not give us bread, but they are a very necessary balance to the great striving for material existence."[38]

And Schwarz acted on these views. A life member of the Save-the-Redwoods League, he donated land for two redwood groves in California, one named for Henry S. Graves, one for Professor James W. Toumey. He also gave a stone lodge on the Muir trail, additional land for the research forests of Yale and Harvard, and contributions to the headquarters building of Cornell's research forest. To his classmates he made no public mention of these gifts. But after his death in 1931, one writer told of Schwarz's philanthropy, his background (his father, F. A. O. Schwarz, founded the well-known toy firm), his writings, his clubs (Sierra, Appalachian Mountain, and others), and his human qualities. Meticulous, a loyal friend, Schwarz was "keenly alive to the beauties of nature and to the best in human life."[39]

***

We have already seen some examples of friendly cooperation between foresters and landscape architects: the elder Olmsted and Pinchot at Biltmore in the early 1890s, Aldo Leopold and Frank Waugh at the Grand Canyon in 1917, Leopold and Arthur Carhart in Denver in 1919. But one conflict cast a long shadow over later efforts to cross territorial lines.

The battles over the fate of Hetch Hetchy in Yosemite National Park have often been described with echoes of impassioned arguments on both sides.[40] The project of damming the Tuolumne River in Hetch

Hetchy Valley was a means to supply San Francisco with fresh water, a need dramatized by the earthquake and fire of 1906. But the dam would be a betrayal of trust, an invasion of national park lands held to be inviolate for the generations to come. It would provide a necessity of life for the people of a great city rather than favoring the few who enjoyed scenic beauty in solitude. But John Muir protested, "These temple destroyers, devotees of ravaging commercialism, seem to have a perfect contempt for Nature, and, instead of lifting their eyes to the God of the mountains, lift them to the Almighty Dollar."[41] To supporters of the dam, the artificial lake thus formed would be beautiful and valuable for recreation. To preservationists, such a lake would impair the scenery and restrict the public's enjoyment of the park. Supporting the dam, Gifford Pinchot testified, "the fundamental principle of the whole conservation policy is that of use, to take every part of the land and its resources and put it to that use in which it will serve the most people."[42]

While opposition to the Hetch Hetchy dam project mounted, languished, and rose again over some thirty years, the issue could not remain local or western; it stirred national debate. A year before the battles were finally resolved, the younger Frederick Law Olmsted served as an intermediary between the leaders on the two sides, Pinchot and J. Horace McFarland.[43] Unable to bring them together, Olmsted tried again with an exceedingly fair-minded letter to the *Boston Evening Transcript* in November 1913. After carefully weighing the merits of "full economic use" and the "highest recreative values," he came out in favor of preserving the entire Yosemite National Park, including Hetch Hetchy Valley. Among his concerns were the increasing strains of civilization and people's need to seek relief in wilder landscapes. His clinching argument, however, returned to first principles: Yosemite National Park was created to preserve its scenery intact for the enjoyment of all future generations. To dam a river in that park for a San Francisco reservoir would be to ignore the purpose for which the park was created. What is more, it would set a precedent of abandoning the purpose of any park whenever it conflicted with "considerable utilitarian interests."[44]

But Olmsted and the preservationists lost. A month later, on December 19, 1913, President Wilson signed the bill granting San Francisco the rights to the dam. Today the wisdom of the strategies employed and the fairness of the outcome are still debatable. The historian Roderick Nash observed that the cause of wilderness was strengthened when Hetch Hetchy became a hotly debated national issue. Yet he also pointed out that the losing side had perhaps placed too much emphasis on scenic beauty and wonder, and neglected to stress the qualities of wilderness.[45] These points hint at another issue at stake—control of turf.

Pinchot's and the younger Olmsted's positions on Hetch Hetchy reflected points of view that were then fundamental to their respective professions. And their concerns for utility and beauty would continue to be debated, particularly in the struggles over who should manage vast tracts of public land—the Forest Service, in the Department of Agriculture; the National Park Service, in the Department of the Interior; or some other entity, created through a reshuffling or transfer.[46] Ultimately these debates were about power and control: about politics, with legal, economic, social, and aesthetic implications. Boundaries, domains, and territorial rights became critical. And as each bureaucracy grew, it could accommodate more domains and divisions, more niches for "experts." As we have seen, Arthur Carhart, a landscape architect trained at Iowa State College (B.S. 1916), entered the Forest Service in 1919 as an entry-level "recreation engineer," then quickly became known as the "beauty doctor."

As an employee of the Forest Service for nearly three years, Arthur Carhart developed a passion for making the experience of wilderness accessible to the public. Trappers Lake, in Colorado, had been a revelation to him. But his feelings for wilderness and wild things had been stirred long before that summer of 1919. Born in western Iowa, in 1892, Carhart came to know fragments of wilderness, some virgin stands of oak and elm that remained among the cultivated fields near home in Mapleton. He also knew a silt-laden creek that carved a gash in overgrazed pasture lands whenever it flooded. As a boy, he was often free to explore that creek with his shepherd dog—that is, when he was not needed for chores, such as turning the grindstone while his father sharpened sickle sections before harvesting twenty acres of native hay on the farm. Years later Carhart recalled details of his homeland, a frontier in transition: the white frame houses on Sioux Avenue in Mapleton; the smell of freshly planed white pine in a neighbor's shop; and the last flock of prairie chickens that he ever saw in Iowa, beating the air over his father's cornfield before they landed and were shot. They made a fine meal.[47]

Some traces of wildness thrilled young Carhart: the heat of the summer sun on his back after a dash through a waterfall in the creek; the nearby valley where wildflowers grew beneath the elms, oaks, and hickory, and where red squirrels and cottontails made their homes. What Carhart knew of wilderness came one day in the mail: an illustrated railway brochure on the wonders of Yellowstone National Park. Wilderness later became an environment, on the job with the Forest Service in 1919, when he traveled throughout the Rocky Mountains and in the border lakes canoe country of northern Minnesota. There he and his guide, Matt, paddled and portaged for more than two weeks without seeing another human being. At sundown they heard loons crying. At dawn they watched moose, mother and newborn offspring, treading the sandy beaches. By day they saw reflections of Norway pines in the quiet bays while waves slapped the sides of their canoe. "Wilderness surrounded us and we were a part of it," he recalled.[48]

However beautiful, wilderness held inherent dangers; there Carhart learned to be alert, attuned to an environment prone to sudden crises. And wilderness was reflected in the men Carhart got to know on the job—the Forest Service field men who took him on pack trips through the Rocky Mountains. The old-timers were former cowboys and loggers, "tough, hard-bitten men" who could go out unarmed and somehow communicate government policies to their intransigent, liberty-loving, well-armed neighbors. These men were the Forest Service's pioneers, blazing trails of forest conservation before the appearance of college-educated young men such as Leopold and Wallace Hutchinson, of the Denver office. Carhart admired both the old-timers and the new men. But he noted that "something was lost" in the transition. "Back country that had been reached before only by laborious trail travel was being opened by new roads," he observed. "More and more the ranger was becoming a trained manager of a block of land of which technical knowledge was more important than saddle calluses and the ability to make sourdough biscuits."[49]

Having entered the wilderness with some of these men, Carhart emerged with a crusade of his own, to make wilderness recreation not only accessible to the public but also recognized as one of the forest's most important "products," along with timber and watershed protection. At stake, he believed, were people's physical and spiritual well-being, as well as the fate of the civilized world. That world had just survived a devastating war in Europe (a war in which he had served by working on sanitation and insect control in a series of military hospitals in the United States). After the war, he sensed that the world was threatened by a kind of overcivilized, luxurious living that had left previous civilizations decadent or in ruins. His solution was to bring people into the wilderness—by auto, on horseback, on foot, by canoe, or whatever means. In the early 1920s, then, while leaders in the Forest Service and the National Park Service continued to compete over domains and appropriations, he proposed a "federation of outdoor clubs" to unite naturalists, sportsmen, foresters, park superintendents, landscape architects, and others in a common cause that might prevail over "political squabbling."[50]

One of Carhart's confidants, the man who for years wrote him long letters of moral support and arranged his appointment to the ASLA Committee on National Parks and National Forests, was the landscape architect James Sturgis Pray, at Harvard. (This connection may have come through Frank H. Culley, a former student of Pray, who was Carhart's teacher at Iowa State and later Carhart's partner in a landscape architecture firm in Denver.)[51] Pray finally met Carhart while on a whirlwind trip through the western states in the summer of 1921. Afterward he thanked Carhart for many courtesies to him and his family, including a drive to the summit of Pike's Peak; from there the views over the Colorado landscape were "glorious."[52]

It happened that the younger Olmsted was also in the West that summer of 1921, mainly around Yellowstone and the southern Sierra. It was the first time that he had "more than a tripper's glimpse" of the National Parks and Forests: two months of real recreation, including long journeys by rail. Fifty-one years old that summer, he came away changed. The scenery was splendid, but he had been most impressed by an overwhelming sense of freedom and independence. Day after day he had been free to wander—whether with or without his wife and nine-year-old daughter is not clear. Afterward he described the calming of nerves and resting of the mind in the presence of natural beauty, not as a hypothetical concern but as a vivid personal experience.[53]

On his return to the East Coast, Olmsted realized that not everyone could know the freedom he had known. Visiting a national park or monument might be akin to viewing a work of art in a museum or a "wild" bird in an aviary. As he noted in a talk before the American Civic Association that fall of 1921, one function of the national parks and monuments was to preserve "supreme museum specimens." Yet, perhaps for the first time, the younger Olmsted recognized the freedom of the wilderness, distinct from scenery, as a unique value, "because it is attainable in large degree only on tracts of vast extent, substantially unimpaired by the intrusion of other functions."[54]

Concluding his talk before the American Civic Association, Olmsted allowed that the nation's superlative scenic wonders could be displayed in relatively small spaces, all for the momentary pleasure of harried, nerve-racked tourists, accommodated in upscale hotels equipped with stock exchange tickers, private telephones, and other amenities. Their busy lives need hardly be interrupted. But now that wilderness, which Olmsted had recently experienced fully for the first time, was approaching the vanishing point, he felt a profound obligation to preserve it. And so he reasserted the need to hold the national parks "permanently free" from the activities and uses proper to national forests. That was one approach. In time there would be others.

***

In 1935 an editorial in the *Journal of Forestry* argued that foresters had no business discussing the beauty of wilderness, for as a rule they were not trained in aesthetics. The writer, apparently Herbert A. Smith, the editor in chief, looked upon the newly formed Wilderness Society as a group of well-meaning but misguided lovers of wild lands who might make a "cult" of the wilderness. Thus he advised foresters to stick to their "good old doctrine of obtaining, through wise use, the largest measure of contribution to the welfare of everybody in the long run," and leave beauty to artists, critics, and landscape architects.[55]

In good time, Aldo Leopold replied, "I suspect there are two categories of judgment which *cannot* be delegated to experts, which every man *must* judge for himself, and on which [the] intuitive conclusion of the non-expert is perhaps as likely to be correct as that of the professional. One of these is what is right. The other is what is beautiful." Reconsidering the familiar concepts of highest use and beauty, Leopold went on to suggest that there was such as thing as beauty "in the broadest ecological sense of that word."[56]

These thoughts about ecology, ethics, and aesthetics, published in 1936, anticipated Leopold's now well-known expression of the land ethic in *A Sand County Almanac* (1949): "A thing is right when it tends to preserve the integrity, stability, and beauty of the biotic community. It is wrong when it tends otherwise."[57] In the interim, before his death in 1948, Leopold could discuss these ideas with colleagues and students at the University of Wisconsin at Madison, where he was professor of wildlife management, as well as with his fellow founders of the Wilderness Society. Some were driven to form that society by a craving for the solitude and rigors of wilderness recreation, something they could experience only in an area free of roads, motorized vehicles, car radios, and other intrusions. Leopold was at least equally concerned about the needs of scientific research in wilderness areas. Generally, he and his fellow founders shared a respect for the beauty of unaltered wild lands and some dawning sense of the rights and needs of all living beings, including wild creatures. The term "ecology" was not yet widely known, yet some nonscientists could intuitively sense a web of interactions in the world around them. As Leopold observed in *A Sand County Almanac,* "An understanding of ecology does not necessarily originate in courses

In the early 1900s Gifford Pinchot's recruits in the Forest Service could have calculated the yield from the redwood being cut here, while landscape architects were more likely to ponder the loss of beauty in the grove. Decades later, Aldo Leopold ignored these distinctions between two professions when he wrote of beauty and ecology. (Image from George Wharton James, California, Romantic and Beautiful *[1914]. Photographer unknown.)*

bearing ecological labels; it is quite as likely to be labeled geography, botany, agronomy, history, or economics."[58]

Whatever the source of their concern, people who mulled over ecological problems and those who cared deeply about the wilderness would eventually cross paths, some via the Wilderness Society. One of that society's most difficult tasks in the early days, however, was to define "wilderness." Those in the inner circle—Leopold and a few others—tended to agree that, to be effective, wilderness had to be substantial—perhaps large enough for people on a portage or pack trip to explore for a week or two without retracing their route. And yet they also saw a need for fairly small "restricted wild areas," located closer to towns and cities, where the popular support for preserving vast tracts of wilderness would have to be found.[59] As one of the society's members, Walter Prichard

OVER TIME

Eaton, noted in 1939, "To appreciate the wilderness one must have seen the wilderness."[60]

Eaton was alluding to people who might not be able to get to a vast wilderness, perhaps for lack of time or money. He himself had hiked in wilderness areas around the country, from Mount Katahdin, in Maine, to the Far West. Now in 1939, in his sixties, he found the more rugged forms of wilderness recreation beyond his reach. On his 200-acre farm in Sheffield, Massachusetts, however, he was allowing wilderness conditions to return. With minimal interference—no thinning, no trails but the roughest sort, most underbrush left untouched—he was watching to see how quickly young pines would grow up by chance; how soon the soil would recover from eroded ledges; which ferns and wildflowers would reappear. And he pointed to other limited yet accessible wild lands, such as bird and wildflower sanctuaries, that might bring a sense of wilderness closer to home.[61]

To set aside these small, accessible tracts of wild land was one of the more modest purposes of the Wilderness Society. The larger threats—roads planned through the vast Quetico-Superior lake country in northern Minnesota, a highway through the Okefenokee Swamp in southern Georgia—absorbed more of members' energies in the early years. In 1946, however, the society's new president, the forester and regional planner Benton MacKaye, urged members to become their own little wilderness societies: to find their own Walden Pond, explore it, and preserve or restore it as a sample of the once primeval local setting. "We must widen the access to the sources of life," he insisted.[62]

The following year, MacKaye welcomed the younger Frederick Law Olmsted to the council (or inner circle) of the Wilderness Society.[63] It was a gracious welcome with a hint of great responsibility; and Olmsted responded with one small project in 1949. To Howard Zahniser, the society's executive secretary, he sent information about a small "wilderness area" in southwestern New Hampshire. It happened that Olmsted's wife, Sarah Hall Sharples Olmsted, had inherited some acreage on Spoonwood Pond, in the little town of Nelson. The land had been farmed and otherwise altered since the late eighteenth century, and some pastures had reverted to forest. From a scientific, ecological standpoint, this was not wilderness, Olmsted noted; but it did have a lovely wild character. His plan was to work out an agreement with two abutters whereby the public could enjoy some access to the pond and wooded shorelands. And with a vision that faintly recalled his father's view of Manhattan a century earlier, the younger Olmsted predicted that summer cottages and resorts would eventually alter the character of other lakes and ponds in the region. His family's little bit of wild land would then become increasingly rare and precious.[64]

The regional development Olmsted foresaw has come to pass, most intensely to the southeast, near the New Hampshire–Massachusetts border, but also along the shores of Sunapee, Winnipesaukee, and other lakes to the north and northeast. Then, too, Olmsted's vision of an accessible half-wild woodland preserve around the 144-acre Spoonwood Pond has been realized in part, although not quite as he suggested in letters to Zahniser and the neighboring landowner, L. Cabot Briggs, in 1949.[65] Both in Olmsted's lifetime and after his death in 1957, parcels of the Sharples-Olmsted land were deeded to his wife's siblings and to others.[66] It would take the efforts of many individuals and organizations— the nearby Nubanusit Lake Association; the Nature Conservancy; the Harris Foundation and its successor, the Harris Center for Conservation Education; and the Society for the Protection of New Hampshire Forests, among others—to work out the details of gifts, land sales at below-development prices, conservation easements, and transfers. The upshot is that a few thousand acres of half-wild wooded land in southwestern New Hampshire remain largely "unimpaired," including the 400-acre Louis Cabot Preserve, set aside for scientific research and the public's enjoyment for generations to come.[67]

SEVEN

Layers of Human
Habitation & Wildness

When Lewis Mumford wrote about American environments and arts in
the 1920s and early 1930s, he did not value wildness for its own sake. He
was more attentive to civilization—cities, trade, manufacturing—and
the level of culture that a civilization allowed to develop. For him "culture" encompassed a great deal: the working of the "raw materials of
existence" into new patterns, including works of art.[1] Nature was more
elusive, something Mumford did not discuss apart from culture and civilization. In his *Sticks and Stones* (1924), for instance, nature is represented mainly by exploited raw materials—land, timber, minerals—by
gardens, and by New York's Central Park.

A native New Yorker, born in 1895, Mumford had known Central Park
since childhood. He used to walk there with his grandfather, arriving
from the Upper West Side. Years later he took shortcuts through the park,
walking to and from high school on the Lower East Side. By 1924, Central Park had become Mumford's exemplar of "nature humanized" and
of "man naturalized, and therefore at home."[2] And this was no mere play
on words. An appreciative reader of Thoreau and Emerson and a leader

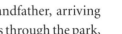

157

in the newly formed Regional Planning Association of America, Mumford was then trying to reconcile noble ideals with practical schemes. His interests lay not in dichotomies but in wholeness, an integration of these things. "'Nature' as a system of interests and activities is one of the chief creations of the civilized man," he wrote in *Brown Decades* (1931).[3]

Today Mumford is known as a discerning critic of these creations, the products of civilization. But for the process whereby people and places became civilized he sometimes showed no sympathy. In one far-ranging study of American culture, *The Golden Day* (1926), he concluded that "the life of the pioneer was bare and insufficient: he did not really face Nature, he merely evaded society."[4] What disturbed Mumford was not only the focus on "conquering" the wilderness but also the continual "reckoning," "calculating," and "figuring," which reduced the pioneers' experiences to numbers and merely utilitarian purposes. Unmoved by the legendary Paul Bunyan, under whose axe fabulous numbers of trees were said to fall, Mumford showed more sympathy for Rip Van Winkle, Washington Irving's character from upstate New York who fell asleep for twenty years, then awoke to find his native landscape changed. "In the bottom of our hearts, we are disconsolate Rips," Mumford wrote.[5]

And yet the source of that remark, *The Golden Day,* is one of Mumford's most reaffirming and hopeful works. If he could not applaud the pioneers' achievements, triumphs over hardships hardly comprehensible to people back east, that was mainly because he traced those triumphs to a devastating war on Nature, a war that left in its wake exhausted soils, forests cut down without thought for the future, and appalling stories of terror and cruelty. Mumford's sympathies lay with the critics of that war, especially with Thoreau and George Perkins Marsh, whom he identified as the leaders in the movement for conservation.[6] Considering Thoreau a poet and Marsh a "scientific observer," Mumford somewhat obscured Thoreau's ambivalent interests in the sciences of his day. But again, Mumford sought wholeness, refusing to choose between Thoreau and Marsh or between poetry and scientific inquiry.

In his early works, Mumford swiftly denounced whole decades of civilization in the making. Though his environmental and cultural values sometimes ran against the American grain, those values have endured and many of his arguments remain persuasive. That said, it is still useful to step back a generation and reconsider the dispassionate observations of Frederick Jackson Turner, the professor at Wisconsin, later at Harvard, who detected among the pioneers in old New England as well as in the West some intriguing patterns of land forms and human settlements. Setting aside for a moment Mumford's ideal of "nature humanized," we can look for layers of wilderness (or mere traces of wildness) interspersed with human habitations, such that they do not blend but rather coexist, the one setting off the other. Here Turner offers more than a thesis about the frontier and the American character. Poring over census maps in 1893, for instance, he found areas of wilderness "interpenetrated by lines of civilization" and "tongues of settlement" advancing among "indentations of wilderness."[7]

During the half century that followed, civilization and wilderness continued to "interpenetrate," but not always as Turner had detected. In the Northeast, where farmers had abandoned their glacier-scoured, boulder-strewn lands for richer, deeper soils farther west, wilderness was overtaking the more remote homesteads. In the South, wherever old plantations had not survived the period known as Reconstruction, avenues of live oaks might lead to ruined mansions—or perhaps to a few chimneys and columns rising up in the forests that had grown back. In Appalachia, settlements that had once advanced the frontier were slipping into a half-wild state. And the result could be very attractive to some people, including one founder of the Wilderness Society, the attorney Harvey Broome, born in Knoxville, Tennessee. "Half-woods say things that whole woods cannot," he wrote. "They are the natural sherds of civilizations—the seeding grounds of wilderness. Half-woods are bilingual, speaking the language of man and shouting the call of the wilds."[8]

It is not clear that Frederick Jackson Turner (who died in 1932) would have appreciated these half-woods or relished Nature's reconquest of lands that had been won through enormous, sometimes excruciating human effort. But he was intrigued by change. "The United States lies like a huge page in the history of society," he wrote in 1893. "Line by line as we read this continental page from West to East we find the record of social evolution." That is, we read from the most recent efforts to explore and settle the land to later efforts—ranching, increasingly sophisticated and intensive farming, and finally manufacturing in cities. The land— the page on which these human activities are written and overwritten— is layered. It is, in Turner's vision of the nation, a "palimpsest," or tablet, on which previous human activities may still be detected beneath later activities written on the land.[9]

As we have seen, traces of wildness could be signs of life and hope to a few generations of Americans who had grown up in rural America toward the end of the nineteenth century and had not entirely adapted to urban life. For some, traces of wildness were links to the simpler, quieter, freer existence they had known as children. But even more invigorating could be the perception of a new frontier in the still-evolving layers of civilization and wildness. What might otherwise have seemed melancholy—abandoned fields and cellar holes reverting to forests in New England, gardens running wild in the old South—led to reflections on culture and nature that now appear fresh, even hopeful, despite hints of ambivalence or regret.

From the end of the nineteenth century through 1949 it was still possible to pursue two kinds of frontier, primeval wilderness and half-wild places, within the borders of the United States. Alaska, a U.S. territory since its purchase from Russia in 1867, did not become a state of the Union until 1959; and it attracted explorers, naturalists, and artists long before the coming of oil pipelines and their access roads. The abandoned farms of New England were featured in the first issue of *Country Life in America,* in 1901. In 1940 an ornithologist recognized a frontier in the marshes obscured by highway billboards in northeastern New Jersey. These items indicate points along our path in time. Professor Turner has already cleared us a path in space, west to east across the country.

***

"Kadiak, I think, won a place in the hearts of all of us . . . so secluded, so remote, so peaceful; such a mingling of the domestic, the pastoral, the sylvan, with the wild and the rugged. . . ." The place was an inhabited island off the Alaska Peninsula (now Kodiak); the writer was John Burroughs, who is not remembered for his love of rugged wilderness. His taste for landscape had been shaped back east, on the family farm among the hills and undulating mountains of the Catskills, in upstate New York. He had spent most of his writing life even farther east, in a country place overlooking the Hudson River and eventually in a woodland cabin nearby. Then in 1899, aged sixty-two, Burroughs joined a group of some forty scientists, artists, writers, and others, all guests on the Harriman Alaska Expedition organized by the railroad magnate E. H. Harriman.[10]

As this was his first journey west of the Mississippi, Burroughs confronted landscapes that to him were new and strange, even sublime. Yet most of the landscapes he recalled from that journey—fertile farms, billowing grasses on the unbroken prairie, stupendous waterfalls—lacked the nestling, sheltering qualities of landscapes that he had grown to love. These intimate landscapes could sometimes be found in nature, but more often they were accidental products of a blend of cultivation and wildness. Interestingly, the "most thrillingly beautiful bit of natural scenery" he recalled from that journey was not in Alaska but in the Pacific Northwest. Multnomah Falls, along the Columbia River Gorge through the Cascades, stirred him as no other landscape ever had. "So ethereal, yet so massive; a combination of a certain coyness and unapproachableness with such elemental grandeur and power," Burroughs exclaimed. "The brief view warmed me up like a great symphony."[11]

But brief views were ultimately unsatisfying. Burroughs liked to live long in one place and know it by the songs of its birds, the imprint of time on its stone, the increasing wildness as autumn gave way to winter. He liked watercourses that were small and might become familiar companions while he was walking or lounging along their banks. A large river, he believed, did not "flow through your affections like a lesser stream."[12] But on this point John Muir could hardly agree. For glaciers, the most glorious of rivers, were his passion—or one of them.

Describing that two-month expedition of 1899, Burroughs did not mention any time spent with Muir in particular, though the coming together of these two white-bearded naturalists in Alaska was remarkable.

*The Serpentine Glacier in Harriman Fiord was discovered by the Harriman
Alaska Expedition of 1899. John Muir, a member of the expedition, thought this
glacier "superb" and found the entire fiord (an inlet of Prince William Sound)
"purely wild—a place after my own heart." (Photograph by Edward S. Curtis,
June 27, 1899. Courtesy of MSCUA, University of Washington Libraries,
Harriman 119.)*

It was an "event in American life," in the view of a much younger fellow
guest, Charles Keeler, the poet and naturalist from Berkeley. Keeler spent
quiet times with both men on that expedition. With Burroughs he went
off to a wooded island near Kadiak, studied the wildflowers and moss-
draped trees, and listened for subtle variations in the songs of a winter
wren. With Muir he shared a stateroom on the ship and came to believe
that the passion of Muir's life was nothing less than "the awakening of
the dull and circumscribed soul of the average man or woman to the
ineffable splendour of the great out-of-doors."[13]

Muir

The 1899 expedition was Muir's fifth visit to Alaska, and he knew exactly what he wanted to study. It was not layers of human habitation and wildness but utter wilderness—the northern part of what was once a belt of glaciers two thousand miles long, from about 63° latitude in Alaska, near Mount McKinley, down to the Sierra Nevada in California. Muir's published notes from the Harriman Expedition are a concise account of the glaciers' natural processes, with only passing mention of celestial light, crystal prairies, and the songs sung by rivers of ice and rivers of water.[14] On his first trip to Alaska, in 1879, he had by chance visited the ruins of a deserted Native American village overgrown with weeds and vines. In the lichen- and moss-encrusted totem poles and wooden dwellings he found excellent workmanship and "skill of a wild and positive kind." The artifacts spoke to him of seriousness, bravery, and truth. And yet Muir's own voice was oddly muted, as if his deeper sympathies could be stirred only by the products of inhuman forces, something truly expressive of divinity.[15]

When Muir and Burroughs came together in 1899 in Alaska, they stood for a wide spectrum of attitudes toward wildness and civilization at the century's end. In the new century, people who shared their concerns might look to Burroughs or to Muir for inspiration yet recognize that emulation was not possible. It was not only a question of receding frontiers, for large areas of Alaska would long remain unexplored. But as the frontier receded in the lower forty-eight states, as people increasingly left rural areas for cities and towns, as autos, radios, steam heat, and billboards became common, the relative values of civilization and wildness had to be reconsidered.

Robert Marshall, for instance, came to Alaska in 1929 with a passion for adventure and discovery that was comparable to Muir's. Disregarding personal dangers in the pursuit of yet another high peak or blank spot on other people's maps, Marshall might remind one of Muir, who once crossed ice bridges across crevasses in a glacier with the terrified dog Stickeen as night was approaching and rain turned to snow.[16] Even Marshall's role as a founder of the Wilderness Society recalls Muir and the Sierra Club. Yet there were some sharp differences.

Marshall, a trained forester, was also an intellectual who craved the rugged outdoor life (and pleaded with friends to call him Bob). Born in New York City in 1901, he grew up there, fearing that the days of physical adventures were over. Lewis and Clark, Thomas Jefferson's explorers, were Marshall's boyhood heroes. Marshall did get to Alaska, midway through a doctoral program in plant physiology. Later he would assume upper-level management roles in both the U.S. Forest Service and the Bureau of Indian Affairs. He was free-spirited, gregarious, and happily solitary at intervals, yet he worked within networks of bureaucratic constraints that Muir never knew. Marshall also shared the environmental and social views of his father, a constitutional lawyer, Jewish leader, and advocate for minorities. These facts help to explain why the first book to bring Marshall national recognition was not about wilderness alone but about human settlement in the wilderness.[17]

Marshall arrived at the gold-mining settlement of Wiseman, just south of the Arctic Circle, in the summer of 1929, more than a decade after the last gold rush had subsided. From there, with a prospector as guide, he set off to study tree growth at northern timberline. The journey yielded nothing Marshall would publish in a scientific journal. But a fascination for the people and the land brought him back for the year 1930–31 to study "civilization in the Arctic."[18] Although not profoundly affected by the Depression himself, he was aware of the suffering and quiet desperation of Americans in other parts of the United States at that time. In contrast, the 127 people who lived in Wiseman and along the watershed of the Upper Koyukuk (77 white [and Marshall included in this category a pale-skinned African American], 44 Eskimo, 6 Indian) struck him as remarkably content on the whole. It took him a book of nearly 400 pages to explain why, writing as a lay anthropologist about geography, climate, history, labor, communal life, philosophy, and more.

In *Arctic Village* (1933) Marshall also wrote as an admiring friend of these people, many of whom had first rushed out to greet his airplane on his arrival in 1929, back when planes were rare in the Arctic. As his lists, tables, transcribed conversations, and black-and-white photographs reveal, Marshall could not separate social from environmental issues, so

OVER TIME

closely were these things intertwined. Anticipating the long Arctic winter of his second sojourn, Marshall had shipped to Wiseman a phonograph and a crate of records and books to share, ranging from Oswald Spengler's *Decline of the West* and Leo Tolstoy's *Anna Karenina* to a work on thermodynamics. The Eskimos responded to Ravel's *Bolero* as if it were the music of nature at its most wild. What Marshall responded to in the Eskimos and their neighbors was a vitality and serenity born of independence, communal interests, a zest for dancing, storytelling, and travel by dogsled, and freedom from any fear of unemployment. There was always work and always time, it seemed, to help out a neighbor or a stranger.

Despite the tables and statistics, one might dismiss *Arctic Village* as an idealized account of a few arduous, impoverished lives in a harsh if beautiful land. Yet even the sharp-tongued H. L. Mencken judged it a good book. He felt the author was shrewd, civilized, sometimes eloquent; and some of the portraits he took were "superb."[19] Marshall's final words bear quoting:

> . . . the inhabitants of the Koyukuk would rather eat beans with liberty, burn candles with independence, and mush dogs with adventure than to have the luxury and the restrictions of the outside world. A person misses many things by living in the isolation of the Koyukuk, but he gains a life filled with an amount of freedom, tolerance, beauty, and contentment such as few human beings are ever fortunate enough to achieve.[20]

***

Two French missionary priests were settling down to Christmas dinner when one paused to observe, ". . . a soup like this is not the work of one man. It is the result of a constantly refined tradition. There are nearly a thousand years of history in this soup."[21]

With these words Willa Cather distills a major theme of her novel *Death Comes for the Archbishop* (1927), set in a land she had first seen and loved in 1912—the American Southwest. The theme is civilization. Here it emerges from the different cultures—French, Spanish, Anglo-American, Mexican, Native American—that meet in the sparsely settled land she never labels "wilderness." Instead, she shows us its wildness in the hardness of sun-baked earth, the aromatic smoke of burning piñon logs, the savage sound of a banjo, the sand that filters through cracks in the walls of a Navajo hogan. A French bishop and his fellow priest, who had been boyhood friends in their native Auvergne, embody the refinement of French culture and, by extension, Western civilization. This is a refinement of soul, not of surfaces. The bishop's friendship with the taciturn Navajo chief is believable, then, despite their differences.

Cather draws some now-familiar contrasts between the Europeans' urge to stand apart from nature, to master it, and the Native Americans' tendency to slip into the landscape and vanish, or to become a part of the landscape, using its resources with restraint, on a relatively small scale. But Cather also depicts an uncommon kinship between the Old World and the New. A spring bubbles out of the parched earth in New Mexico and creates an oasis overhung by cottonwoods. It is an ancient refuge for humanity, the bishop reflects. "It was older than history, like those well-heads in his own country where the Roman settlers had set up the image of a river goddess, and later the Christian priests had planted a cross."[22] In both the Old World and the New, human desires have long ago been written and overwritten on the land, yet the New World still retains a simplicity and freshness—at times crude, at times austerely beautiful.

The Old World and the New, cultivation and wildness, all come together in the bishop's garden. There he finds his recreation, his opportunity for making again and renewing. A row of old tamarisks with hardened, twisted trunks, left over from before the bishop's arrival, has its counterpart in a row of young poplars. Both common trees and rare varieties yield apples, cherries, apricots, quinces, and French pears—a shared harvest, in that cuttings from these trees are bearing fruit in many Mexican gardens. A place of mingled beauty and utility, the bishop's garden contains vegetable plots, an orchard, a grape arbor, and native wildflowers such as the purple verbena that he has domesticated and then let run up a hillside to form a solid mantle of rose-violet and blue-violet glowing in the sun.

As he tends his garden and attends to the spiritual needs of his people, the bishop becomes attached to the sparse, dry landscape around Santa Fe, with its plains, mountains, villages, and encircling hills. In time, about to retire, he goes back to the misty mountains and deep valleys of his native Auvergne. But the morning air is heavy there, just as it is heavy in all lands where the plow and harvests have replaced the open range. The bishop reflects on what happens to the human spirit as wildness gives way to cultivation and as the fresh, light air of grassy unbroken plains and sagebrush desert is lost. "That air would disappear from the whole earth in time," he imagines. Meanwhile, he knows that the New Mexico air, light and fragrant, still makes him feel young: "Something soft and wild and free, something that whispered to the ear on the pillow, lightened the heart, softly, softly picked the lock, slid the bolts, and released the prisoned spirit of man into the wind, into the blue and gold, into the morning, into the morning!"[23] And so the aging bishop returns to Santa Fe, where the cathedral he has had built of a golden ochre stone will remain a fortress of civilization after he is gone. The story is moving, exhilarating despite traces of ambivalence about cultivation and wildness. What lingers is the bishop's graceful acceptance of change, which is not only inevitable but also a sign of life.[24]

* * *

Forty-six years separate two books on wilderness and half-wild places in the Gulf Coast country, Maurice Thompson's *My Winter Garden* (1900) and Henry Hazlitt Kopman's *Wild Acres* (1946). What brings them together is a common fascination with birds and an overlap in the authors' years of leisurely yet purposeful exploration along the Mississippi Delta and its coast.

Thompson, an Indiana lawyer who left his profession in mid-career to write poetry and prose, had grown up in Georgia and fought for the Confederacy. With pioneer ancestors in the South since the seventeenth century, he was perhaps more alert than some to the overlays of human aspiration and wildness in his winter environs on the Gulf Coast. Yet each winter on arrival from the frigid Midwest he had to readjust to a "thermal dream," a drowsy atmosphere in which all Nature appeared to nod and blink, never quite sleeping, while all sense of boundaries vanished. Even the line between land and water kept shifting, as one seemed to merge into the other.

"All the adjoining lands are yours," Thompson announces early on. "What you can see you hold." He chooses a marsh meadow frequented by herons. And as he surveys his ever-expanding domain—a territory limited only by the imagination—he believes he sees something rare. It is the "blending of savage nature with the most advanced results of landscape culture." Centuries ago, he muses, the Indians probably arrived to camp there in winter, bringing with them exotic plants. Later white people did likewise. Over time the tenderly cultivated exotics would have slipped beyond the pales and into the woods and marshes, adapting to the soil and climate and finally becoming what Thompson would call "indigenous." This thought leads to the idea of a palimpsest, "vague records upon records stamped in the soil" by Spaniards and Frenchmen, buccaneers and planters. As an example, he describes a flowering acacia that seems to flourish in a primitive pine forest. But a closer look reveals row upon row of cotton ridges running through that forest. Where he stands, then, was once a vast open field, cultivated by slaves.[25]

In the spirit of Montaigne, his master, Thompson uses the open-ended literary form of the essay to philosophize now and again. His tone is genial but his words can be sobering. In one aside, he declares that the "return to nature" is really about following one's genius, uninfluenced by fashion or the critics. And this applies to birds as well as to humans when Thompson distinguishes among the songs of different mockingbirds—the resident, the migrant, and the one in a cage. Defying a contemporary expert, Thompson insists that in brilliance, power, purity, and sweetness the songs of both the free resident and the migrant are far superior to the song of the lonely captive bird. And only the migrant is truly wild. "There is no mistaking the joyous, triumphant strain of him whose life has been perfected in the broadest freedom of nature," Thompson writes. "It is the strain of genius, audacious, defiant, untrammeled—a voice of absolute independence crying in the wilderness."[26]

Kopman's tone is not so assertive as he describes the creatures and environs of the Gulf Coast. Perhaps it was a question of sensibility, or of minds differently shaped and furnished. Thompson had once worked as a civil engineer and had served as state geologist of Indiana in the 1880s, yet there was more of Chaucer, Montaigne, and the ancient Greek poets in *My Winter Garden* than the method of a scientist. In contrast, Kopman, a graduate of Tulane University, worked for the U.S. Bureau of Biological Survey, became active in ornithological societies, and organized seabird nesting colonies in Louisiana, Mississippi, and Florida. Although written for a lay audience, his *Wild Acres* is informed by decades of patient observation for scientific purposes during a period of rising professionalism and specialization. All the more welcome, then, is the graceful literary tone of his writing, which calls to mind the early writings of his younger contemporary Rachel Carson.[27]

Born in New Orleans, Kopman came of age about the end of the nineteenth century. The Gulf Coast he recalls from that era was a place of repose, with comfortable houses, a few fishing wharfs, a sandy beach road, but no seawall. It was not a wilderness, nor did it suggest the tensions of a town. Remembering the time when vacationers began arriving, Kopman gives no dates, only the sounds of rustling in the tops of pines, the odors of resin and something like wintergreen, the colors of wildflowers, and the activities of woodpeckers, nuthatches, warblers, pelicans, and other birds.

New Orleans, he explains, was once a city that could sustain one's zest for studying birds, so rural were certain parts of the city. In an area of uptown called Blue Alley, an uncovered drainage canal was bordered by a dense hedge of Cherokee rose on one side and a pathway lined by Osage orange trees on the other. The buildings and sounds of the city were nearby, yet the pathway had the atmosphere of a country lane. In fact, he and a few city-bound friends used to gather there and trace the migrations of birds that were rare in Louisiana, including the Philadelphia vireo, the purple finch, and the white-crowned sparrow.[28]

Studying habitats, Kopman notices when some particular alteration by humans has accidentally changed the birds' movements or the composition of species overall. Formerly submerged or swampy surfaces may have become a rich woodland with dense undergrowth—not quite a jungle—because of a drainage project elsewhere. In these woodlands, birds seem to move about with leisure; "a strange secrecy covers the life of thrushes, vireos, warblers, and other woodland kinds; their voices advance and recede deceptively among leafy masses."[29]

On the whole, Kopman seems willing to accept the human alterations to the land-and-water continuum that he describes. Yet he admits that the sugar plantations were less obtrusive, more welcoming to birds, around the turn of the century than in the 1940s. "Improvements and cultivation, instead of dominating the outlook, sank into it as a token of truce between man and nature," he recalls. "Even though the needs of civilized living were there, the wilderness was always within touch." With their blend of new cultivation and old growths, the sugar plantations offered a variety of habitats: the old drainage canals overhung with vegetation, the live oaks and pecans near the house, and the "batture" between the levee and the river, formed by silt deposits and covered with a bower-like deciduous forest.[30]

This batture could serve as a symbol of all the half-wild places that Kopman explores. It offers what might not exist along the Gulf Coast had people never built levees there—an "illusion of upland country," and thus an attraction for shy migrating birds from the North.

Kopman finds more half-wild places in the ribbon of land shored up by levees along the final reaches of the Mississippi and among the river's bays, mudflats, and mainstream. This strip of land in Plaquemines Parish, barely a mile wide, lies mostly west of the mainstream—or did at the time Kopman was writing. He explains that among these watery lands, east and west are difficult to separate.[31] And in his account of this "realm apart," neither countryside nor wildness, what is past and what is present are not always clear as things and people intermingle. He writes of a few English-speaking families among the Creoles, the migrating birds, and the seasonal movements of people who tend the fields and orchards and harvest the rice, sugar cane, oranges, and pecans. A steamer, a passing train, or the crack of a hunter's gun pierces the quiet now and again. But once alerted, furtive birds such as the king rail and purple gallinule, hidden among wild coffee and indigo and water plants, may escape by rising up just at the moment when the hunter is struggling for a foothold in the watery ground. Without idealizing the place, Kopman simply observes, "Life in these surroundings rose seldom above the level of simple activities, an all-enveloping tranquillity, and an inert, inarticulate beauty stamped here by nature."[32]

***

Moving on from the languid Gulf Coast to the more bustling Eastern Seaboard, we could linger in the wild lands of the Carolina Low Country or the beaches and barrier islands, bays and marshes extending for hundreds of miles farther south or north. But for the most unexpected layering of human habitation and wildness we go straight to the heart of a coastal city.

"Into any garden, no matter how artificial or how tame, some wild things will find their way," wrote the essayist Herbert Ravenel Sass in 1935. In a desert of roofs and streets, he noted, a city garden could be an oasis, more densely filled with wildlife than a square mile of country. Looking up from weeding his own garden in Charleston, Sass once saw something glorious in the darkening sky: a pair of eagles flying south. Another time he gazed at three low-flying Canada geese. For the birds' sake, he welcomed some weeds in the garden, along with a variety of trees, shrubs, vines, and grasses. "Nature—wild Nature—dwells in gardens just as she dwells in the tangled woods, in the deeps of the sea, and on the heights of the mountains," he insisted, "and the wilder the garden, the more you will see of her there."[33]

Of all the eastern cities, few can have stirred the imaginations of people who care for wildness more powerfully than New York. A whole volume could be written about the city's creatures, habitats, and transformations due to weather, the seasons, the rivers, and the sea. Between 1897 and 1949 alone, the writings of Charles M. Skinner, Mabel Osgood Wright, Margaret McKenny, Lewis Gannett, Walter Prichard Eaton, Charles Downing Lay, John C. Van Dyke, Donald Culross Peattie, John Kieran, and others would appear in such a volume. Katharine S. White's garden articles did not appear in the *New Yorker* until 1958, but her husband, the essayist E. B. White, might occupy a page or two in a book about "wild" nature in New York through 1949.[34]

In the summer of 1948, noting the Popsicles and remembering the literary giants, White saw New York as a poem, a compressor of all life into a small island. If he detected more irritability and tension there than in years past, New York still offered the "gifts" of loneliness and privacy. Toward the close of his wry meditation, White reflected on the prospects of annihilation from the air just as the new United Nations headquarters was about to rise. And he ended his essay *Here Is New York* with an old willow tree in a garden a few blocks west of the future UN headquarters. For him this willow, held together by wires and reaching for the sun, was a symbol of the city, of persistent life and growth against all odds. "If it were to go," White mused, "all would go—this city, this mischievous and marvelous monument which not to look upon would be like death."[35]

If our journey in space and time were to end in New York at the dawn of the Cold War, a yearning for the old frontiers charted by Frederick Jackson Turner would be understandable but futile. Yet by mid-century there remained a few frontiers that Turner may never have recognized— though E. B. White possibly did, wandering afield from his old farmhouse in Maine.

One frontier lay practically undisturbed in the early twentieth century, and such writers as Sarah Orne Jewett, who was born and reared in South Berwick, Maine, were among the first to see a glimmer of its potential. It was largely a New England phenomenon, in part a result of the late nineteenth-century decline in whaling, shipping, and agriculture. It was recognizable in the unkempt yards around dilapidated wooden farmhouses, in the ungrazed pastures overtaken by shrubs and trees, in the stone walls that seemed to run without purpose through dense forests. Sometimes the frontier was in the forests themselves, formidable even in their second growth. Or the frontier lay in abandoned structures and half-wild fields, calling out for human efforts to mend, reshape, and tame again.

In Jewett's "Dunnet Shepherdess" (1899), set in the land "up country" from a village on the Maine coast, a visitor from the city asks why people don't raise more sheep on the exposed, sloping ground, which seems fit for little else. The elderly native's answer lies in one exception to the rule of decline and decay—a successful, intelligent woman farmer (his sweetheart of forty years) who is willing to give her waking hours to herding sheep and caring for her widowed mother.[36]

The New Yorker Edith Wharton, who lived for half the year in Lenox, Massachusetts, in the early 1900s, also wrote about the declining rural landscape and its people, most of them poor, some lawless, some dutiful. But her vision of their lives is dark, and lovers just about destroy one another. One of her most highly regarded novels, *Ethan Frome* (1911), is predominantly keyed to winter, its isolating storms, frozen feelings, memories snowed under, ambitions buried. In Jewett's *Country of the Pointed Firs* (1896) and later, in "A Dunnet Shepherdess," the moods of summer prevail; a wise widow can use cultivated and wild herbs to cure illnesses, and sweethearts blessed with inner resources and stamina can marry at sixty. Wharton dismissed Jewett's renderings of country life, seen through "rose-colored spectacles."[37] Yet Jewett's characters seem genuine, drawn from childhood memory and depicted with a sympathy untroubled by Wharton's grimmer sense of reality. Perhaps somewhere between their two visions lay the frontier that actually beckoned.

In any case, Wharton revealed that a distant glimpse of Bear Mountain, some twelve miles south of The Mount, her elegant home in Lenox, had led her to expand an earlier, unfinished tale into the chilling *Ethan Frome* we know today.[38] A closer look at Bear Mountain also inspired Walter Prichard Eaton's vision of hope for the declining rural landscape of New England. As we have seen, Eaton had spent some eight years as a drama critic in New York before settling permanently in the Berkshires in 1910, to live there year round by his writing, lecturing, and teaching. For nearly thirty years he served on a state planning board, the Mount Everett Reservation Commission. From 1940 until his death in 1957 he also wrote a weekly column for the county's largest daily newspaper, the *Berkshire Eagle.* Eaton had a range of opportunities, then, to influence public opinion and to help shape and maintain his environment.[39]

About ten miles north of Eaton's farm in Sheffield, Massachusetts, was the summit of Bear Mountain, a high plateau some ten miles long, where a once-viable farming community had dwindled to a few families living among unplowed fields that were reverting to forests. Here and there an old colonial dwelling was sinking into a pile of lumber and bricks. While there was talk of "redeeming" some hill towns, Eaton made one suggestion in 1917: In a place such as Beartown, where the old independent agricultural life could no longer be restored (for lack of abilities, imagination, economic incentives, or whatever), why not welcome the forest that was clearly winning out over the farms—a state forest, with splendid trees, properly harvested, along with hiking trails, game preserves, and perhaps a mountain inn? Rather than die, the old settlements might thrive as "human centres in the busy wilderness." Eaton thought his dream might be realized even in Massachusetts, "which has a quaint faculty of every now and then kicking clean over the traces of tradition in which it usually plods, and doing something radical and eminently sane."[40]

The dream was realized in part. Although the community of Beartown has disappeared, Eaton may have had something to do with its successor, Beartown State Forest. Within the boundaries of that state forest there now runs a segment of the Appalachian Trail; and its route corresponds to the general outlines Eaton recommended in 1922, shortly after his friend Benton MacKaye first published the original idea of an Appalachian Trail.[41] Hiking and trail-blazing were among Eaton's greatest pleasures; and while others might detect only sadness and degeneracy in New England's agricultural decline, Eaton seems to have found there a kind of new yet old frontier. "The West remains conquered," he wrote in 1933, thinking of the celebrated American pioneers and their agricultural triumphs. "But the high New England hills did not remain conquered."[42]

By the 1940s two more frontiers had emerged on the Eastern Seaboard, within the city and at its ragged edges. Two men, both seeking to regain their health, went out alone into a wilderness most people never imagine. And in each case, an ornithologist saw in their personal quests something universal.

"Every country dweller with trained ear and eye may discover a frontier of which his pioneer ancestors were largely ignorant," wrote Dr. Frank M. Chapman, curator of ornithology at the American Museum of Natural History, in New York. He was alluding to birds and other wild creatures that were still thriving, even in the unkempt fringes of urban New Jersey. And so, in the foreword to *Modern Wilderness* (1940), by the amateur naturalist William A. Babson, Chapman encouraged readers not to lament the passing of the frontier, but to go out and look for it. In the late 1930s Babson had done just that, exploring the river valleys of the Passaic and the Whippany. Within a stone's throw of highways and billboards yet hidden from the motorist's view were swamps, marshes, and forested islands where summer canopies were so dense that sunlight barely penetrated and outside noises were hushed. This was Babson's frontier, a sanctuary for wildlife—and for people.[43]

Two woodcocks spiral up into the air to sing their courtship, oblivious of the distant rumbling traffic. Two downy gray barred owls—barely hatched and helpless—stare up from a crotch in a tree into the lens of a camera. The delight in such discoveries is eventually interrupted by the sounds of steam and clanking machinery. A WPA flood-control project is under way, to dredge the bottom of the Passaic and dump the remains on a bank denuded of its trees. "Why is this little wilderness a paradise only to a few?" Babson asks, wondering if youth no longer finds nature beautiful, mysterious, with all the allure of a great adventure. He thinks of shiny speeding cars, radios, the news of bombs shattering Warsaw, all seemingly far away. Close by and real are the feeding waterfowl and the call of a horned owl. Babson has no answers but concludes that "life goes on as it did before the white man came. There is beauty here. There is serenity. There is peace in the evening sky."[44]

In *Modern Wilderness* we never learn what kind of illness had sent Babson, a New York lawyer, into the swamps of New Jersey. But, seeking health in his boyhood haunts, he found a reality of wildness and peace to counter that other reality of war, which was already tearing Europe apart. A few years later, in the winter of 1944–45 in Washington, D.C., Louis Halle found that his eyesight was deteriorating while he worked long hours at the U.S. State Department. Prescribed tonics and advised to start wearing glasses, Halle instead began to go out in all kinds of weather, cycling, walking to work, wading through marshes, always looking for birds—in the tidewater, along Rock Creek Park, at the National Airport, in the sky.

In the process, Halle's normal eyesight returned. But when friends chided him for escaping reality, he tried to explain the feeling of getting outside after a long confinement, like awakening after a nightmare. "This is reality, this meadowlark singing in the sunlight," he wrote, "not the artificial banging and clatter that, mistaken for life itself, had made life seem meaningless."[45]

Halle's *Spring in Washington* (1947) is a joyous revelation of the miracle that is spring as it slowly unfolds in the midst of a great city. It contains such close and spirited observation of bird life that Halle's friend Roger Tory Peterson was moved to write an eloquent foreword for the second edition.[46] And yet Halle obliquely observes human life as well, routine human life in the offices and city streets of the nation's capital.

No stranger to bureaucracy, Halle chides those "workers in the hive" who are attuned only to "news of the hive"—perhaps the arrival of some French functionary—while the news of arriving ducks goes unrecorded. "Our civilization, apparently, has become divorced from the universe and is feeding on itself," he muses.[47] His allusions to the weapons of war and the death of President Roosevelt are only indirect. For he is sketching in a world, a whole universe, as seen by something he associates with eternity—a flock of migrating geese, perhaps, or two violets blooming in a crack in the pavement of Rock Creek Parkway. And so he rewrites geography from the point of view of wilderness and wild creatures. Surveyed by an eagle, Washington is a wandering tribe's campground, a temporary usurping of the eagle's "immemorial domain." Washington is also a frontier town, seen by some fish and fowl—for, as they move upriver, their saltwater habitat ends at the Tidal Basin and the Falls of the Potomac. Georgetown is "where the West begins." Below it is the cultivated piedmont; above it the Potomac flows in rapids.

Where do these perceptions come from? From the first mention of

Thoreau, Halle sets up expectations. In time it appears that his Washington is Thoreau's Concord, Massachusetts; his Rock Creek or Tidal Basin is Thoreau's Walden Pond. The logic is straightforward. "An appreciation of nature is the proper expression of our urban civilization," Halle observes, noting that Walden meant a great deal to Thoreau because of nearby Concord. And wilderness means a great deal to Halle because of New York and Washington. Though he cannot live entirely within a human-centered world, neither can he take these cities for granted. He notes, "I would have them serve no better purpose than to direct the attention of men outward to the world of nature, to be the shadows that frame the sunlight."[48]

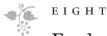

EIGHT

Ecology along the Roadside, by the Water, & in the Garden

A man in a bowler hat and a dark business suit stands behind a low pile of sand and sparse vegetation, his back to the water. The caption beneath the photograph identifies the pile of sand as an "embryonic dune" along the beach at Cheltenham, south of Chicago; the vegetation is *Ammophila*, a sand reed. In another photograph, a woman in a light-colored blouse and a long, dark skirt stands in the wheel rut of a country lane. On the left, a swath of sunlit grass forms an opening among roadside shrubs and deciduous trees. To the right, masses of sunflowers rise above the flowers of the woman's narrow-brimmed straw hat. With wildflowers spilling over one arm, she stands erect, her gaze fixed on the sunflowers, *Helianthus annuus.* Both images appear in works of 1901. But from the texts we learn nothing of the man in the bowler hat; he simply gives scale to the dune. The woman, "Flower Hat," knows something about classical music, likes to paint out-of-doors, and annoys an elderly farmer and naturalist by her indiscriminate picking of wildflowers.[1]

These photographs represent two different ways of introducing ideas about ecology to the general reader. The first photograph had already appeared in 1899, in a series of more technical articles on Lake Michigan's dune vegetation, written by a young plant ecologist at the University of Chicago, Henry Chandler Cowles (1869–1939).[2] In 1901 Cowles summarized his studies of the dunes for a wider audience, while he also described other plant associations, or "plant societies," that he had studied along ravines, river bluffs, prairies, swamps, and sand hills in and around Chicago.[3] For this wider audience he gave detailed directions so that others could retrace his journeys, getting around by railway and streetcar. And yet his approach was not popular but scientific. Methodically he focused on land forms, watercourses, erosion, water-borne deposits of sand and silt, and the border lines, or "zones of transition," between one plant association and another. Above all, he was interested in change: how a sand dune encroaches on a swamp or a forest and eventually buries it; how an island in a river migrates downstream, its upriver portion slowly eroding, its downriver portion enlarging as sand bars form; how one plant association succeeds another as the conditions of light, soil, moisture, wind, and other phenomena change.

In 1901 Cowles credited European scientists with introducing the fairly new field of plant ecology—the relations between plants and their environment.[4] In turn, the historian Donald Worster has recognized Cowles as America's first professional ecologist, who worked independently of the Nebraska ecologist Frederic E. Clements but thought along similar lines. Cowles and Clements were both founders of what became known as the tradition of "dynamic ecology," or studies of succession from one plant society to another.[5] As Cowles asserted in 1901, "There must be, then, an order of succession of plant societies, just as there is an order of succession of topographic forms in the changing landscape. As the years pass by, one plant society must necessarily be supplanted by another, though the one passes into the other by imperceptible gradations."[6]

These insights could stimulate professional landscape designers, such as Cowles's friend Jens Jensen, as well as informed amateurs. But to some readers a scientist's latest finding about the natural world would not in itself be compelling. To interest them, the man in the bowler hat had to be made real, part of a story, a human story—at least, that is the impression we get from turn-of-the-century nature writing by such best-selling authors as John Burroughs and Gene Stratton-Porter, and by those with smaller but significant followings, such as Bradford Torrey, Mabel Osgood Wright, and Dallas Lore Sharp. As Sharp observed in 1911, nature writers were not detached, like scientists, but personally engaged with nature, "domesticating" it for themselves and others. The best were sincere, joyous, sensitive to the pulse of life, and motivated by a "large love for the earth as a dwelling-place."[7] Among them are the writers considered here—those who mediate between scientists and nonscientists, professionals and amateurs.

***

It was Mabel Osgood Wright who photographed the woman in the flowered straw hat, gazing at sunflowers along a country lane. In her *Flowers and Ferns in Their Haunts* (1901), Flower Hat is a product of modern urban civilization, a fashionable woman too restless to sit still while her friend the narrator slowly scans the Connecticut countryside for something worth photographing. What the narrator seeks, beyond the native plants that grow in hidden places, is the spirit of the woods and fields, marshes and streams. One day she finds that spirit embodied in a man she calls "Time o' Year," a native with roots in the soil that go back two hundred years.[8]

This elderly man's ancestors had tamed the wilderness, cultivated the land, and handed it down. Now he appears to be the end of the line, a widower and reluctant farmer whose son left home some forty years earlier. From a book left behind by a schoolteacher who once boarded at his farmhouse, Time o' Year has picked up some botanical names, but much of his deep knowledge of plants has come to him from dwelling among green living things. A recluse, he rarely speaks. When he does, his words tumble out in a rough country idiom. He also camouflages his botanical and spiritual quests by carrying a fishing rod, something "purposeful." Ironically, in a land of abandoned farmhouses and forests overrunning the old fields, there are few neighbors to question his apparently idle wandering. The narrator, whose husband is mentioned but never around, also enjoys wandering, driving her one-horse carriage alone or with her friend Flower Hat. Slowly the narrator gains the confidence of the reclusive old man, who knows the time of year when all sorts of plants are flowering but hesitates to share his knowledge for fear that callous weekenders from the city will pick the flowers. The narrator shows her good faith by carrying no shears or pruners, only a camera. Time o' Year accepts her as a kindred spirit, tolerates her fashionable friend, and shows both of them places of unexpected beauty.

At first this fellow with rough country speech seems to be a narrative device that allowed Wright to give fairly painless lessons in ecology. Without using the terms "plant association" and "habitat," she simply let their meanings unfold within the story. She also took about half of the book's many photographs; the others were credited to her printer, J. Horace McFarland. Wright wrote from experience, then. And what she knew through her senses she underscored: that many fine plants should be sought out in their native haunts, where their colors, fragrances, habits, and neighbors—flora and fauna—could be appreciated; that to pick a flowering plant or transplant it in a different habitat would be to change it, however subtly.

While Henry Cowles focused on complex linear changes, writing of "progressive" and "retrogressive" phases of change in plant societies, Mabel Osgood Wright gave more attention to cyclical changes, diurnal and seasonal. And so the environs of her country home in Fairfield, Connecticut, seem fairly stable, despite hints of urban development encroaching from her native New York City. Cowles's world seems more dynamic. Viewing the retrogressive phases of change as relatively ephemeral, he asserted that progressive changes, however slow to develop, should be recognizable over long periods of time. He borrowed terms for four major plant groups—hydrophytes, xerophytes, mesophytes, and halophytes—from the recent work of the Danish ecologist Eugenius Warming.[9] And the idea of progress, so pervasive in his time, Cowles seems to have accepted without question.

Meanwhile, Wright referred to the "so-called progress" that had silenced most of the water wheels of old mills along a river. She wrote of ancient hemlock woods that men had cut down or burned. And she lingered over the middle ground: the half-wild places of second- and third-growth woods and the chance roadside gardens where natives mingled with "wayfaring" plants that had escaped from household gardens and become naturalized. Now all seemed to belong, natives and wayfarers alike.

To write of these things Wright didn't need fictional devices. But with Flower Hat and Time o' Year she could expand her ecological studies to include humans, who were not only agents of change in the landscape but sometimes wayfarers, like plants, seeking a place to call home. Thus a Hungarian couple with many children try to reclaim an old abandoned farm in Connecticut. The long-lost son of Time o' Year, who has made his fortune in California, marries a Hispanic Catholic. This son and his wife die young, leaving a daughter who is engaged to be married. So the lineage of Time o' Year may be carried on, after all. The intricate plot is somewhat improbable; some readers might prefer to focus on the ferns and wildflowers. Yet the people and the plants keep intermingling, mirroring one another. Time o' Year's self-image, "only a stalk of wayside Silkweed goin' to seed," plays off the narrator's view of him as a "half wild wood spirit in his haunt." And Wright the amateur ecologist plays off Wright the social critic, attuned to the forces of civilization that are changing her world. Protestants might marry Catholics, people and plants might become naturalized, but the concept of a native haunt—a habitat where plants, wildlife, and people seem to be at home—lives on.
***

To appreciate Bradford Torrey's accounts of sauntering along valley roads in the White Mountains of New Hampshire or drifting down a river in Florida's Everglades, we don't need to know that he was a co-editor of Thoreau's journals. But once alerted to that fact, we realize that Torrey's own manner of writing about birds, trees, and habitats may have been influenced by what he had noticed while looking over Thoreau's shoulder, so to speak.

In 1899 Torrey noted that Thoreau needed to know something about botany, ornithology, entomology, and other fields to pursue his outdoor studies. Like any scientist, Thoreau needed a sharp eye, patience, diligence. But he also aspired to sympathy. He wanted to become intimately aware of the life around him, to perfect his own sympathy with things in nature so that he could be moved by them. He gathered facts not to form theories, Torrey observed, but to "know when in the year to expect certain thoughts and moods."[10] In 1906, the year Thoreau's fourteen-volume *Journal* appeared, Torrey tried to clarify once again Thoreau's attitude toward science. "He had by nature a bias toward the investigation of natural phenomena," Torrey explained, "a passion for particulars, which, if he had been less a poet and philosopher, might have made him a man of science." But Thoreau's stronger impulse was toward sensibility, not science; toward seeing, tasting, smelling, hearing, and feeling more than abstract thinking. These seemingly contradictory passions and impulses set up tensions that Thoreau sometimes released through humor and extravagant language. For these Torrey made no apology. Rather, he saw Thoreau and his wild apples as kin; what was sharply acidic and "puckery" in Thoreau's books was in part the quality that preserved them so well in "Time's literary cellar."[11]

Bradford Torrey's own writing was milder, more congenial, and his stories of informal exploration along two coasts of the continent and in the American Southwest reveal none of Thoreau's inner tensions. As a literary journalist with a keen interest in birds, he reported on a range of natural history topics, now and again slipping in some curious fact that might interest a scientist. It happened that he and the botanist John Torrey had a common ancestor. But Bradford Torrey, born in the South Shore town of Weymouth, Massachusetts, in 1843, was not a scientist. Whenever he described his travels with a botanist or some other scientist, he presented himself as an observer, less intent on a scientific quest than broadly curious about all the strange and lovely things in his surroundings.[12]

Torrey was often drawn to half-wild places and the edges of wilderness rather than to its core. In Florida, some five miles south of Miami, he once ventured into a dense, dark jungle but found it too terrifying to linger. On another occasion he came across an unfamiliar glossy-leaved shrub. No white man who happened to pass by could identify it. But the first two African Americans he came across knew it instantly—the cocoa plum, an identity later confirmed in a manual of plants. After more encounters with these people, Torrey noticed that the African Americans were much more observant of natural things than white people. Perhaps, he mused, that was because their forebears had come from the islands, where many of Florida's plants were more at home.[13]

A bachelor, Torrey spent the last three years of his life in Santa Barbara, attracted by the mild climate. There, at the meeting place of sea and land, he was glad simply to be alive among coastal mountains, ocean waves, seabirds, land birds, verbenas, and yellow primroses. Even a smelly tide pool by the railroad tracks, known locally by the Spanish term *estero,* appealed to him because it was a resting place for migrating birds. He knew the *estero* was safe for them, for it lay within the city limits, where shooting birds was prohibited. But how, he wondered, did the birds know it was safe? And why did the small, seemingly frail titlarks that wintered in Santa Barbara fly to the Colorado Rockies every spring? He recalled his own exhilaration as he stood on the summit of Pike's Peak with titlarks for company. If he was drawn to that high, lonely place, could it be that those tiny birds, too, were drawn there by some "irresistible attraction?" Without speculating on what scientists might say, Torrey turned his thoughts back to the Santa Barbara beach and its sanderlings, plovers, scoters, northern phalaropes, and other birds. Sympathetic to those creatures, he recalled a phrase from Keats—who explained that he "takes part in their existence."[14]

The same could be said of Gene Stratton-Porter, wading in the Limberlost Swamp near the Wabash River in northeastern Indiana. There she sought out moths and birds, photographed them, studied their habits, and gleaned details of their lives for her books of fiction and natural history. Born in 1863, the youngest in a family of twelve children, Geneva Stratton grew up on a farm along the Wabash, where she was often free to wander afield. When her mother became an invalid, older siblings took charge, leaving Geneva to amuse herself with a corn doll, some live butterflies, a few classic novels, a wildflower garden. On finding a new bird's nest, Geneva would help feed the chicks without frightening the mother bird. On finding goose quills and arrowheads, she would tuck them away and later sell them for pocket money. From details like these came novels for which the movie rights would be sold.[15] But who could ever film the "carnival" of cecropia moths, which she described in a work of nonfiction? Moonlight shone on the apple trees in bloom; and as she stepped out onto the porch of her cabin, the moths came floating down on her "like birds down the moonbeams," covering her hair, her shoulders, her gown, and her outstretched hands.[16]

Stratton-Porter was a phenomenon in her day, writing books that sold in the millions and were translated into seven languages. One novel, *A Girl of the Limberlost* (1909), was the first American book to be translated into Arabic.[17] Appreciative letters to the author poured in from around the United States, from military camps during World War I, from Asia, from London.[18] In 1921 the Yale professor of English William Lyon Phelps stepped lightly around questions of literary style to proclaim Gene Stratton-Porter one of the foremost naturalists in America, "a public institution, like Yellowstone Park."[19]

Ironically, like Yellowstone, Stratton-Porter's beloved Limberlost Swamp could not endure the impact of modernization and remain unimpaired for future generations. People began to drain the swamp in 1913. In time, rows of celery and sugar beets, oil wells, new roads, bridges, and barbed-wire fences rendered the swamp and its roadsides useless for her fieldwork. Undeterred, Stratton-Porter and her husband left their cabin by the Limberlost Swamp and moved north, to Sylvan Lake.[20] She also took up the nature writer's familiar cause, preservation. Toward the end of his life, for instance, Bradford Torrey had argued that Santa Barbara's eyesore *estero* did not need to be "improved," for it already served a distinguished band of travelers clad in feathers.[21] Toward the end of *her* life, in the 1920s, Stratton-Porter wrote a column in *McCall's* magazine, where she once lamented the increasing scarcity of wild animals and fine hardwood trees that she had known as a child. Arguing that there may be limits to the earth's coal and iron, and making connections between the increasingly dry midwestern summers and the loss of forests, she called for a "nation-wide movement" to preserve areas of natural beauty and conditions favorable to human life. Where birds were abundant, she added, spraying to fight insect pests was unnecessary.[22]

***

Walter Prichard Eaton's native haunts were the rural fringes of Boston, from Malden, where he was born in 1878, to Roxbury and, later, Reading. While he was a boy, those haunts were also extended to include Franconia Notch, in New Hampshire, where his father, a schoolteacher, had acquired an old farmhouse for a summer place. The family's barn door framed a view of Mount Moosilauke, to the south. And three or four miles to the north lay the resort town of Franconia, where, one summer evening, young Eaton watched a performance of *Uncle Tom's Cabin*, then walked home in starlight. Along the way he studied the caravans of the itinerant actors as they passed him on the road, with a lantern swinging from tent poles in the last caravan. He heard a cry—from Eliza's baby, he guessed. It was her real baby onstage, then, not a prop![23]

Years later, as a drama critic in New York, Eaton would not rank the stage adaptation of *Uncle Tom's Cabin* with *Hamlet*. He did, however, reveal a fondness for Harriet Beecher Stowe's people and places. As a boy he had read her later antislavery novel, *Dred: A Tale of the Great Dismal Swamp* (1856); and from then on, the swamp in Reading that he and his friends used to explore grew so vast and frightful in his dreams that he developed a "secret passion" to visit the Dismal Swamp.[24]

Eaton finally went there with an artist friend in early May 1910, taking a night boat from Manhattan to the mouth of the Chesapeake Bay, then a steamer out of Norfolk, Virginia, bound for the Dismal Swamp Canal. Eaton knew something of the swamp's natural history (as part of the ancient bed of the Atlantic Ocean) and its human history (as the site of many drainage projects, including one that George Washington and other Virginia planters had organized in 1763). The "Washington Ditch" seemed to him almost tropical and "beautiful beyond belief," with patches of filtered sunlight like jewels on the black water as he and his friend explored it by canoe. About a third of the swamp's thousand square miles had been reclaimed, he noted, mainly along the edges. What the two men encountered, then, was the remains of a wilderness. Yet despite the logging roads, occasional farms, hunters' camps, canal locks, and a dam on Lake Drummond, the Dismal Swamp still seemed a vast jungle, with an abundance of giant cypresses (*Taxodium distichum*), birds, and other creatures. They saw none of the swamp's notorious snakes or mosquitoes. One day a party of men, women, and children rowed in from Suffolk to enjoy a picnic. One moonlit night Eaton and his friend gazed at the mist rising up from Lake Drummond, while cypresses towered over the mist like white phantoms in a prehistoric forest, their roots lapped by unseen waters. "The scene was poignantly lovely," Eaton wrote, "yet lonely, too, with the soft forgetfulness of a Lotus Land."[25]

Having read Nathaniel S. Shaler's 1888 monograph on the Dismal Swamp, prepared for the U.S. Geological Survey, Eaton disagreed with some of his findings and opinions. Shaler had given only a modest estimate of the bird life, for instance, and predicted that transverse ditches across the swamp would help farmers raise crops worth millions. But Eaton insisted that the swamp was a "paradise of birds" (in spring, at least); and their calls made up a continual symphony. Among other birds, Eaton spotted cardinals, chickadees, a mother ovenbird, a flicker, a Carolina wren, and the rare water thrush. And so, aware that some Virginia lawmakers were thinking of establishing a state reservation around Lake Drummond, Eaton heartily urged them to do so, for the sake of the birds and other wild creatures as well as for the public, who could benefit from such a refuge, wild, beautiful, and imbued with historic significance. "There are thousands upon thousands of square miles in the South still uncultivated which do not require costly drainage," he noted, "and there is only one Dismal Swamp."[26]

If Eaton could dispute the opinions of the late professor Shaler, this was in part because the eminent geologist and geographer was not necessarily an expert on ornithology, agriculture, engineering, and economics. Then, too, scientists in 1910 did not enjoy the unchallenged authority that some may hold today. Although their power and stature were on the rise, it was not out of the question for a layman to question a scientist's thought or the direction it seemed to be taking.

This kind of self-reliance permeates the later writings of John Bur-

This view across the Washington Ditch in the Great Dismal Swamp reveals many hardwoods among the cypresses, a sign of increasing dryness. In 1910 Walter Prichard Eaton found a "paradise" of birds here; and although he knew this was no virgin wilderness, he urged its preservation. The Great Dismal Swamp National Wildlife Refuge, in Virginia and North Carolina, was established in 1974.

roughs. Better known for his accounts of quiet rambles along country lanes and streams in upstate New York, Burroughs turned increasingly toward some of the weightier, more troubling questions of his age. How, for instance, could a person of faith accept Charles Darwin's theory of evolution? In 1912 Burroughs's reply was straightforward: whenever he accepted on the "authority of science" things that transcended his own experience and that of other humans through the ages, he considered his acceptance an "act of scientific faith."[27] In 1916 Burroughs saw that scientific faith—or "faith in the universality of natural causation"—was rising in proportion as religious faith was declining.[28] Rather than declare a crisis, however, Burroughs considered the benefits of improved sanitation, medicine, and machinery against the drawbacks of Nature stripped to bare bones, dehumanized, demystified, and reduced to component parts, no longer a whole. In the end he would still look to literature, art, religion, and philosophy for something that science could not explain, the whole of human life.[29]

Burroughs found Darwin's concept of evolution intriguing but disturbing. In his seventies and eighties, looking for clues and perhaps some reassurance, he would often turn to the works of Darwin, Thomas Huxley, John Tyndall, and the less strictly scientific, more philosophical Henri Bergson. On his own Burroughs had spent a lifetime getting to know the ways of wild honey bees and the hiding places of speckled trout. He had leafed through other pages in the book of nature as well, patiently reading the fine print. What troubled him in Alaska and at the Grand Canyon was not only the large type, the vastness. It was the lack of human scale in time. So with evolution. "I confess that I find it hard work to get on intimate terms with evolution," he wrote in 1912.[30] Yet he kept on mulling over its implications, "grazing" among classic texts and scientists' recent findings, not for final answers but for some means to bridge the widening gap between the scientific method and his own approach to nature, through observation, sympathy, love, and the precocious, poetic insights of his mentors, Emerson, Thoreau, and Whitman.

Without using the term "ecology," Burroughs brooded over the ways by which living things adapted to their environment. As chemical and mechanical explanations failed to satisfy him, he preferred to believe in a life force (or Bergson's élan vital) that could explain living beings' power to adapt to environments.[31] In 1916 he believed that "man can and does alter his environment to a limited extent, but not so radically as his environment alters him."[32] With that statement, and with his serene belief in progress, he seems remote from our time. But Burroughs also anticipated the views of a later age. On the question of whether humans appeared on the earth by accident or as lords of all creation, Burroughs noted in 1919, "In our pride we say it is all for [man], and all our theology has been for centuries trying to explain away this apparent hostility or indifference of the natural forces. . . ."[33] Even his close friend Whitman had exclaimed,

> All forces have been steadily employ'd to complete and delight me,
> Now on this spot I stand with my robust soul.[34]

But Burroughs, aware that microscopic germs in the universe might "pounce" on him at any time, could not adopt Whitman's proud stance. And so he turned to a caterpillar crawling on his porch: a sample of blind Nature, seeking a place to weave a cocoon, endure metamorphosis, and emerge a creature with wings.

***

Landscape architects and foresters could glean something about ecology from *Garden and Forest* magazine. How plants and other living things were adapted to their environments was a frequent subject, treated sometimes from a scientific point of view but often to emphasize the beauty of compositions in the wild or the economy of planting natives and other hardy plants where they were most at home. Wealth from tourism, as well, could flow into villages that offered city dwellers restful scenery and luxuriant vegetation along back roads, beneath centuries-old oaks, elms, and maples, and by the moss- and lichen-covered stone walls. Between 1888 and 1897, these were among the lessons that *Garden and Forest* pointed out, from the Coast Ranges west of Ukiah, California, the swamps of Arkansas, and the dry upland prairies around Ames, Iowa, to New

England villages and Charles S. Sargent's country place in Brookline (which was featured in the magazine but not identified).[35]

With reports from so many regions, by professionals and amateurs alike, *Garden and Forest* did not express a single point of view. Yet in time, as editorials repeatedly favored native plants over exotics and as more articles were focused on the flora of a single region, the magazine acquired a certain tone—not entirely scientific or technical, not particularly poetic or entertaining, but practical, informed, earnest, often with an underlying reverence for the simple beauty that only Nature in her wild and half-wild states could offer.

Garden and Forest thus prepared readers to appreciate plant associations before the word "ecology" was generally known. An editorial in 1888 explained why forsythias, lilacs, and other nonnative shrubs should be removed from the edges of natural woods in Brooklyn's Prospect Park: "We have become accustomed to see certain plants adapted by nature to fill certain positions in combination with certain other plants in a given region; and . . . all attempts to force nature, so to speak, by bringing in alien elements from remote continents and climates, must inevitably produce inharmonious results."[36] Nine years later, editorials still underscored the artistic and economic benefits of planting trees and shrubs that seemed natural in their setting and needed little attention. In August 1897 one E. J. Hill, of Chicago, contributed "Oecological Notes upon the White Pine." In September 1897 William Trelease, of the Missouri Botanic Garden, told about the flora and fauna he found in the swamps of southeastern Missouri and Arkansas, where the Mississippi River and its ancient delta once flowed. There he noted changes in the combinations of plants as water levels rose and fell; and his evocation of the swamps' great silence, an otherworldly calm ruffled by the occasional call of a mallard or plunge of a turtle, was more lyrical than most contributions.[37]

And so the appeal for native and hardy plants continued. In the fall of 1897 one editorial noted "the current preference for exotics and garden varieties," then argued for the subtler kinds of variety that could be found among ordinary American plants in the wild. Mariana Griswold Van

Rensselaer, among others, agreed. She recalled the striking effect of a clump of sumac overrun by a tangle of *Clematis virginiana* and wild grape (*Vitis aestivalis*) beside a country road north of New York.[38]

After *Garden and Forest* ceased publication in 1897, Jens Jensen in Chicago would carry the message of native plants to his clients and readers, at first tentatively, later with conviction and warmth, as a philosopher and poet of the land. In these later roles he was an unusual professional, but not unique.

Jensen's closest counterpart on the East Coast may have been Warren H. Manning, the horticulturist on whom the elder Olmsted had often relied for expertise in plants.[39] After working in the Olmsted office in Brookline from 1888 to 1896, Manning developed his own successful design practice and also wrote now and then for *Country Life*. There, in 1908, he described what he had done with an old farm that had been in his family for two centuries, in a township north of Boston. The farmhouse, built in 1696, was run down, but close by were some fine old elms and locusts, and along one boundary were wetlands—a swamp and a sphagnum bog. He bought the farm and restored the house for a summer home and place for family reunions. He also bought more land to control the wetlands.[40]

Manning knew that many plants would thrive in his "muck swamp," including the cardinal flower (*Lobelia cardinalis*), fringed gentians, marsh marigolds, tall blue lobelia, and loosestrife (*Lysimachia thyrsiflora*). But his prized possession was his sphagnum bog, which differed from the swamp because of its springy peat, its acidic waters free of bacteria, and its nitrogen-poor soils—so poor, in fact, that the native pitcher plants (*Sarracenia purpurea*), sundew, and butterwort had to capture insects and other minute creatures to get their nitrogen. While pointing out the limitations of the sphagnum bog, Manning insisted that it was precious; and that all such bogs in America should be preserved, for they could never be reproduced. "Every one of them should be a botanical garden for these ineffably precious flowers that will perish from the face of the earth if these bogs are drained for farm lands, or filled in to make building lots," he wrote. But he did not preserve his own bog just as he found it; for near the bog's native huckleberries, blueberries, orchids, and sheep laurel he grew pitcher plants (*Sarracenia flava* and *S. rubra*) gathered from Pinehurst, North Carolina. At the bog's edge were also hepaticas from central New York State, lady's slippers from Camden, Maine, and other hardy plants from somewhere else.[41]

Dan Kiley, a landscape designer in Manning's office in the 1930s, recalled him as a "lovely, wonderful man," not a designer but an expert horticulturist and a philosopher of the land.[42] Jensen became that sort of mentor, too, for Genevieve Gillette, Alfred Caldwell, and other landscape architects. The story of Jensen's development from a young park superintendent who planted natives or bold, bright exotics, depending on the situation, to a white-haired sage and poet of the native landscape has been told with sensitivity to Jensen's needs as an immigrant and manual laborer moving into professional roles and as a relative newcomer to the specialty of native plants. If Jensen did, in fact, assume a leading role in the native plant "movement," Stephen Christy has given one plausible reason: the others were professionals; Jensen was an artist.[43]

In 1908 Jensen extolled the virtues of concrete for structures in public parks. Used honestly, not to simulate some finer material, concrete might be covered by rambling vines and "some of our climbing friends," Jensen observed, alluding to climbing plants.[44] A few years earlier he had published his own diagrams for displaying bold, bright tulips, salvias, and cannas in geometric beds "not unlike the rug on the parlor floor."[45] A few years later he wrote about soil temperature, climate, the prairies in flower, the crabapple as a street tree for midwestern towns, and the prairie river, which, like life itself, "flows along a winding way, beautiful in its variety, constant in its ever-changing presentation of new scenes, new hopes, and some renewed and worthy purpose."[46] These and other pieces by Jensen suggest the development of an artist's vision, sharpened rather than dulled by his daily struggles as a professional.

As we have seen, Jensen could learn from friends and colleagues— O. C. Simonds, Frank Lloyd Wright, Henry C. Cowles, and others—then move on, developing his own particular feelings for plants, habitats, and land forms. He may never have attained the horticultural expertise of

Warren Manning, but his emotional responses to living things could be startling in their intensity. One friend and colleague, the weaver Mertha Fulkerson, related a story Jensen told her from his Chicago days. Visiting a job site one day in December, he was shocked to see some large, beautiful elms left unplanted, their roots exposed to subzero temperatures for the night. "No feeling of responsibility to those beautiful elms!" he exclaimed. "No feeling of responsibility to life itself!"[47]

Another story recalls Jensen's self-effacing notion that gardens need not be restored once the maker was gone. In a woodland clearing among the hills and limestone cliffs of Kentucky he had once built a swimming hole of stratified rock, with deeply raked joints of cement mortar that were filled in with earth for chance seeds to take hold. Many years later Jensen returned to find the client gone, the house partly ruined, the swimming hole nestling against the ancient cliff. There Nature had absorbed Jensen's handiwork and reclaimed the spot as her own. The sight brought tears to Jensen's eyes; he was simply, profoundly grateful.[48]

***

In the early twentieth century, many landscape architects viewed themselves as artists. Like Jensen, they would have set out not to copy nature but to idealize it in some way.[49] They also had to know something about plants. By the late 1920s, when the landscape architect Elsa Rehmann joined Edith A. Roberts, professor of botany at Vassar College, in writing a series of *House Beautiful* articles on plant ecology for the Eastern Seaboard, these women extended the perhaps rudimentary but fairly common knowledge of plant associations that many landscape architects already had. Still, those articles, slightly revised and brought out in book form in 1929, represent a major pioneering effort.[50] It was an attempt to bring together science and art at a time when specialists within disciplines and professionals within a field (including landscape designers and city planners) were moving apart.

In hindsight, we know that Roberts and Rehmann's *American Plants for American Gardens* (1929) appeared at the end of an era, before the Depression, another world war, the modern movement, and advances in technology, urbanization, and specialization transformed the way most

landscape architects would practice. Within months of the book's publication, the stock market crash would effectively eliminate a prosperous
clientele—private homeowners—for whom some consideration of form,
color, texture, and "spirit" among native plants might be worth paying
for in their own gardens and grounds. Depression-era jobs in reforesta-
tion and camp building, followed by wartime needs for the more technical engineering and planning skills of landscape architects, all tended
to direct the professionals' priorities away from an aesthetic appreciation of plants and the land. Then, too, in an increasingly urban and
mechanized environment, "bush planting" did not carry the status or
command the fees of engineering, planning, and building. For these and
other reasons, many professional landscape architects have long downplayed the land, soils, and plants commonly associated with their field.[51]

Today *American Plants for American Gardens* reads like an Indian
summer idyll, oblivious of the storms and hardships that would soon
follow, as chapter after chapter unfolds, calling attention to the tiniest,
most fragile ground covers and palest tints and blushes on wild berries
and leaves. With an artist's sensibility the authors notice subtle, often
fleeting effects as the trees and the spaces are seen in changing lights and
seasons. And the scientist's eye and mind are ever present. Among the
plants listed for each association, some are starred; although not native,
they have been so well naturalized in the Northeast and Middle Atlantic
states that they are included as options, sometimes a bit reluctantly.
Strict environmental correctness, which Rehmann would later discuss
among landscape architects, is waived for this book—which is, after all,
drawn from engaging articles in *House Beautiful*.[52]

In its own time, *American Plants for American Gardens* must have
been a welcome, unpretentious invitation to explore eleven plant associations, from the open field and the juniper hillside to the bog and the
seaside. Roberts and Rehmann express such delight in the gossamer-like
quality of gray birches in any season, such concern for preserving old-
growth and even second-growth forests of beeches, maples, and hem-
locks, such interest in tiny gardens as well as large estates, that they may
have led more people to take up an already popular activity in their day,

"wild gardening." What they did not do was transcend or question inherited notions of the place of humans in all this half-wild nature. Often referring to boundaries, possessions, "flower pictures," and picturesqueness, they imply an owner looking at a scene, not someone living with and within an environment. Even at the seaside, where they recognize something "fundamental" in the vegetation, the discussion soon turns to boundaries, borders, edgings, and groupings. Ideally, all the plants are native. The house is sited, shaped, and clad so as to be harmonious in its setting. But birds and other creatures of sea and land, including humans, fall outside the frame.

This image of a storm at sea appears on the cover of the original manuscript of The Outermost House, *by Henry Beston. Inside, written in a careful, legible hand, are the thoughts of a man who pondered the mystery and presentness of creation during a year on the outermost sands of Cape Cod. (Artist unknown. Reproduced by permission of Catherine Beston Barnes. Courtesy of Dartmouth College Library.)*

To widen that frame—to consider not only natural processes but technological, social, and economic processes as well—was not the task that Roberts and Rehmann set out to accomplish. Nor was their notion of plant ecology complicated by what others would later recognize as "human ecology."[53] For a glimpse of a human figure in the wild and half-wild landscape of the late 1920s we can turn instead to a work that celebrates the beauty and wonder of living things and cosmic forces in ways that transcend property lines and disciplines.

Henry Beston's *Outermost House* (1928) is a classic of nature writing, memorable not only for fine storytelling but for joy, reverence, and the melancholy tinged with hope that now and again surfaces from the dark undercurrents of modern life.[54] In the fall of 1926 Beston went to spend a few weeks at his cabin on the easternmost stretch of sand dunes on Cape Cod. Lingering, he decided to stay a full year. He had a stone fireplace for warmth, an oil stove for cooking, an outhouse, and an indoor water pump. Friends with a car helped him get to a market for food twice a week. His nearest neighbors were the Coast Guard at Nauset, two miles away. Most often he was alone, with notebooks, pencils, and field glass, at the meeting place of sea and land.

From the outset Beston views the sea and land as primordial adversaries, poised at a shifting edge where the world ends and begins again, endlessly. Plants advance toward the sea, take hold in a mound of sand, then perish in wind and waves as the sea reclaims more territory in a storm. A great storm in midwinter unearths a shipwreck from its grave in a dune, then leaves in its wake another wreck and nine men dead. One night a summer storm sweeps away many birds' nests but spares one, in a shrubby tangle of dusty miller, not quite buried in sand. Next morning the mother song sparrow still broods over her eggs, "resolved and dutiful." The chicks are born. In July the family flies away.

Having lived through a world war, Beston knew something of wreckage and death. In 1915 and 1916, in his late twenties, he had driven an ambulance for the French Army. In 1918, at age thirty, he had served as an "official observer" for the U.S. Navy in the submarine zones near the British Isles.[55] Now, based at his cabin, the Fo'castle, and nearing forty,

Beston once again sees life and death at close range and feels them as great rhythms, like day and night or the ebb and flow of the tides. He regrets that his civilization, obsessed with power and given to explaining the entire world in terms of energy, has lost touch with elemental nature—things like fire before one's hands and the earth beneath one's feet. In pitch-black night he sees poetry. In a school of "herring" (or alewives) huddled at one end of Eastham brook and struggling to swim beyond some natural barrier, back into the pond where they were born, Beston recognizes a natural urge: "That immense, overwhelming, relentless, burning ardency of Nature for the stir of life!"[56]

One day, walking inland from the ocean to Cape Cod Bay, Beston notices a fine group of trees at a turn in the road. He learns that these nonnative western cottonwoods, *Populus deltoides,* were planted by Cape Codders who had moved to Kansas, then came back, "homesick for the sea." Later that day, pausing on a moorland cliff over a marsh, he reflects on the English starlings that winter there in flocks of perhaps fifty to seventy-five birds. In England, he recalls, these birds gather in flocks of thousands. Were they to multiply on Cape Cod, he realizes, the starlings would upset the region's natural economy, for they would leave no food for native birds that return in spring.[57]

These notes on the ecology of the Cape's flora and fauna reveal Beston as a reasonable man, sympathetic to both "Nature's eagerness to sow life everywhere" and the needs of natives. To many readers of Beston these views are familiar. But some of his probing, brooding thoughts on science, art, and endless creation were cut from the original manuscript before publication. Toward the end, after insisting that *"Creation is here and now,"* Beston had continued:

> Like Hudson, I have never been able to believe that natural selection and our other brave and enormous generalities are the whole answer to the diversities and transformations of plant and animal life. There is something more. These endless experiments, this incredible creative pageant, is not wholly the invention of environment and the caprice of atoms.[58]

In another deleted passage Beston wrote:

If you would have life, then, and touch life, open your doors on Nature and reverence. If you have not watched and known the ritual of the sun, you have not lived a year. Do not be afraid of a little solitude. Every spirit which respects itself needs to be alone part of every year and part of every day. Let no laboratory, extending knowledge, rob you of the poetry that Nature is sacramental. Man has need of the sky.[59]

Why were these passages cut? And did Beston cut them or an editor? One clue may lie in Beston's foreword to the first edition—an edition with many photographs, for which he thanked several people. More recent editions omit the photographs and retain Beston's 1949 foreword, an eloquent statement about Nature and the human spirit. But we need the foreword to the first edition to find Beston's appreciation of the ornithologist Edward H. Forbush as both a "literary artist" and a scientist. There, too, Beston thanked a local congressman for responding to his "frequent requests for scientific studies published at Washington."[60] Evidently Beston wanted to be kept informed of scientists' findings. Was he wary of offending them? More clues may surface in chapter 9, where another of his deleted passages appears. Clearly, as a writer who once declined to describe himself as a "naturalist," Beston was seeking something that science alone could not explain.[61] Reflecting on what he had learned during a year on the outermost sands of Cape Cod, he declared, "Poetry is as necessary to comprehension as science. It is as impossible to live without reverence as it is without joy."[62]

NINE

Spirit of the Landscape,
Humanized & Wild

Doonerak, an Eskimo word for "spirit" or a mischievous devil, was the name Bob Marshall gave to one of the highest peaks of the Brooks Range, north of the Arctic Circle in Alaska. He felt insignificant when he first gazed upon that peak in 1929, and he never managed to reach its summit, neither that summer nor on later trips during the next ten years.[1] Still, lured on by the very idea of Mount Doonerak when it was obscured by clouds or a blizzard or by the sight of its sharp crest against an impeccable blue sky, Marshall continued to explore the Arctic wilderness. He also gave more names that remain on maps today, including Frigid Crags and Boreal Mountain. Their configuration he called "the Gates of the Arctic," the name later given to our northernmost national park, established in 1980 and recognized as the nation's "ultimate wilderness."[2]

Marshall took pleasure in naming mountains, passes, creeks, and other natural features in Alaska, drawing upon traditional names, the language of local people, and their given names. But beyond that pleasure, he was exhilarated simply to be in wild lands, whether exploring unmapped terrain, studying white spruces at timberline, enduring the cold, the heat, the wind and rain, or savoring a bite of grayling caught at daybreak.

Writing of those "glorious" days, Marshall gave much of the credit for avoiding disaster to his companions: Al Retzlaf, his guide the first summer; Nutirwik, a Kobuk Eskimo, and several white men, among them Ernie Johnson, Kenneth Harvey, and one-armed Jesse Allen. They were self-reliant old-timers, familiar with some of the watersheds from hunting and prospecting, and quick to get a fire started in a rainstorm or in fresh snow, several feet deep. While someone else went off in search of the next meal, Marshall might study tree growth at timberline and speculate on whether the trees' frontier was affected more by climate or by the recession of the last glacier. One summer night when the mosquitoes were driving their horses mad, he and Retzlaf broke camp to find a better site, and around 1:00 A.M. the light of dawn revealed a moose standing by a pond before a hillside covered with pale-yellow reindeer moss. The eastern sky turned pink and reflections of spruce were black in the still water. Another night, after rain had flooded the two rivers that flowed together around their island camp, Marshall and Retzlaf barely avoided being stranded by a series of quick, wise moves and lucky breaks.

Marshall was not only a good storyteller; the stories were true, as one of his companions asserted after reading a copy of *Arctic Wilderness* (1956), Marshall's posthumously published work.[3] Yet one small detail from that first Alaskan journey remains a bit of a mystery. Sometime during the days of endless rain, swollen rivers, and efforts to build a raft sturdy enough for an escape from the peninsula near the shrinking island camp, Marshall found time to mull over the impact of modern science on faith and jot down his reflections. Earlier in the narrative, he mentioned reading Joseph Wood Krutch's new book, *The Modern Temper*. Now, unable to rely on prayer in the face of danger, Marshall recorded in his journal that he and Retzlaf would have to trust "nine logs and the torrent of the Koyukuk."[4] As it turned out, farther upstream along the Clear River, where a new channel was being cut by the force of the current (a force in part resisted by boulders that had begun to fill in the main channel), Marshall and Retzlaf were able to ford the river without entrusting their

[handwritten margin note: always books published]

lives to the raft. But the question remains: Why was Marshall reading *The Modern Temper*? And why did he think it worth carrying for twenty-five days of exploration in the Brooks Range?

Krutch's *Modern Temper,* which first appeared in the spring of 1929, tells of one New Yorker's malaise over the prospect of a pervasive materialism, traceable to scientific methods and the application of modern science to human needs and desires (genuine or fabricated). That materialism, born of science, in turn threatened to smother just about every other trace of intellectual and spiritual life, whether expressed in art, religion, love, philosophy, or literature. Erudite, profoundly pessimistic, yet remarkably detached for a work subtitled *A Study and a Confession, The Modern Temper* represented a position and point of view that caused an immediate stir in literary circles. Lewis Mumford and Bertrand Russell, among others, publicly expressed their appreciation for the book.[5] But in many respects Krutch's point of view was sharply at odds with that of Bob Marshall, forester, doctoral candidate in the Laboratory of Plant Physiology at Johns Hopkins University, and determined optimist, a lover of life in its myriad forms, human, animal, and vegetable. For instance, Krutch treated Man, Nature, Science, and Art as grand abstractions. He did consider concrete details in novels and treatises, but not in regard to any living being; whereas Marshall's interests always seemed to be grounded in the details of something very much alive and, to him, infinitely interesting. So why did Marshall add the physical and mental burden of Krutch's *Modern Temper* to his heavy pack in Alaska—particularly if he had already taken exception to something in Krutch's conclusion to the book before leaving Johns Hopkins at the end of the spring term in 1929?

As his brother George Marshall later noted, Bob Marshall's influential essay "The Problem of the Wilderness" (1930) was written before the summer of 1929 in Alaska.[6] And in that essay, among supportive quotations from Willa Cather, William James, Aldo Leopold, Emerson, Thoreau, and others is a line from Krutch's *Modern Temper* that Bob Marshall evidently found irritating. He could agree that certain learned people "come inevitably to feel that if life has any value at all, then that value lies in thought," as Krutch had written. But Marshall objected to the context of Krutch's remark—the notion that the physical pleasures of people "too absorbed in living to feel the need for thought" were somehow inferior; that those pleasures—eating, begetting children, conquering—were things barbarians indulged in as they stormed over once highly cultivated but now effete civilizations with their naive animal desires, annihilating all that was once fine and exquisitely subtle even as they laid the foundations for "animal rejuvenation." Marshall could have come across such a view in the past, among intellectuals in his native New York, in Cambridge, in Baltimore; but Krutch expressed it in such forceful language, with such stoical acceptance of what he called a "lost cause," that Marshall may have considered it a view to be reckoned with, briefly, in his essay on wilderness, then more slowly in Alaska, perhaps on a day unfit for exploring a new watershed.[7]

Marshall's essay and Krutch's book were influential in different ways. The Wilderness Society's origins and national wilderness policy to this day owe a debt to Marshall and his essay.[8] Krutch, having won wide recognition and critical acclaim for *The Modern Temper* just before the Depression set in, would move on to other topics and other roles in life, eventually that of a nature writer. It will be useful, then, to pause a moment in the spring of 1929 and sort out a few disagreements and overlaps between these two temperamentally unlike people.

Bob Marshall, a man of astonishing physical energy, was also highly intelligent and articulate, able to argue a case in a way that might please his father, a lawyer, but also skilled in something that a U.S. Supreme Court justice and family friend once identified. "How deftly you blend the concrete and the abstract," Justice Benjamin M. Cardozo wrote to Marshall, before quoting a passage from one of Marshall's letters from Alaska: "Almost everything in life seems to be at least somewhat blurred and misty around the edges and so little is ever absolute that there was a genuine satisfaction in seeing the flawless white of those summits and the flawless blue of the sky and the razor edge sharpness with which the two came together."[9]

In the experience of wilderness, beyond the material comforts of the city that could become cloying or stifling, Marshall found what people still find and value to this day: physical well-being; a sense of freedom; a chance to be self-sufficient, often with other self-sufficient people, sometimes alone; incentives to independent thought; extraordinary beauty; and an experience of vastness in a world constantly changing—not something merely looked at but enveloping and gratifying to all five senses. As a forester he knew well the arguments of those who, like Gifford Pinchot, objected to "locking up" resources by barring all logging, road building, mining, grazing, and other forms of industrial development. But as one familiar with the philosophical arguments of Tom Paine, Thomas Jefferson, and John Stuart Mill, Marshall argued for the rights of one often overlooked minority—those physically able and temperamentally suited to endure the rigors of wilderness recreation. As civilization continued to spread out and "conquer" the land, as city dwellers grew increasingly restless if not crushed by the artificial structures in their midst, the need for wilderness would grow, he reasoned. Today some might deny that any human traces—trails, telephone lines, lookout cabins—could exist in a true wilderness. But for Marshall the issue was clear and urgent: people needed to come together to fight for wild lands and preserve them for the sake of human well-being. And on that note he ended his essay "The Problem of the Wilderness."

In the decades that followed, the rights of nonhuman life would also enter this argument—to be picked up below. Here, we need to recognize a substantial overlap between Marshall's and Krutch's concerns; that is, the growing sense of surfeit with material comforts, most readily available in cities but beginning to penetrate the entire continent by means of highways, telephone wires, private automobiles, the tourist industry, and a whole web of supportive industries, extractive, manufacturing, marketing, and more. The Depression and the Second World War took the gloss off some of their arguments. But their yearning to preserve the freedom of the wilderness or somehow to escape from a "mechanistic universe" (Krutch's words) would grow more intense over time.

Ironically, Krutch's own escape seems unlikely as he deploys one abstraction after another. Pitting humanism against science and against nature, Krutch did not allow for any creative interactions among the people, environments, and aspirations only vaguely implied by these terms. He could not imagine what a scientist such as Loren Eiseley or Rachel Carson would soon create from the desiccated remains of life on ancient sea bottoms or out of the Sargasso Seas of living things—that is, poetry. "Time was when the scientist, the poet, and the philosopher walked hand in hand," Krutch wrote. "In the universe which the one perceived the other found himself comfortably at home. But the world of modern science is one in which the intellect alone can rejoice."[10] And with these thoughts, Krutch, the disillusioned humanist, struck a sympathetic chord among many contemporaries in 1929.

From his autobiography and from the further probing of his biographer, John D. Margolis, we learn that Krutch, born in Knoxville, Tennessee, in 1893, grew up with a leaning toward the sciences and thought of becoming a mathematician.[11] Instead, he turned to literary pursuits at the University of Tennessee in Knoxville, then moved to New York, did graduate work at Columbia and in London, lingered in Paris, became a drama critic for the *Nation,* and spent many years gradually overcoming his sense of provincial origins and socially conservative values. In this context, *The Modern Temper* can be read as an acceptance of loss by a fairly young man who has deduced that modern science has left him "no place" in the "natural universe."[12] Or it can be recognized as an expression of dismay by a man who on some level would still like to be able to believe in the myths, the religion, the literature, art, and philosophy of his forebears.

Looking back on that book three decades later, Krutch set it in a context that seems plausible but reveals nothing of his physical illnesses of the late 1920s, or any deep emotion. As he explained, he had rejected the optimism based on science that seemed pervasive in the 1920s. Yet he had felt that to reject all that seemed to be errors, superstitions, and fears in the light of modern science would not work, "because it left man too bleakly and hopelessly alone in an alien universe." And that, he added, was the "rock bottom of skepticism."[13] In time he would rise from it, his spirit renewed in ways that some of his urban and highly intellectual friends could not comprehend.

***

Somewhere between the peaks of exhilaration and the rock bottom of skepticism and despair lie those middle grounds of equilibrium—nothing to write home about, perhaps, but satisfying. So it is with certain people and places important to this study, yet often overlooked. John C. Van Dyke and *The Desert* (1901) may long be remembered; but what about *The Meadows* (1926), his affectionate study of backwaters in his native New Jersey?

There an older, more mellow, less prickly Van Dyke goes out to explore brooks creeping beneath the watercress, shallow pools flecked by darting fish, and abandoned farm fields reclaimed by nature and returned to goldenrod, aster, yarrow, cedar. In a leisurely, meandering way he begins to question the idea that all about him can be explained by some principle of mechanics or instinct. "The same intelligence runs through all life and varies only in degree," he insists. Pondering the possible extinction of certain wild creatures, he moves on to the traces of a garden, now overgrown, which must have flanked the path down to a springhouse whose stone foundations lie half buried in mud. The spirit of the garden was, he imagines, the lady of the house, who once carried milk and butter down to the springhouse. She may have been "radiantly happy." Now no monument tells her story, and her house and garden have vanished. From these glimpses of the Raritan Valley of New Jersey Van Dyke moves on to national issues that seem to be attracting little concern at that time—pollution of the air and streams, diminishing numbers of fish and birds, and consumption of the earth, or development, "which is too often only another name for flaying the face of things for present profit."[14]

Whether Van Dyke's protests would have been more effective in the newspapers or at the factory gates than in discreet little clothbound books can be debated. But throughout a long writing life, Van Dyke was at least consistent, holding up certain values—the beauty of landscape, the importance of memory, respect for life holding out against adversity, the idea that there is nothing really commonplace in nature. "Everything is shaped to an end, in a mould and pattern of its own, and for a specific purpose," he concluded in *The Meadows*. "The fault is in man's lack of vision and want of comprehension."[15]

The landscape architect Charles Downing Lay would have had some sympathy for these thoughts of Van Dyke. His own lyrical descriptions of marshes on Long Island Sound, their abundant life, and their beauty in the changing light of a midsummer's day are comparable to Van Dyke's reflections on the Raritan.[16] But Lay rarely sustained that mood in his writing. It seems that he was determined to keep his private life and certain personal feelings separate from his public, professional life.

We have already considered Lay's vision of a habitable city of some 60 million people, perhaps extrapolated from the New York he knew in the mid-1920s.[17] Here we need to see how his interests in art and science came together, if somewhat tentatively, in the garden. In his *Garden Book for Autumn and Winter* (1924) Lay showed some interest in the "new study" of ecology but a bit more interest in space composition and modern design. "Like all scientific studies," he wrote, "ecology must be the servant not the master of the artist and every gardener should be in some degree an artist."[18] From Bernard Berenson's writings on paintings of the Italian Renaissance Lay derived his own ideas of space composition.[19] And, reading Clive Bell on cubism, Lay reasoned that a landscape architect, too, could be modern, expressing "abstract ideas in aesthetic terms."[20]

Lay's designs for small gardens, published in the 1920s, do not differ much from the work of many of his contemporaries in the Northeast. Typically he provided rectilinear terraces and lawns, straight paths and borders (planted with perennials in "drifts," which he credited to Gertrude Jekyll's influence), and trees in allées and orchards, all aligned with the geometry of the house or of an outlying structure. He enjoyed seeing these areas of geometric order contrasted with the "more or less wild and unkempt spaces beyond."[21] Although Elsa Rehmann's book *The Small Place* (1918) includes no works by Lay, his gardens could have easily fitted in with those she did include—gardens by the Olmsted Brothers,

Warren Manning, Marian Coffin, Elizabeth Bootes Clark, Pray, Hubbard, and White, among others.[22]

If Lay stood out, it was not as a designer or plantsman but as a professional who tried to engage the minds of people—clients, general readers, his peers—in ideas both practical and philosophical, traditional and forward-looking. The topics of his *Garden Book for Autumn and Winter* ranged from soils and styles to the time of year for transplanting magnolias and the place of human constructions in nature. Man's works were as much a part of the natural environment as the homes of beavers and muskrats, he asserted; and so the city and the railroad were not such artificial intrusions after all.[23] Lay also thought the growing interest in ecology was a positive sign; people would learn to see the beauty of otherwise neglected plants of their own regions and locales. In fact, what others casually referred to as "wild" gardens Lay considered "ecological trial grounds." Rather than limit himself to natives exclusively, however, he preferred to plant things that he found lovely or interesting, things that at least appeared to be native. In the end, what appealed to him more than scientific precision was the spirit of the landscape, something many people could sense intuitively but few could articulate.[24]

Lay also touched on professional matters, such as the value of a landscape architect's services. In a nation of independent-minded people who considered themselves as able as the next person to handle a spade and read a manual, landscape architects sometimes needed to explain why their knowledge and skills were worth paying for. Familiar with horticultural sciences, design arts, engineering, and construction, these professionals might claim expertise in some area. Yet, short of advertising, it was difficult to get that message across to homeowners, who might prefer to experiment and make their own mistakes.[25]

We have seen a trace of this self-reliance in California. In *The Simple Home* (1904) the poet Charles Keeler advised his readers to make the most of their gardens, studying them as an art form. In the Bay Area they could use a range of indigenous and exotic plants. They could learn from Italian and Japanese garden traditions, then adapt certain features to their own life and landscape. Some sort of enclosed, habitable area in the garden would be appealing. But Keeler made no mention of engaging a professional to lay out or plant the garden.[26]

At that time, this sort of self-reliance was also evident in New Hampshire. In *Our Mountain Garden* (1904) Mrs. Theodore Thomas described the cottage and gardens that she and her husband had designed for a south-facing slope in the White Mountains. The twenty-five-acre site was wild land, with woods, rock ledges, a brook, a swamp, and views of fields, a few farm buildings, and Mount Lafayette. But more than scenery, the land offered two city people the chance to regain their health. Mrs. Thomas, recently an invalid, plunged into the work of planting "wild" gardens, aided by her imagination, a feisty spirit, a good-natured neighbor's boy, and works by William Robinson and Liberty Hyde Bailey. Her husband, the conductor of the Chicago Symphony Orchestra, suffered from overworked nerves and insomnia; and during a few sleepless nights in Chicago he worked on plans for their garden in the White Mountains. "Under his artistic hand, the rough, unkempt aspect of the land was softened to a graceful wildness," noted his wife. She was delighted that they could do as they pleased in the garden, "undisturbed by the disapproving eye of a professional gardener."[27] Then, after a summer in the mountains, she would return with her husband to Chicago. She felt fortified for her strenuous urban winter, and life had for her a "new meaning."

So what could a professional offer people such as the Thomases—imaginative, independent-minded people, fond of things wild and free? Charles Downing Lay's tastes ran closer to the cultivated than the primeval. And he had no mountain views from his place in Stratford, Connecticut, only a glimpse of Long Island Sound. He could have cautioned the Thomases about the swamp that they had, with help, made into a pond. In swamps, where Mrs. Thomas had seen only ugliness, Lay found whole "worlds of their own," with spring peepers (*Hyla crucifer*), bullfrogs, turtles, muskrats, luxuriant plant growth, and other living things to explore. Then, too, Lay saw in the salt marsh a "delicately balanced organism" with a flora and a fauna of its own. And yet he saw no reason why a landowner should not alter a swamp or drain a marsh. As a professional, then, he explained why he preferred to leave wetlands intact before discussing how they might be drained or otherwise altered to achieve a certain aesthetic or economic result.[28]

If in the 1920s Lay offered no scientific arguments to preserve swamps and marshes but only preferences based on aesthetics and the pleasures of an amateur naturalist, this may tell us something of the general state of environmental awareness in his day. But another issue is involved here, one that runs deeper than the landscape architect's interests in art and scenery. Krutch alluded to it in *The Modern Temper*—the fear that modern science and its reductivist methods were undermining the legitimacy of spirit, or a certain way of being in the world. "If I speak of the spirit of the garden I may be thought sentimental or mystical," Lay admitted, before trying to explain that spirit by analogy with a quality sometimes found in a home—the "expression of souls in equilibrium."[29] Something of that equilibrium shines through Lay's best writing. What throws it off balance is his suspicion that scientists are gaining the upper hand in areas where he, the artist, wants to lead.[30]

By 1924 Lay could see that the "old systematic botany" was giving way to new ideas about ecology. He knew that ecologists would save him time and trouble with their facts about soils, climates, and conditions. Meanwhile, he would continue to write about matters of the spirit and experiences so common that they often went unnoticed. Country scenes stimulate our spirits, perhaps because we live more in cities, he mused. "The loveliest scenes which I know have been so altered by man's interference," he wrote, "that it seems almost as if his interference were necessary to produce a beautiful landscape." As examples Lay cited a temple at Paestum, in southern Italy, and the landscape of dairy farms, fields, and woodlots in New York State's Chenango River Valley. In his summer travels he did not enjoy looking at densely forested peaks in the Adirondacks and the White Mountains. In fact, he preferred the wildness of the seashore, where winds and waves had done the "organizing" work of eroding, battering down, smoothing, and polishing, leaving dunes, marshes, and a "delicately modelled surface of sand."[31]

When Lay jotted down these thoughts, it happened that Henry Beston had not yet lived a year on Cape Cod. And when Beston's *Outermost*

House appeared in 1928, a passage reminiscent of Lay's delight in the "organizing" work of natural forces had already been deleted. It would have appeared in the chapter titled "The Year at High Tide," where Beston describes the shell- and pebble-incrusted nests of a miniature tern, the "leastie." There Beston had written:

> I should like to digress here, and begin to write on a topic almost never treated, to write, that is, on animals as artists.
>
> For the last fifty years, our understanding of Nature has been mechanical, and this conception has mastered every other. Science, having stolen the clothes and the manner of theology, has itself become dogma. Nowadays, when we study the bodies of animals and animal behaviour, we look for some "practical," some mechanical answer to all problems. A blue bird is blue because of this, a crow black because of that, a parrot differs from a finch because the tiddleywink trees in tropical countries grow nearer the moon.
>
> Against this mechanicalism, I would protest. The spirit behind nature is more than a celestial engineer. The sustaining soul of things works toward beauty for pure beauty's sake; it works decoratively as well as "practically,"—whatever that quoted word may mean,—and again and again the whole mechanical scheme goes to smash for a chance at a colour or a sound. As a practical matter, this world of ours is really an experimental chaos; it is only as beauty that it is incomparable. Let us begin to rid our brains of the notion that the beauty of living things and the beauty they create is only a by-product of the mechanics of keeping alive. For instance the leasties and these mosaic shells. I ought to be writing with scientific awe of Nature's profound purpose of protective colouration or of the mechanics of sand and nests. Were I to do so, I should be indulging in purest fiddledeedee. These birds (however crude their performance) put in the stones because they liked them. The impulse to beauty is one of the fundamental r[h]ythms of all life, and like the impulse to the dance, touches more than man.[32]

Why was this passage deleted? Did someone consider it an unwarranted attack on modern science? Other deleted passages from Beston's manuscript tend to challenge orthodox scientific beliefs or to personify forces in nature—the sun, the earth, the impulse toward life—as if they were characters on a cosmic stage. Would those passages have marred *The Outermost House*? Or enriched it? In any case, the pared-down text became a classic.

Meanwhile, the battles at the frontier of sea and land continued. The Cape Cod writer Robert Finch recalls that in 1978 (ten years after Beston's death) a great winter storm swept Beston's house out to sea. In the aftermath, all that turned up was the outhouse and the plaque that had designated the house a National Literary Landmark.[33]

***

In Petersburg, Virginia, south of Richmond, there are still some traces of a sanctuary for wildflowers and birds in Lee Memorial Park, a largely wooded landscape named for General Robert E. Lee. That sanctuary, funded mainly by the federal Works Progress Administration (WPA) in the mid-1930s, came into being mainly through the work of women, African American and white. The story of the sanctuary and related efforts to document the wildflowers through pressed, dried, and labeled specimens and a collection of watercolors has come to light in a book by Nancy Kober.[34] And in her text is no hint of conflict between science and art. Rather, the sanctuary and its documentation represented both a labor of love and a means of supporting one's family at a time when jobs were scarce.

Drawing upon government records, Garden Club publications, oral histories, and interviews, Kober has written a story about women who took on "men's work" as laborers, supervisors, and administrators; in effect, the Depression opened a few doors for them. It is a moving story, with familiar, painful details of racial discrimination and segregation; the supervisors were white, for instance, while the outdoor laborers were black. And yet there was evidence of heroism and persistent hard work on all sides. The woman who did watercolor "portraits" of the wildflowers was Bessie Marshall, mother of nine children and wife of a minister whose failing health eventually left her the breadwinner. Marshall was not a trained botanical illustrator; yet, as one officer of the Garden

Club of Virginia observed, she "captured the soul of the flower in her work."[35]

Today those watercolors suggest the species diversity that the Lee Park sanctuary once offered—some five hundred species, once identified by metal markers in the ground. The markers have since disappeared; in and around the sanctuary, however, Kober's botanical consultant, Donna M. E. Ware, continues to locate specimens that represent the original herbarium collection, including the laurel-leaved greenbrier (*Smilax laurifolia* L.) and the delicate large whorled pogonia (*Isotria verticillata* Raf.).[36] And as members of the Petersburg Garden Club work toward the long-term effort of restoration, the old archival photographs are of human as well as botanical interest. In one photograph, laborers and supervisors pause in their work to pose for the camera, their backs to the "bog" and Lake Willcox below. Surely the spirit of those women remains in that landscape, a place already layered with memory by the 1930s. Once farmland, it was the site of defensive earthworks during the Civil War. Decades passed, and some of the land became Lee Park. There the town dammed a stream for a reservoir, which later became a swimming area for white people only. In the 1950s, pressures to integrate the swimming area led to its closing; eventually other park facilities were integrated. Perhaps the efforts to create a sanctuary in the 1930s were the beginning of a healing process, long overdue.

Meanwhile, other divisions were forming. At the sanctuary in Petersburg women were engaged in a kind of work that male landscape architects were turning away from, whether by preference or because of Depression-era constraints. As their private clientele declined and as their public work during the Depression and World War II increasingly called for planning and engineering skills on large-scale projects, practicing landscape architects—then predominately male—tended to move away from any intimate engagement with plants, their habitats, and the spiritual qualities associated with the earth.

There were exceptions, of course. The Boston-area landscape architect Arthur Shurcliff worked on the restoration of Colonial Williamsburg from 1928 to 1943, striving to authenticate not only the historic street plans, walkways, and garden layouts but also the actual species of plants known and valued in colonial times. That collaborative effort with the architects Perry, Shaw & Hepburn, supported mainly by funds from John D. Rockefeller Jr., was complex yet relatively intimate in scale; and the plants remained important elements of the whole.[37] But on some of Shurcliff's later projects, such as Boston's Storrow Drive, from 1949, plants and their habitats were not top priorities. Shurcliff was reluctant to take on that particular job, in any case; for it intruded on a historic, livable urban setting that the Olmsted firm and he himself had helped to shape.[38]

Born in Boston in 1870, Shurcliff worked for Olmsted, Olmsted & Eliot, later Olmsted Brothers, after earning degrees from "Tech" (MIT) and Harvard. He also taught in Harvard's new program in landscape architecture from 1900 to 1906, assisting the younger Frederick Law Olmsted, before opening his own office of planning and landscape design in Boston. Years later, like many of his generation, he did not welcome the new architecture of the Bauhaus and other bold expressions of modernism. Form and style had something to do with it. And Shurcliff did not drive a car—although his son and partner, Sidney, was fond of cars and intrigued by modern design.[39] But more important, Shurcliff feared that, in the progress of human alterations on the surface of the earth, something precious was being destroyed.

In 1930, as president of the American Society of Landscape Architects, Shurcliff urged his colleagues to recognize the strongest of their common bonds—the "loveliness of the earth," which had to be protected *and* created, whether in the mountains, by the sea, in a city, or in a garden.[40] In his journal, published in 1931, he again took up that theme as he praised the work of his New England forebears, who had cleared land for arable fields and pastures. Scanning a landscape of farms, mill wheels, small dams, bridges, and roads, he saw its loveliness as the result of human effort and natural forces working together. "Our kin were partners with the sky and earth," he wrote, "as the birds who build nests of grass with the faith of birds are partners with the heavens and the ground."[41]

A few years later, Jens Jensen expressed a similar thought in *Siftings:*

"Nature and man's hand must go together." But the context of this line was less serene than Shurcliff's journal entry. Mingled with Jensen's evocation of a garden in harmony with the elements of nature were his jabs at the "prison-like space of the city" and grim thoughts on life in a machine age. He envisioned a splendid tree, grown from a seed that a bird once dropped over the grave of a man; and the image remains ambiguous. Was that a single human being whose decaying remains nourished a tree? Or was it all humankind that had passed away? "So nature goes on without any vengeance," Jensen concluded.[42]

Certainly the Depression lay in the background of Jensen's and Shur-

This orchid, a large whorled pogonia (Isotria verticillata *Raf.*), *grows in a woodland just outside the Lee Park Wildflower and Bird Sanctuary in Petersburg, Virginia. Only a few inches high, blooming in April, it was spotted by Donna M. E. Ware, a botanist with a sharp eye and long familiarity with the site.*

cliff's darker thoughts. Yet those two were fortunate in some deeply satisfying jobs that came their way in the 1930s. While Shurcliff was busy with the restoration in Williamsburg, Jensen became involved in a project comparable to the sanctuary for wildflowers and birds in Petersburg. In the mid-1930s, for the Garden Club of Illinois, Jensen was honored to work out a plan for the Lincoln Memorial Garden, in Springfield—one of the great commissions of his career. As in Petersburg, the Springfield site bordered on a reservoir created from streams; and the garden was, to a great extent, conceived, planted, and maintained by local women. (Girl Scouts, Boy Scouts, and garden club members from other states would also contribute acorns and garden benches.)

To express the spirit of President Lincoln in a garden, Jensen conceived of something great in scale yet intimate in feeling. Instead of one grand entrance, there would be three of equal importance, each marked by a pair of boulders, just off the boundary road. From these entrances a web of grassy paths would lead through groves backed by denser woodlands to a clearing, or to one of eight stone council rings, or to the shore of Lake Springfield. Plants would be mostly native, either to the Springfield area or to the states in which Lincoln had lived. On the nearly treeless original site the garden would only gradually reflect Jensen's vision, taking three-dimensional form both from his designs and by chance; that is, from Jensen's broad-brush planting schemes and basic principles; from young saplings, bulbs, and wildflowers; and from those relatively few white oak acorns (among the many planted) that happened to sprout and grow. In the Lincoln Memorial Garden there would be no sense of hierarchy among the paths and spaces, no single beginning or end, or any perfect moment of completion. Rather, it would be a living, growing memorial to a man and a people, something slow to evolve and—Jensen predicted—longer lasting than even the presidential faces on Mount Rushmore.[43]

As Robert Grese has observed, the Lincoln Memorial Garden now offers "a model of design as a partnership with natural processes and succession to create landscapes with at least some of the function and beauty of natural ecosystems."[44] The garden is also a model of design as

For Jens Jensen the ring was a symbol of strength and friendship. His council rings, designed for storytelling, song, and other shared experiences around a central fire, were also reminders of primordial needs and desires. This council ring, one of eight, appears in the Lincoln Memorial Garden, in Springfield, Illinois, designed by Jensen in the mid-1930s.

an art devoid of arrogance, touched by a refreshing humility, open to chance and change.

***

At one time Frank Waugh would subordinate all concerns of landscape architecture—form, materials, soils, climate, even ecology—to one all-encompassing concern, the "spirit of the landscape." Yet he pleaded the poverty of language to explain his lack of precision in writing about spirit in *The Natural Style in Landscape Gardening* (1917). The spirit of peace, of fury, of beauty, joy, energy, all were inherent in landscapes of the world, he wrote. But first among them was the spirit of life. "There may be a perfectly dead landscape on the moon," he allowed, "but that is not our planet. Our world teems with life. From the infinitesimal microbe, swarming by millions in the drop of water, to the crowding trees in the forest there is life—growing, urgent, irrepressible life. Even the inanimate ocean and the tumbling clouds and the singing brook are so nearly alive that they tell the same story to our listening ears."[45]

Moving on to consider the spirit of the prairie, of the pine woods, of the palmetto swamps, and more, Waugh suggested that the Indians had been right all along in their belief that each tree and shrub had its "living soul." In 1917 that view alone would give some readers pause. They might also look upon the evocative photographs in Waugh's book as vestiges of a world that was rapidly disappearing: the horse-drawn carriage along an unpaved woodland road; the little boys with homemade fishing poles; the woman hiking along a leafy mountain trail in an ankle-length skirt; and a backyard garden where two women in long white dresses lingered by a naturalistic pool while time seemed to stand still. In any event, Waugh's critics were not persuaded. Professor Waugh, writing of tragic seas and mountains, had been misled by the old "pathetic fallacy," it was said. Then, too, his terms were "old-fashioned." At least he was "sincere" in his appreciation of scenery.[46]

Waugh was not alone in attracting this kind of criticism from his peers. Jens Jensen, whose work in landscape design Waugh much admired, would draw similar criticism for the seemingly unprogressive views in his book *Siftings* (1939).[47] But Jensen, living in semiretirement in remote Elison Bay, Wisconsin, from the mid-1930s onward, was not about to swerve from a path chosen earlier in life. Waugh, teaching not far from Boston, was still broadening his interests; and his writer's voice would change.

For many years head of the Division of Horticulture at Massachusetts Agricultural College (now University of Massachusetts at Amherst), Waugh was at heart a midwesterner. Born in Sheboygan Falls, Wisconsin, in 1869, he grew up in McPherson, Kansas, south of Salina, where he could see for twenty miles in any direction and was thrilled to see the land set ablaze by prairie fires at night. His degrees in horticulture were from Kansas Agricultural College (now Kansas State University at Manhattan), while some of his ideas about ecology came from the German theorist Willy Lange and his own observations at Dahlen, in Berlin.[48] Waugh also came to know Aldo Leopold and Arthur Carhart on his stints as consultant to the U.S. Forest Service from 1917 onward. Carhart later credited Waugh with insisting early on that recreation was an essential concern of the Forest Service.[49] But by the early 1930s Waugh's interests had veered toward research. He did ecological studies on the edges of ecosystems, looking at roadsides in different regions of the country, and also at the margins of forests, where he detected "highly significant transition zones" with ecologies of their own.[50]

In light of his more personally revealing and lyrical early writings, Waugh might have tried at some point to fuse his perceptions of landscape spirit and landscape ecology. There is a trace of this impulse in his "Ecology of the Roadside" (1931), where he concludes that a scientifically accurate planting plan for the margins of roads and paths might lead to an artistically more pleasing result. But an idea he had picked up from Liberty Hyde Bailey apparently kept him from attempting any real fusion of science and art or ecology and poetry. Bailey, the well-known professor of horticulture at Cornell, had insisted that scientific and poetic interpretations of nature, although equally legitimate, should never be confused; and Waugh had adopted this view as early as 1910.[51] In 1926 Waugh was still repeating it; and in passing he revealed his frustration that "the obsession of our age is science—something quite different from art." He insisted all the more strongly, then, on the value of landscape architecture as *art*.[52] But that attitude would soon change. Perhaps the Depression had something to do with Waugh's shift toward detailed ecological studies, away from his interests in art, soul, and spirit. In the process, his lyrical language gave way to plain, impersonal prose.

Meanwhile, a new voice, at once poetic and scientific, rose to put in a word for life at the water's edge and beyond.

A promising young writer, Rachel Carson had turned to the sciences at what is now Chatham College, in Pittsburgh. Her years of graduate work at Johns Hopkins overlapped with Bob Marshall's; and she would have gone beyond her master's degree in zoology but for the Depression and her need to be the breadwinner for her extended family. A part-time job, a salable feature story or essay—anything would help. And so it was the general public, not fellow scientists, that Carson wanted to reach in her much-revised essay "The World of Waters." Edward Weeks, editor of the *Atlantic Monthly*, was delighted with the piece, suggested a few changes, including the title, "Undersea," and accepted it for publication in September 1937. In that way Carson, by then a junior aquatic biologist with the Division of Scientific Inquiry, Bureau of Fisheries, in the U.S. Department of Commerce, began to reach a wide audience with her uncommon perceptions of life beneath the sea.[53]

In "Undersea" Carson invites us to "shed our human perceptions of length and breadth and time and place." That accomplished, we linger by the tide pools among starfishes and sea anemones, crabs and sea slugs, shorebirds and seaweed. Space has no boundary. Time becomes an interval between one dawn and another. From this perspective, humans are introduced, calmly and almost casually, as plunderers and predators. The rhythms of the language rise and fall as with the tide, and soon we are slipping beneath the "boundless pastures" of surface waters into deeper, dimmer regions of chance phosphorescent glimmers, then primeval, endless night. "What human mind can visualize conditions in the uttermost depths of the ocean?" Carson asks. Her vision is of a vast underwater landscape of ravines, valleys, plateaus, submerged islands, hillsides, all on the continental shelf; then a precipice and the abyss. Some creatures are more fantastic than others—plankton, cuttlefish, sea spiders, blue whales. But the point of the story is their interdependence and their participation in a "material immortality" as a fine, slow rain of disintegrating fragments of once-living creatures filters down to nourish creatures below. Here, rather than offer a selection of individual life stories, Carson presents a "panorama of endless change."[54]

The echo of Henry Beston's *Outermost House*, evident in the phrase "uttermost depths" of the ocean, is no coincidence. In 1937 Carson had only recently read the book. Years later she told Beston of her profound pleasure in reading and rereading it.[55] Less evident at first but clearer over time was Carson's sense of the unity of the waters, the land, and all of life. In "Undersea" she visualized an entire landscape submerged under the sea. A decade later, on an Audubon Society field trip in Pennsylvania, she visualized another landscape submerged—but not in her lifetime.

That story came to light in Carson's "lost writings," edited by her biographer Linda Lear. Against an exposed rock on Hawk Mountain in the Appalachians, in October 1945, Carson was resting during a lull between sightings of hawks. She leaned back, thought of the nearby hill streams in their descent to the sea, and recalled the ancient seas that once covered the land beneath her. Half closing her eyes, she then imagined herself lying on the ocean floor—"an ocean of air on which the hawks are sailing."[56] A fleeting thought, this one had eons of time behind it. It revealed a flexible mind and perhaps a hint of the creative imagination that would be inseparable from her most lasting contributions as a scientist.

TEN

A Land Ethic for a
Plundered Planet

Just as the land ethic in Aldo Leopold's *Sand County Almanac* (1949) evolved over many years, so the book itself evolved through a series of revisions, criticisms, and rejections. Apart from his physical ailments, Leopold had to contend with two disparate tendencies in his writing: to probe memory, tell a story, and delight in a well-turned phrase; and to probe the tangled issues of a problem, analyze them, and develop a philosophical stance. As we will see, some editors pushed for more narrative, less philosophy. But Leopold's own voice persisted. "There are some who can live without wild things, and some who cannot," he began.[1] Before long, drawing upon what he knew of rural Wisconsin and other parts of North America, he was describing land as community—soil, water, pines, birches, trailing arbutus, alfalfa, weevils, pileated woodpeckers, meadow mice, wolves, and humans, all part of an interconnected whole. In the end, he dealt with the intertwined issues of ecology, aesthetics, and ethics. And he showed why that land should be loved, respected, admired, and valued.

Meanwhile a comparable though less personal work appeared, encompassing geological time and several continents. In *Our Plundered Planet* (1948) Fairfield Osborn noted, "It is amazing how far one has to travel to find a person, even among those most widely informed, who is aware of the processes of mounting destruction that we are inflicting upon our life sources."[2] As he had begun to write that book, Osborn, president of the New York Zoological Society, was troubled by two grave conflicts—the Second World War, which was then winding down, and a silent war that he considered more deadly, man's conflict with nature.

Today, whether we are any closer to adopting Leopold's land ethic and winding down Osborn's silent war is not yet clear. In any event, these two works of the mid-century, along with Jens Jensen's *Clearing* (1949), seemed promising, as high peaks to keep in view while on a quest for traces of wildness. I imagined that Jensen's work, tinged with an after-glow of nineteenth-century romantic fervor, would have no counterpart in 1949. But I did not foresee the range of insights that would in some way anticipate Leopold's land ethic and Osborn's plundered planet. What follows, then, is a kind of geological road cut, through layers of time rather than sedimentary rock, that reveals more foundations beneath our peaks of environmental writing. These foundations include once-familiar books and essays that should be better known today. And at their base is the work of one geologist who offered long, sweeping views across time and space.

***

Toward the end of his life Nathaniel S. Shaler wrote a fairly short non-technical book, *Man and the Earth* (1905), in which he set out to change the prevailing view of the earth's natural resources. His focus was the "material foundations" needed for human development—water, soils, forests, metals, sunlight, winds, waves, and other sources of energy, along with the living creatures of sea and land.[3] He was moved by the beauty of these things, seen as a whole. And, touching on the interrelations of moral, political, and material concerns, he proposed an ethic based on notions of kinship and duty.

It was an ethic that read like an epic, gradually unfolding until, in the end, Shaler returned to his main purpose: to emphasize the nobility and dignity of man's relation to the earth, a relation that implied a grave duty.[4] As dean of Harvard's Lawrence Scientific School, Shaler was in touch with scientific developments beyond his fields of geology and paleontology—and, a generalist by inclination, he regretted the relentless increase in specialization. Rather than teach such subjects as astronomy, geology, physics, and biology in isolation, each "as a little world in itself," Shaler would have preferred to dwell on the unity of nature, a realm in which man was both the highest product and the master.

As an educator writing of people's duty toward the earth and its creatures, Shaler was not thinking only of superbly trained people working at the frontiers of human knowledge. He had in mind a revised system of popular education. Beyond learning things that would be economically useful or intellectually stimulating, the "ordinary man" needed a deeper understanding of his place in nature. From that understanding, informed by science, would come his sense of kinship with other creatures and "duty by the great inheritance of life."[5]

The resources of the earth were not the possessions of a single person, Shaler noted, but the inheritance of all people and their descendants. As any individual could have only a "life estate" in those resources, to squander them was an act of barbarism. To conserve them—that is, to use them wisely—was man's duty. As human populations expanded, more lands would be put under cultivation and mining or timbering operations. Yet over time, in all civilized countries, Shaler predicted, some portions of the national domain would be preserved in its natural state for the sake of the earth's natural beauty. Many birds and mammals, too, might find refuge in such areas as America's national parks, which would remain as samples from a time "when the earth was free."[6]

Aware of the extinction of some wild creatures in the United States in the brief time since Europeans had first arrived, Shaler saw the need to preserve *most* of the creatures that remained. He also articulated the rough outlines of an ecosystem, writing of organic life as "a group of vast associations in which the species, each representing certain capacities and powers, are united as in a commonwealth." He did admit one price to be paid for humanizing the earth—the loss of some species. But he cautioned that "this life of the earth is the record of the greatest work of the world," the product of endless trials throughout the geological ages; that "when a species dies it goes forever"; that organic life was precious to present-day science and would be even more precious to science in the future. Hence humanity's duty to take care of living creatures, especially birds, which seemed to be disturbed more than other creatures by the advance of civilization.

Had Shaler limited his observations to those mentioned here (and in the introduction), he might be better known among conservationists today. His biographer, David N. Livingstone, found it an enigma that after Shaler's death in 1906, no one who contributed to President Theodore Roosevelt's National Conservation Commission, set up in 1909, even mentioned Shaler's writings. Perhaps, as Livingstone suggests, Shaler's work became lost in a no-man's-land between certain positions and values—aesthetic and empirical or spiritual and utilitarian. In any event, Livingstone finally settled on one reason for Shaler's later obscurity: his awkward position, straddling two intellectual traditions—an earlier religious perspective on science and a later secular scientific view.[7]

Now our quest for wildness may uncover another reason for the neglect of Shaler—aside from his tendency to let ethnic and racial identities determine one's place in a hierarchy, with man of Northern European extraction at the top. Those prejudices, common in his day, might alienate people of later generations who would otherwise find his ideas persuasive. But something else was dawning on people in the early 1900s, in small but widening circles—a sense of the preciousness of wild lands and wild creatures. Perhaps some people were offended by Shaler, the utilitarian conservationist, who alluded to a time when the earth was free, then wrote calmly of subjugated waters of the Nile and subjugated Egyptian people. He could foresee a time when forests would be gone, "save those that may be preserved in order to insure the flow of streams." And he could look upon swamps, bogs, lakes, and tidal marshes as "reserves of land to be won"—that is, to be drained for cultivation when the earth's growing population might demand it.[8] However rational these notions—given the state of environmental awareness in 1905—they hinted at a lack of feeling for things wild and free, especially from a man who emphasized feelings of kinship and "tides of affection" between humans and their parent, the earth.

Child, master, tyrant, kindred soul, subjugator, caregiver: these were all roles that Shaler identified for man in relation to the earth. He knew that the science of his day did not have all the answers. In fact, he thought that someday people would look back on him and his kind with a generous sympathy, for those much more knowledgeable people would surely feel an even stronger bond with all of life on earth, past, present, and to come. Yet who could fault an ardent preservationist for thinking Shaler too utilitarian, or a hardheaded conservationist for resisting Shaler's appeals to emotion and a quasi-religious sense of duty toward the earth? Either way, his usefulness to one cause or another might

This walkway above a salt marsh leads to a creek (Castle Neck River) near Plum Island, north of Boston. Reporting on these tidal marshes over a century ago, Nathaniel Shaler found "beautiful exhibitions of natural forces" in the landscape, as well as good prospects for drainage and cultivation. Since Shaler's time, others have emphasized the intricate webs of life in half-wild lands such as these.

OVER TIME

be diminished. Then, too, Shaler was overly optimistic, assuming that oceans and the Arctic tundra would be preserved from human depredation by their vast depths and remoteness from civilization. With great vision, he did look beyond specialized disciplines toward an integration of scientific and cultural perceptions within a widely shared ethical framework. But others would have to point out connections among the logging of old-growth forests, the draining of swamps, the loss of habitat, and the extinction of species that Shaler had urged us to save for posterity. Others, too, would develop a land ethic based on an understanding of ecosystems that was perhaps unavailable to scientists in 1905.

***

As we have seen, a contemporary of Shaler, John Burroughs, shared some of that geologist's inclination to mediate between science and religion, as well as between science and culture. If Burroughs's niche in history is more secure, that may be in part because no one would mistake him for a scientist and judge him as such. Whatever his immediate purposes, as a farmer, literary critic, or observer of life in half-wild places, he remained an accessible, genial author with a gift for a particular medium, the familiar essay. Perhaps a land ethic could be reconstructed from passages in his essays. In "Grist of the Gods" (1908), for instance, he listed natural resources—coal, oil, fertile soils, wild creatures, primeval forests—that civilization was using up at a rate that would eventually leave the earth depleted, like a "sucked orange." But Burroughs's purpose tends to be more broadly philosophical, less strictly ethical. Here he exults in our connection to the air, the soil, the cosmic dust, the cosmic mind coursing through all things without end. And he remains grounded, rooted. "To have a bit of earth to plant, to hoe, to delve in, is a rare privilege," he writes; "one cannot turn it with his spade without emotion."[9]

Another contemporary of Shaler, William T. Hornaday, will be remembered for his vigorous crusade to save wildlife from extirpation, mainly at the hands of sportsmen with guns. A "reformed" sportsman turned preservationist, he ran the New York Zoological Society's Bronx Zoo and raised an endowment for his Permanent Wild Life Protection Fund. He also wrote a book, *Our Vanishing Wild Life* (1913), to expose the extent of damage with statistics, lists, quotations from experts, and photographs of a single day's catch or kill contrasted with photographs of living birds that were being shot for the plumes and feathers in women's hats. The New York Zoological Society supported the book's publication and distributed 10,000 free copies, as Hornaday later recalled.[10] And the society's president, Henry Fairfield Osborn (father of Fairfield Osborn), wrote a foreword that singled out America as a leader in destroying nature. "We no longer destroy great works of art," he noted, "but we have yet to attain the state of civilization where the destruction of a glorious work of Nature, whether it be a cliff, a forest, or a species of mammal or bird, is regarded with equal abhorrence."[11]

Moving up a layer in time, we reach the generation of people born in the 1870s—Frederick Law Olmsted Jr., Dallas Lore Sharp, Willa Cather, Walter Prichard Eaton, Benton MacKaye—people who were moved by wild and half-wild places in different ways. Cather, writing of pioneer farmers, and MacKaye, writing of loggers and watershed protection, could not ignore utilitarian concerns; nor could Olmsted, when he spoke with Stephen Mather about the national parks or wrote about regional parks for Los Angeles.[12] Sharp and Eaton could not have written about birds without consulting a manual or scientific report once in a while. But all these people came to value wildness as something irreplaceable and precious, apart from purely scientific or utilitarian interests. Having come of age toward the end of the nineteenth century and grown up with some intimacy with the earth and its creatures, they learned to trust their intuitions. And in their own aesthetic and emotional responses they found some basis for proceeding with confidence, with or without the backing of science—at least for a while.

Dallas Lore Sharp, a Boston University professor of English, grew up in southern New Jersey, among woodlands and wetlands where the Maurice River flows into Delaware Bay. In his forties he recalled migrating snowy herons that lingered in the Maurice River marshes. Then, around 1916, he heard from a friend in Oregon about all the snowy herons along the shores of tule lakes. They lay dead, in heaps, minus their lovely plumes. "A few men with guns—for money—had done it," Sharp explained.[13]

Such facts, like passing clouds, sometimes darkened the pages of Sharp's otherwise sunny, sprightly essays about life on his fourteen-acre farm in Hingham, Massachusetts. In "Mere Beans" (1916), one of Sharp's neighbors, a working farmer, asserted that "a farmer has got to get all he can and keep all he gets, or die." Sharp countered that a farmer has to give if he's going to get. Then he elaborated, sketching in a land ethic for farmers. It happened that Sharp, who kept chickens, also kept a gun, which he used rarely and without accuracy, especially when a fox began to catch more than the occasional chicken. Now, to the neighboring farmer a fox was a varmint. To Sharp a fox was "something primitive, something wild and free and stirring," a poem, a shadow that tempered the glare of a tame day. True, he noted, a farm was a place to grow beans, raise chickens, make a living. And American farms needed better ma-chinery, methods, buildings, roads, and schools. But Sharp would not be content until he saw much more give-and-take, "until the farm is run on shares with all the universe around, until the farmer learns not only to reap the sunshine, but also to harvest the snow; learns to get a real and rich crop out of his landscape, his shy, wild neighbors, his independence and liberty, his various, difficult, yet strangely poetical, tasks."[14]

In that essay Sharp drew support for his views from Thoreau ("The Beanfield," in *Walden*) and the Bible (Genesis). In the end, he persuaded the neighboring farmer to look upon his own farm in a new light, to enjoy the beauty of his meadow and listen to the bobolinks now and then. And Sharp continued to mull over the places of foxes and humans in the universe. Despite lost chickens, he admired the fox, a cunning, beautiful, resourceful, deliberate, cool creature. He was also proud to count seventy-five species of wild things (fourteen in fur, thirty-six in feathers, and more) with whom he shared a small plot of cultivated ground on a single day in June.[15]

What Sharp did for Hingham, Massachusetts, Walter Prichard Eaton did for rural Stockbridge and Sheffield, at the western end of the same state. Both helped to develop what Eaton called "the literature of place," each with his own distinctive voice. As Eaton explained in 1918, "you try to tell why it is that your small corner of the world is so fair to see, so intimate, so dear, so like a human spirit ever brooding by your side."[16]

That effort may lead, of course, to insights that transcend the particulars of a place. In "The Harvest of the Wild Places" (1914) it is maple-sugaring time, with snow still covering the ground, when Eaton walks out one morning to the distant pasture on an old farm that he is renting in Stockbridge. Cleared by New England pioneers, that farm is now half wild, its pasture slowly reverting to forest. Eaton identifies the previous night's visitors by their tracks in the snow. Then he is struck by the beauty of weed tops above the snow, some with pods full of seeds for the birds and mice. He reflects on other seasons, other harvests for wild creatures: the wild cherries for robins and rose-breasted grosbeaks, the wild apples for the squirrels and deer, pine buds for the pheasants, wild sunflowers for the goldfinches and butterflies. The lack of quail reminds him of whole flocks of them, back when he was a boy, on the edge of a wood in eastern Massachusetts. A few dark thoughts about the barbarism of hunting soon pass, and Eaton's attention returns to sugaring and the smell of wood smoke, the light of a golden afternoon and the pure strains of a thrush. Reflecting on the little creatures in his midst, he feels for them a "curious kinship": "To shoot the least and smallest would be to break with murderous hands the bonds which link Nature into unity."[17]

That essay appeared during the first tremors of "the earthquake," as Eaton later described the First World War. A member of a wartime Committee on Public Information, he wrote articles on why Americans were fighting in the war. Afterward he was overwhelmed by a sense of horror, then by sadness. He saw too much concern for power, too little compassion, too little sense of real democracy and its potential.[18] For a while a wistful, faintly tragic note slipped into his otherwise genial essays, as in "Landlord to the Birds" (1920), which contained a fair amount of statistics on the birds' utility in eating noxious weed seeds and insects. The U.S. Bureau of Biological Survey and Edward Howe Forbush, ornithologist to the Massachusetts Board of Agriculture, were among Eaton's quoted authorities. But when his own advice on habitats by the roadside and food in the feeders began to sound too utilitarian for his liking, Eaton paused, then admitted his affection for the little creatures. "The air without birds would be an aerial desert, cold and void," he cried. Without their songs, "a silence would settle over my garden which would seem like the silence of the grave, as if the life breath had gone out of nature."[19]

***

"Shucks, there ain't no place to play here, there ain't no street." That was one of the more memorable lines from the proceedings of the National Conference on Outdoor Recreation, held in Washington, D.C., in May 1924. Major William A. Welch, general manager of the Palisades Interstate Park of New York and New Jersey, was telling about busloads of city kids who had been taken to a country park for two weeks of summer camp. It happened that the boy who at first missed his city street managed to extend his two-week exposure to grass and trees into an eight-week holiday, for he could never be found when buses were ready to take the children back to the city.[20]

Major Welch's stories, and those of medical doctors, park superintendents, women from the Girl Pioneers of America and the Federated Women's Clubs, men from the National Ski Association and the National Parks Association, all reinforced the value of outdoor recreation for people's physical and mental well-being. "Life in the open is a great character builder," observed President Calvin Coolidge, who initiated the conference and called on Assistant Secretary of the Navy Colonel Theodore Roosevelt (the former president's son) to organize it.[21] In all, 309 delegates from 128 national organizations attended.[22]

In his opening address, President Coolidge noted that as Americans moved to the city, they tended to take up clerical work or manual labor that was increasingly specialized, often a form of "drudgery." They needed outdoor recreation for their health, then, but also for certain intangibles. In a nation of people of many cultures and races, Coolidge saw recreation as a potentially unifying interest, a chance to develop greater solidarity. Different forms of recreation—hunting, fishing, gardening, team sports, exhibition games—would elicit different skills and personal qualities. Right living, useful lives, good citizenship, the appreciation of nature, even a "truer insight into the whole affair of existence," might come from their time spent in outdoor recreation. One of the president's statements drew applause—that next to every industrial plant there should be a gymnasium and an athletic field. In closing, he noted that Americans were the joint inheritors of a country full of wonder and delight. With effort, they could make it a land of vision, of work, of "wholesome enjoyment and perennial gladness."[23]

Some of the American inheritance had already been squandered, however. Speakers at the conference told of polluted rivers, the wild fowl and other creatures hunted to extinction, the breeding grounds lost through use of the axe, the plow, and the dredging machine, the film of oil on the waters of the New Jersey shore where oyster beds once flourished, and the Alaskan village where inhabitants dumped their wastes on the spawning beds of salmon. Will Dilg, president of the Izaak Walton League, cited some of the nation's environmental losses: 85 percent of American waterways polluted; 75 million acres of lowlands and marshes drained, leaving wild fowl to die along their migration routes. Dilg also told of his current lobbying efforts to prevent the drainage of 343,000 acres of lowlands along the upper Mississippi, bordering on Minnesota, Wisconsin, Iowa, and Illinois. Among those lowlands was "the last stand of warm water game fishes, especially black bass." Shortly thereafter President Coolidge signed into law a bill to make the lowlands a federal wildlife refuge.[24]

But other issues raised at the conference could not be resolved by the stroke of a pen. William T. Hornaday identified the automobile as a "fearful scourge" to wild game, giving hunters a vastly wider territory than ever before to penetrate with their sophisticated guns. The University of Illinois professor Henry Ward recalled that as a boy he used to swim in the Hudson, a river that had since become polluted; and he stressed the longevity of that pollution—the chemical industrial wastes, evident not only in the nation's rivers but also along the Gulf and the Atlantic and Pacific coasts. John C. Merriam, paleontologist and director of the Carnegie Institute, noted the inevitable conflict between civilization and the large tracts of "unmodified" wild lands that scientists needed long before they could predict the practical value of their research.[25]

Henry Vincent Hubbard, professor of landscape architecture at Harvard, saw the need for large roadless areas and recommended that portions of the national reservations be limited to certain kinds of access—some by train or by auto, others by pack train or on foot. H. H. Chapman, professor of forestry at Yale, recommended that forests along waterways and roads be left unaltered in quarter-mile-wide swaths (known today as "beauty strips") to preserve scenery and protect watersheds, while allowing timber to be cut in the hinterlands.[26] And so the arguments for one cause or another were given a hearing, sometimes to extended applause. As chairman, young Colonel Roosevelt occasionally mentioned an incident from his boyhood in the out-of-doors. And some in the audience may have been aware of President Coolidge's boyhood on a farm in Plymouth, Vermont. "I love those hills," Coolidge had replied when a journalist asked if he would ever return.[27]

Aware of a lack of coordination among the various state, municipal, and private agencies and federal bureaus with interests in outdoor recreation, Coolidge had hoped that this conference would lead to a "definite and clearly prescribed national policy." Rather than dominate these efforts, however, he believed the federal government should simply provide inventories and opportunities. The real work, he implied, would be done by existing bodies and bureaus. The common goals would be lofty, inspired by the Greek ideal of a sound mind in a sound body and adapted to a modern industrialized democracy.[28]

The president's conference on national recreation became an annual event for a few years. Then on July 1, 1929, during the Hoover administration, it died of insufficient funds and lack of interest.[29] In the intervening five years, the members of committees formed at the 1924 conference compiled a great many surveys and recommendations. That alone reflected a goal of one of the conference participants—the landscape architect Warren Manning's call for national planning and studies of the national park system. Another participant, Dr. Charles C. Adams, of the New York State College of Forestry at Syracuse, recommended that the staffs of the national parks and national forests should include wildlife scientists and educators. This, too, has since come to pass. And a third goal has been realized. Benton MacKaye, speaking for the Regional Planning Association of America, explained the social and environmental purposes of the Appalachian Trail.[30]

***

As we have seen, MacKaye conceived of the Appalachian Trail as a path through mountain fastnesses that could lead to an understanding of the great drama of the earth, the story of evolution. The adventure could be intellectual as well as physical, not only for trained scientists but for anyone alert to certain clues in the "primeval" wilderness. Like Shaler, his former teacher, MacKaye saw the study of geology as a broadening, basically cultural pursuit. And they were not alone. In the 1920s the British mathematician and philosopher Alfred North Whitehead recommended to a general audience some comparable adventures not to be found at the cutting edge of knowledge.

At Harvard in February 1925 Whitehead delivered a series of public lectures about certain adventures of the mind, mainly mathematical and scientific, that had far-reaching consequences for modern life. With additions, those lectures appeared in his book *Science and the Modern World* (1925). Roaming across time in the Western world, from the late Middle Ages to the age of relativity and quantum theory, he managed to make fairly abstract subjects come to life. But along the way he uncovered some dark sides of Cartesian thought, including abstraction.

One advantage of abstraction, Whitehead noted, was that it limited one's attention to clear-cut things with clear-cut relations. But by focusing on certain abstractions—numbers, concepts, cause and effect, rates of production, margins of profit—scientists and others ignored much that was of value to society in the long run. "A civilisation which cannot burst through its current abstractions is doomed to sterility after a very limited period of progress," Whitehead warned.[31] And he did so not with the wrath of a William Blake or a Thomas Carlyle but with the equanimity of some broad-minded, informed, and generous soul such

OVER TIME

as Shaler had envisioned—someone who, by looking upon all of life with a feeling of kinship, would not judge the people of an earlier age unkindly.

Clearly Whitehead felt some kinship with his predecessors, those adventurers of the mind who did not confuse civilization with mere security and thus willingly took risks. Noting the limitations of abstraction, he suggested that the next field of intellectual adventure might be the concrete realm of the organic, with its implication of wholeness and its dimensions of aesthetics, morality, and ethics. He pointed to the forest, with its associations of trees, soils, microbes, and natural processes, as "the triumph of the organisation of mutually dependent species."[32] He looked upon the factory, too, as a kind of organism, with its machinery, workers, and some social and enconomic functions which should be considered as a complex whole rather than be judged by abstract calculations alone. And so, not with entirely new observations but with a fresh synthesis, Whitehead pointed to certain imbalances in the capitalist, materialistic, increasingly specialized and professionalized Western world of the 1920s.

If they ever happened to read *Science and the Modern World,* such foresters as Aldo Leopold, Bob Marshall, and Benton MacKaye may have found some support for their own views on ethics and wilderness recreation. Whitehead's notes on the necessity for wandering were largely metaphorical yet rich in suggestion. "When man ceases to wander, he will cease to ascend in the scale of being," Whitehead remarked. "Physical wandering is still important, but greater still is the power of man's spiritual adventures—adventures of thought, adventures of passionate feeling, adventures of aesthetic experience."[33] Earlier he had described the opposite of wandering: the specialization and professionalization of knowledge, which produces "minds in a groove." These minds could add to a profession's progress, but that progress would be restricted to its own groove. And the upshot was unfortunate; Whitehead saw an increase in knowledge at the expense of wisdom, vision, a grasp of the whole. Hence the need to shift attention to the concrete, the organic whole.

The landscape architects Frank Waugh and Charles Downing Lay, each pursuing an art form in an era that seemed to be succumbing to the momentum of science and technology, may have found some comfort (though not security) in Whitehead's *Science and the Modern World*. Or perhaps on their own they may have realized that the organic aspects of their art form—the plants, the soils, the ecology of the whole—could give greater weight to their professional standing and accomplishments. Waugh probably did realize that. And yet Whitehead, warning against narrow professionalism, would have them wander beyond the pale of their own field. Rachel Carson, for one, went beyond the limits of *her* scientific discipline. She did so with serenity in "Undersea," in 1937, then with great force and eloquence when she described the pervasive threats of pesticides in *Silent Spring* (1962). But what if Carson had stayed within the confines of marine biology as her superiors in the Bureau of Fisheries understood it?

It happened that two leading American drama critics, Walter Prichard Eaton and Joseph Wood Krutch, were troubled by some aspects of modern science in 1929. Eaton, who had left the theaters of Broadway for the hills of western Massachusetts in 1910 and turned increasingly to nature writing, found that the market for his familiar essays was drying up in the late 1920s. Reflecting on this change in the spring of 1929, he pointed to two factors. First, the war in Europe had divided the generations, leaving younger people more concerned (and vocal) about their souls and their sex, "and apparently quite too restless to contemplate the quiet places where I love to roam." Second, Eaton had come to believe that "in nature writing, nature is more important than writing." Then he elaborated: "I am too well aware of my lack of scientific equipment for significant observation. A vague love of nature isn't enough."[34] In time Eaton overcame his sense of inadequacy and had more nature essays published—some cheerful, some elegiac. But the fact that he had been caught up short and humbled by the accumulation of scientific knowledge in his time sheds light on some dilemmas of his contemporaries.

Joseph Wood Krutch, younger than Eaton by fifteen years, was a somewhat estranged member of the restless, more vocal younger generation.

In *The Modern Temper* (1929), ranging far beyond the theaters of Broadway yet lingering within the abstractions of many fields, Krutch confessed his intellectual anxieties about the modern world that science was ushering in. And, given his own early leanings toward mathematics and the sciences, he was able to follow the implications of developments in those fields to a logical conclusion—that is, to the "rock bottom of skepticism" and alienation, if not despair.[35]

We have seen that Krutch's book drew praise from prominent critics when it first appeared, and that it caught the attention of Bob Marshall that spring of 1929. After the stock market crash in October, Krutch's arguments against a stifling prosperity and the optimism born of modern science fell flat. In early 1930, physically ill but determined, Krutch set off on a cross-country lecture tour to promote his book. Then on the train journey home from Los Angeles he read Thoreau's *Walden* for the first time, and the impact was profound. Both the social criticism and the experiences of wildness as described by a civilized man, Thoreau, intrigued him. In time Krutch would write a biography of Thoreau and turn to nature writing.[36]

Meanwhile, Marshall's essay on wilderness, written by the end of the spring of 1929, lost none of its validity when it appeared at the onset of the Depression, in the February 1930 issue of *Scientific Monthly*. If anything, the essay gained a sense of urgency from the more sobering realities of unemployment and psychological as well as economic depression. Marshall had read at least one of Aldo Leopold's two articles on the need to preserve wilderness, both of 1925; but he put somewhat less faith in the work of existing government entities than did Leopold, who cited progress made by the Forest Service and the National Conference on Outdoor Recreation and its committees.[37] Instead, with allusions to Tom Paine and Thomas Jefferson and phrases that rang like a call to arms, Marshall asserted the people's last chance to repulse "the tyrannical ambition of civilization to conquer every niche on the whole earth." That chance—that hope—would lie in "the organization of spirited people who will fight for the freedom of the wilderness."[38]

Marshall's essay was like a spark that smoldered before igniting a blaze.

Shortly after it appeared, Harold C. Anderson, secretary of the Potomac Appalachian Trail Club, read it, was impressed, and recommended it to Benton MacKaye.[39] MacKaye read it and was also impressed. But nothing came of that call to arms for a while. Then Herbert Hoover stepped aside and Franklin D. Roosevelt took the oath of office. To many conservationists the future looked bright. From 1934 to 1936 MacKaye served as a regional planner with the Tennessee Valley Authority in Knoxville. But he soon noticed that primeval wilderness was not high on the list of New Deal priorities. Labor-intensive road building in the nation's forests and the "skyline drives" that began to parallel and overlap the Appalachian Trail all ranked higher. MacKaye proposed the alternative of "flank-line" roads—that is, roads that wound around slopes and in the valleys, offering varied scenery yet leaving intact the wilderness of the high peaks.[40] But in private he saw that he and like-minded people would have to heed Marshall's call, band together, and fight for that wilderness. They did. "To meet the emergency of a sudden excessively dangerous decline in America's unequalled wilderness," eight men—Marshall, MacKaye, Anderson, Leopold, Harvey Broome, Robert Sterling Yard, Bernard Frank, and Ernest Oberholtzer—formed the Wilderness Society on January 21, 1935. It was formally organized on April 24, 1937.[41]

How the history of the Wilderness Society and that of the Appalachian Trail intertwined in the mid-1930s is already known; Stephen Fox outlined it brilliantly, from several points of view.[42] In the first issue of the society's quarterly, *The Living Wilderness,* for example, Leopold's "Why the Wilderness Society?" appeared opposite MacKaye's "Why the Appalachian Trail?"[43] And the two were complementary. More philosophically, tentatively, Leopold pointed to the value of wilderness for scientific research and called for an "intelligent humility toward man's place in nature." MacKaye's piece, written to defend the AT against skyline drives, auto horns, and other intrusions, was a spirited call to action.

Years later, on the thirtieth anniversary of the Wilderness Society, MacKaye reflected on how the group had come together. Recalling Marshall's article "The Problem of the Wilderness," he wrote, "What the Koran was to Islam let Walden be to Wilderness. Well, I consider Marshall's article as the 'Walden' of our own particular movement and Society. So let's place the source of this Society to Marshall's article of 1930."[44]

***

The title of Fairfield Osborn's book *Our Plundered Planet* may owe something to Bernard DeVoto's astringent blend of history and social criticism in "The West: A Plundered Province," which appeared in *Harper's* in August 1934. Citing grizzly political cartoons and popular mythology (the West as escape, freedom, sanctuary, manifest destiny, a last chance), DeVoto soon cut to a definition of where the West begins: "where the average annual rainfall drops below twenty inches."[45] He told of the obstacles posed by an arid climate and Americans' determination to ignore or overcome them for many reasons, including greed and empire building. At first the villains seemed to be bankers, industrialists, and middlemen from the East who plundered the West as if it were a resource-rich colony. But in the end all Americans were implicated. The essay ended with a reappraisal of the American Dream, which DeVoto viewed as both a product and a condition of the grand westward movement across the continent.

DeVoto saw in that vague concept, the American Dream, a belief that there are no limits to American willpower, energy, and ingenuity, nothing to hinder a swamp from becoming another Chicago or a plot of 160 acres—anywhere, even in the desert—from yielding a decent living from farming or grazing. But that dream was shattered in the arid West. "Of the Americans, it was the Westerners who first understood that there are other limits than the sky," DeVoto remarked.[46]

A westerner himself, born in Ogden, Utah, in 1897, DeVoto had lived for many years in the Midwest and the East, studying, writing, and teaching. Before the mid-century he would write histories of the West that would win the coveted prizes of the East—a Pulitzer, a Bancroft—and a few honorary doctorates. He would also stress the impact of scenic beauty on people's lives and urge that some areas of wilderness be preserved.[47] But one of his most important contributions dated from 1934, when he pierced the myth of the West's rugged individualism; emphasized cooperation, without which human society could not have survived in its arid land; and insisted that the West was a land of limits. Years later, acting on those convictions, DeVoto alerted the public to a sweeping land grab in the public domain that stockmen and "wool-growers" were on the verge of carrying out. His *Harper's* article of January 1947 was a kind of first alert. In time he and others, including Arthur Carhart, stirred the interest and political will to keep the coveted Taylor Act grazing lands and national forests in the public domain.[48]

In February 1947, when Aldo Leopold rose to sum up the Twelfth North American Wildlife Conference in San Antonio, he obliquely alluded to DeVoto's recent article in *Harper's* and the land-grab effort.[49] Later that year, however, when Leopold outlined the tradition of writing in which he would place his own "Great Possessions" (later retitled *A Sand County Almanac*), he did not mention Bernard DeVoto's feisty writings on conservation.[50] Nor did he cite Dallas Lore Sharp, Rachel Carson, or Henry Beston. In a draft foreword dated July 31, 1947, Leopold recognized a dividing line drawn by modern science, with its revelations about ecology, animal behavior, and endangered species. On the far side of that divide, he noted, were Thoreau, Muir, Burroughs, W. H. Hudson, and Ernest Thompson Seton. On the near side were the company of authors to which he aspired: the British writers Fraser Darling and R. M. Lockley and the North Americans Sally Carrighar (*One Day on Beetle Rock*), Theodora Stanwell-Fletcher (*Driftwood Valley*), and Louis Halle (*Spring in Washington*). Why these authors and not others? For years this question was not asked; after setting aside his 1947 foreword, Leopold wrote a new one for the book that was finally published (posthumously) in 1949.[51]

The historian Roderick Nash has identified a good reason for publishers' and readers' hesitant or delayed responses to *A Sand County Almanac* in the late 1940s: Leopold's ideas were radical, calling for a restructuring of American priorities and behavior and a radically new definition of progress.[52] Consider the context. After enduring the Great Depression, the Second World War, rationing and limits of all kinds, how many Americans would welcome the prospect of yet more limits to their freedom, all because the land, which they had long taken for granted, had rights as well? Then, too, there was the promise that science and technology would release people from pests, diseases, chores, even from their ties to the land, the planet. Wary of that promise, Leopold confessed to a frustration with science in his draft foreword of July 31, 1947. "This concurrent growth in knowledge of land, good intentions toward land, and abuse of land presents a paradox that baffles me, as it does many another thinking citizen," he wrote. "Science ought to work the other way, but it doesn't. Why?" Again, most readers could not know that Leopold had ever asked that question until 1987, when a fine collection of essays about *A Sand County Almanac* appeared; for appended to that collection was his previously unpublished 1947 foreword.[53]

By now we might have some intuitive sense of why Leopold would want to identify with an author such as Louis Halle. Not a scientist but an amateur naturalist, Halle could envision Washington, D.C., from the point of view of migrating Canada geese and the fish and fowl that need a saltwater habitat. As we saw earlier, in 1947 Halle looked upon the natural world through the window of a great city. And, aware of the limits of science, he got down to the roots of a deeper, more pervasive problem—a people alienated from nature; a civilization divorced from the universe, "feeding on itself."[54]

Sally Carrighar was another observant nonscientist who could write about the natural world with uncommon sympathy. Born in Cleveland in 1898, she had a gift for writing but did not find a compelling subject until she reached her forties. She had learned something of zoology at Wellesley College and later from conversations with Dr. Joseph Grinnell, head of the Museum of Vertebrate Zoology at the University of California at Berkeley. In time she went to Sequoia National Park and rented a cabin on the western slope of the High Sierra. There a whole community of wild creatures impressed her with their stability, sanity, alertness, and vitality. Among them she found her home, and from that home came her first book of nature writing, the much-reprinted *One Day on Beetle Rock* (1944).[55]

It is difficult to extract a single gemlike passage from Carrighar's *Beetle Rock,* so closely does one idea, one incident follow the one before it. The language is understated, the writing transparent. Behind it is a naturalist's desire for accuracy: to depict a whole animal community in the sugar pine belt of the Sierra Nevada at an altitude of 6,500 feet as observed on a single day, June 18. As she explained in what appear to be notes for a publisher, this was a transition zone with much interaction among the wild creatures. And, as an indication of how closely she observed these creatures, there remains among her papers a large, detailed, hand-ruled graph in which the horizontal axis charts the twenty-four hours of the day. The vertical axis lists weather conditions, the actions of nine featured animals, other animals, humans, and incidents.[56] Drawing on these minute details of the animals' lives, Carrighar wrote a book of many episodes, all tending to underscore the animals' interdependence and a code of behavior that was rarely broken.

The ethical relations among people, other creatures, and the land in works by Carrighar and Halle are often implied, not defined. Either way, the message can be understood. But Leopold, it seems, wanted it both ways. He aspired to tell stories of land and wildlife with vivid, spare prose that had literary value. At the same time he wanted to explore complex issues of wilderness, wildlife, ethics, and aesthetics, using whatever analytical or rhetorical tools seemed necessary. The librarian and scholar Dennis Ribbens has explained how various editors, including those at Knopf (Carrighar's publisher), had tried to guide and shape Leopold's manuscript. After some six years of correspondence, the editors at Knopf were still pressing for more objective narratives, without the ecological arguments.[57] But Leopold persisted in seeking his own fusion of narrative and polemic, literary art and scientific content.

Leopold did make some shifts toward objectivity, setting aside a long, personally revealing foreword (that of July 31, 1947) and writing at least two versions of a shorter one.[58] In a foreword dated December 5, 1947, he referred to what he did at his weekend refuge, and certain ideas whereby he as a dissenter rationalized his dissent. In this version the threats to wild things include "mechanization," "population increase," and "civilization." In the foreword of March 4, 1948, however, the one actually published by Oxford, Leopold reached for a bit more universality; he would write of what his family did at *their* refuge; of ideas whereby *we* dissenters rationalize our dissent. And threats to wild things were summed up as "progress."[59]

With equal intensity, Jens Jensen, too, wanted it both ways. Writing of gardens that might slip back into nature and of forests as the last stand of wilderness along prairie rivers, he wanted to lead readers beyond the arrogance of possession and control toward a simple, reverent love of the land. At times he subtly implied his message. At other times he was didactic: "That all life is one Life, that all heart beats are one Heart Beat, that all expressions of the living quality of love creates [*sic*] a wholeness is the music of flowing waters."[60]

That passage from *The Clearing* (1949) survived the cuts made before the work reappeared in a small volume of Jensen's collected writings, published posthumously in 1956. And that passage was typical of the writing that survived an editor's deletions. As a result, later generations of readers might hastily assume that Jensen was a remnant from some remote romantic era, a gentle soul, but somewhat irrelevant in modern times. Unfortunately, the editor deleted Jensen's sharp critique of materialism; his story of an explorer in Greenland who felt connected to the universe; his memory of a family in Appalachia who looked upon their foothills as something human, with a soul; his evocation of a sense of well-being shared by a prairie farmer, an Asian, a black man, and an Eskimo; and his vision of science reoriented toward life. One of Jensen's sentences was edited to a platitude: "Works of the scientist must begin at the root of all wisdom." Only those with access to the now rare first edition could see what Jensen meant: "Works of the scientist must begin at the root of all wisdom, Life's rhythmic pattern, if science is to be a pillar upon which are compiled findings upon findings."[61]

Another item cut from Jensen's original text in *The Clearing*, evidently to pare down the book for the collected writings, was the dedication. "This book is dedicated to the soil." That summed up Jensen's feelings succinctly. But how many American readers at mid-century were prepared to appreciate those feelings? And how many were prepared for the more probing and intellectually challenging *Sand County Almanac*?

Let others speculate. Here we have simply tried to uncover traces of how people once felt about wildness and wild land, especially in Leopold's sense of a biotic community. In his time, evidently some kind of land ethic was beginning to develop among a range of people and groups. In our time the task Leopold identified remains a challenge: to preserve the land's integrity, stability, and beauty; and to do so with "an intelligent humility toward man's place in nature."[62]

Epilogue

For weeks now the "Whee-you!" of an unseen bird has caught my attention and held it to the end of his song. There it is again—a clear whistle and fragments of melody from deep in the moist woods nearby. With help from a friend, the New Hampshire Audubon Society, audio tapes, and digital recordings, we can identify these haunting sounds as the song of a wood thrush. In the early 1900s, however, before that sophisticated technology existed, people tried to capture the sounds of birds with musical notation and the written word. Some wrote of thrushes that breathed "the spirit of the dying day" or expressed the "wondrous mysteries of the woods." In the song of the wood thrush the ornithologist Edward Howe Forbush sensed the mystery of the universe. And, as we have seen, the poet and essayist Maurice Thompson was thrilled by the song of the truly wild migrant mockingbird. "It is the strain of genius," he wrote, "audacious, defiant, untrammeled—a voice of absolute independence crying in the wilderness."[1]

A century ago independence and mystery were qualities that people could hope to find in the wilderness. They might also look for perma-

e, some glimmer of the eternal. Later, in the midst of more unset-
changes in a modernizing land, even mere traces of wildness, far
any vast wilderness, could be reassuring signs of nature's persis-
...ce. Living in Washington, D.C., during the Second World War, Louis
Halle was encouraged by the sight of Canada geese flying overhead and
violets sprouting up through cracks in Rock Creek Parkway. By 1948
Aldo Leopold had seen so many traces of wildness vanish in the path of
logging, cultivation, drainage, and development that he relished one
special pleasure on evenings in spring at his family's worn-out farm
in Wisconsin—the dance of the woodcocks. In 1932 Benton MacKaye
wrote of something that people might discover as they traced the story
of evolution in remnants of wilderness along the Appalachian Trail.
They might feel a "vital spark," something that belonged to the ages.[2]

These experiences need no further justification. And yet among them,
and elsewhere in these pages, there may be evidence of some trends or
patterns, perhaps even a sign of reconciling a love of wild things with a
life fully engaged in a modern industrial technologically advanced society. We have seen that E. B. White was heartened to see an old willow
tree, held up by wires, persisting in the cold shadow of airplanes during
the hot summer of 1948 in Lower Manhattan. At that time Rachel Carson was writing a series of bulletins on national wildlife refuges, including Mattamuskeet, near Pamlico Sound in North Carolina. There,
where humans had tried many times to drain the land for cultivation—
and failed—Carson delighted in the sights and sounds of swans, geese,
ducks, herons, egrets, bitterns, loons, and grebes that came for the winter, the summer, or for year-round homes among the old drainage canals
and newly restored marshes.[3] These and other instances of nature's per-
sistence, however, with or without assistance from humans, may not
amount to a trend toward reconciling the civilized and the wild. They
may simply reflect the tendency of all forms of life to try to thrive in a
given environment.

In any event, some Americans evidently cared a great deal about wildness and wild places during the first half of the twentieth century, especially in the early years. That period opened with widespread popular

interest in getting "back to nature" by hunting, camping, hiking, and learning about wildflowers, birds, and other wild creatures. It closed, however, with anxiety about other kinds of primal forces, the nuclear weapons that were released toward the end of the Second World War and tested during the Cold War that followed.[4]

On balance, the half century between 1900 and 1949 was not known for the active defense of wilderness in the United States, apart from the efforts of a few individuals and organizations, rowing against the currents of a modernizing, urbanizing society that was increasingly dependent on the findings of science and the advances of technology. Some of those individuals, including John Muir, Nathaniel S. Shaler, Aldo Leopold, Frank Waugh, Rachel Carson, and Bob Marshall, contributed to the scientific knowledge of their time; yet their concerns reached far beyond science and the scientific method, into areas of experience where emotions, feelings, a sense of well-being, and a perception of beauty could be more significant than fact, proof, or prediction.

General theories derived from facts, proofs, and predictions may be essential to the structure of what we commonly refer to as "science," whether natural, social, or political; but they are virtually absent here. Instead, we have focused on sensuous experiences of particular places, interactions among people and nonhuman creatures, and relations to the land in the widest sense of the word. The publications that frame this book—*Garden and Forest* magazine in the 1890s, Leopold's and Jens Jensen's late works of 1949—were all devoted to issues of land. And within that frame of time we paused to notice Walter Prichard Eaton's essay on the "literature of place" (1918), a literature informed by knowledge of local flora and fauna and of the experiences of local people over generations. Its authors were driven by some inner compulsion to communicate their love of a place, regardless of how large their audience might be. They wrote for the sake of their local mountain or prairie grove or seaside town, for the enjoyment of their neighbors, and most often for love of the land.[5]

The first half of this book gives more attention to that sort of literature, local or regional in scope, rooted in a place and informed by scientific understanding, intuition, or both, as in the writings of Mary Austin and Donald Culross Peattie. The second half of the book, ranging more freely in time and space, considers issues of broader, sometimes national interest. Perhaps it also reflects the way many of us have been taught to think about ideas and issues, unhampered by local or provincial concerns. It could be that this dual focus—on geographical region or place and on historical issues or ideas—has split the book in two. But at the time I saw no better way to approach environmental issues than from a broad perspective and also at close range. We need both approaches; if one is ignored, I doubt that we will ever accomplish much in the way of defending wildness and wilderness against the forces of economic development in the evolving global capitalist system.

Among the more compelling works about environmental degradation in our time, a national or global perspective is usually implied if not underscored. Consider just two books that appeared at the end of the twentieth century: Colin Woodard's *Ocean's End: Travels through Endangered Seas* and Mark Hertsgaard's *Earth Odyssey: Around the World in Search of Our Environmental Future.*[6] Woodard and Hertsgaard, both journalists, integrate vivid, unforgettable details of a place within a global perspective; and each recommends some measures applicable here and there around the globe. These measures are thoughtful, creative, and practicable for the near future. And yet we may still come away dazed by the enormous destruction now evident in the sea, on land, and at the point of their endless give-and-take at the water's edge. We may feel angered, overwhelmed, or energized, determined to contribute in some way, personally and significantly, toward repairing the damage. But how?

In *Plundered Promise: Capitalism, Politics, and the Fate of the Federal Lands,* Richard Behan addresses national problems of land use that he believes require locally sensitive solutions. He detects in recent reformist literature on economics and the environment a common thread of decentralization. He also discusses Daniel Kemmis's notion of a "politics of place," by which people might exert some control over the fate of the lands they inhabit. The poet Gary Snyder, too, noted Kemmis's idea of a politics of place (or "inhabitation"), then described a "culture of place" that may emerge from the process of engaging in political action at the local level.[7] Here, as in other recent works that address environmental problems, the global and the local perspectives turn out to be mutually reinforcing and illuminating.

Clearly there are some advantages in integrating global and local perspectives, particularly in a world growing steadily more interlinked through technology, more interdependent politically, economically more uniform—as a "single market"—and culturally more homogenized. But what are our chances of resisting those vast, coalescing forces insofar as they are opposed to (or oblivious of) wildness? And what are the chances of the grizzly, the caribou, and the innumerable organisms not yet identified by humans in some of the rapidly disappearing wild places of the world?

Perhaps our chances and those of our fellow creatures would be somewhat better if we knew intimately what it was that we were defending and why it was so special—how, as Jens Jensen learned, a few mountains in one small part of Appalachia could speak to a family that lived among them; how a garden could be so charming and so natural that, as the landscape architect Fletcher Steele once recognized, "it hurts to leave home for a day."[8] In his case, the garden's charm grew out of love of the land. The garden was natural because it was a place of play, work, and mild leisure for people of different generations. And it was unique for its inhabitants, unlike any other place in the world.

To articulate this uniqueness we need not only a broad, inclusive culture of place but also an informed and intimate literature of place, which may be layered over generations of thought and experience. That literature never ceased to be written, but at times it has been eclipsed by other kinds, other preoccupations. On balance, it appears that the main currents in economic, political, social, and cultural developments of the first half of the twentieth century in the United States were moving against a literature of place, encouraging people in many ways to be more mobile, more inured to the continual building up and tearing down of structures, more abstract in their thinking, with national and international perspectives.

The literary critic Malcolm Cowley gave a broad yet personal overview of changes he lived through in the first two decades of the twentieth century. Once institutions and enterprises—publishing, finance, theater—became centralized after 1900, he observed, unified markets for cars, soaps, and clothes (and entertainments of all kinds) came into being. As a child in rural western Pennsylvania in the early 1900s he came to know the woods and its creatures through his summer wanderings; but as a schoolboy in Pittsburgh and as an undergraduate at Harvard he learned very little about the places around him. "Looking backward," he wrote, "I feel that our whole training was involuntarily directed toward destroying whatever roots we had in the soil, toward eradicating our local and regional peculiarities, toward making us homeless citizens of the world."[9]

Cowley went on to describe the experiences of a rootless or "lost" generation of writers—his contemporaries Ernest Hemingway, F. Scott Fitzgerald, T. S. Eliot, and others—who moved back and forth across the Atlantic, driven by shattering world events and their own desires. They survived, became exemplars of the modern writer, and earned the respect of the transnational Western world in which they were born. But now Cowley's reflections on his generation's unrooted education and training may apply equally well—and eerily—to the rearing of new generations in other parts of the world, even those once isolated by conditions of geography and climate. As Helena Norberg-Hodge discovered in Ladakh, on the high Tibetan plateau in northern India, many forces, including the media, tourism, global economic patterns, and education, have isolated Ladakh children from their culture and from nature. These forces have denied them self-esteem and local pride, weakened family and community ties, taught them to crave Western gadgets and fast food, and trained them for narrow, specialized work in a Westernized urban setting. Norberg-Hodge's emphasis is on the psychological costs of Western-style development, especially the loss of a "deep-rooted contentedness." But she also mentions the environmental costs—environmental problems that, "if unchecked, will lead to irreversible decline."[10]

Extrapolating from Cowley's experience of education that helped to create "homeless citizens of the world," from Norberg-Hodge's critique of modern education in Ladakh, and from newspaper articles about the economy, the environment, and expanding webs of communication, we can foresee an increasingly homogenized global economy and culture in which disparities of wealth and poverty may long persist. This world may prove to be one without the biological diversity that E. O. Wilson and others have shown to be precious beyond any price.[11] It may lack the social diversity that Bill McKibben brought to our attention in 1995.[12] It may also lack the grace of gardens and landscapes that are unique, much loved. This would be a world without the cultural diversity that T. S. Eliot defended as early as 1948.

At that time Eliot was mainly concerned about the different cultures within the British Isles, his adopted home. But his vision extended around the globe, for there were already signs of some form of world government in the making; and the notion of a uniform world *culture* appalled him. Noting that cultures tended to vanish under modern conditions, he suggested a few alternatives—"to grow a contemporary culture from the old roots," to keep alive the mutually beneficial interactions between "strong" cultures and local "satellite" cultures, and to give more attention to "the ecology of cultures."[13]

Here Eliot was on to something as critical for our well-being as biological diversity—or biodiversity. He called it the "ecology" of cultures, apparently to emphasize the intricate web of interactions among people, their land, and their artifacts that make up whatever culture we inherit. Now it appears that cultural diversity and the love, pride, and caring that we feel for our own special portion of that diversity may become part of our defense against the forces that would—even with the best of intentions—destroy the integrity of places on earth and homogenize the remnants. Other parts of our defense may come from a literature of place or a politics of place. Yet another part of our defense will surely be biodiversity and its sustenance—land and waters allowed to remain wild and free.

Notes

ABBREVIATIONS

AHC Papers   Arthur Hawthorne Carhart Papers, Conservation Collection, Western History/Genealogy Department, Denver Public Library

AL Papers   Aldo Leopold Papers, Conservation Collection, Western History/ Genealogy Department, Denver Public Library

FLL   Frances Loeb Library, Harvard University Graduate School of Design

FLL/SC   Frances Loeb Library, Special Collections, Harvard University Graduate School of Design

HB Papers   Henry Beston Papers, Dartmouth College Library, Special Collections

HUA   Harvard University Archives

MKF Papers   MacKaye Family Papers, Dartmouth College Library, Special Collections

SC Papers   Sally Carrighar Papers, Dartmouth College Library, Special Collections

TWS Papers   The Wilderness Society Papers, Conservation Collection, Western History/Genealogy Department, Denver Public Library

USGPO   United States Government Printing Office

WPE Collection   Walter Prichard Eaton Collection, The Clifton Waller Barrett Library of American Literature, The Albert and Shirley Small Special Collections Library, University of Virginia Library

Preface

1. Praise for *Garden and Forest* in *Harper's Weekly,* quoted in *Garden and Forest,* no. 463 (Jan. 6, 1897), ii.
2. *Garden and Forest,* no. 514 (Dec. 29, 1897), 518. On the history and significance of this periodical, see "*Garden and Forest* (1888–1897)," pts. 1 and 2, *Arnoldia* 60 (2000), nos. 2 and 3.
3. See Virginia Tuttle Clayton, ed., *The Once and Future Gardener: Garden Writing from the Golden Age of Magazines, 1900–1940* (Boston: David R. Godine, 2000).
4. Melanie Simo, *100 Years of Landscape Architecture: Some Patterns of a Century* (Washington, D.C.: ASLA Press/Spacemaker Press, 1999); Simo, *The Coalescing of Different Forces and Ideas: A History of Landscape Architecture at Harvard, 1900–1999* (Cambridge: Harvard University Graduate School of Design, 2000); and Peter Walker and Melanie Simo, *Invisible Gardens: The Search for Modernism in the American Landscape* (Cambridge: MIT Press, 1994).
5. Henry Vincent Hubbard and Theodora Kimball, *An Introduction to the Study of Landscape Design* (New York: Macmillan, 1917), 74–75.
6. See Frank Waugh, *The Landscape Beautiful* (New York: Orange Judd, 1910); and A. Donald Taylor, "Frank Albert Waugh: A Biographical Minute" (1943), in *Landscape Architectural Education,* ed. Gary O. Robinette, 2 vols. (Dubuque: Kendall/Hunt, 1973), 1:133–34.

Introduction

1. Arthur H. Carhart, "This Way to Wilderness," 60, unpublished ms. in AHC Papers, CONS 88, Box 2:100, Folder: "Manuscripts—Biography, This Way to Wilderness." See also Carhart, *Timber in your Life* (Philadelphia: Lippincott, 1955), 137–48; Carhart, "Historical Development of Outdoor Recreation," in *Outdoor Recreation Literature: A Survey,* Report to the Outdoor Recreation Resources Review Commission by the Librarian of Congress, (Washington, D.C., 1962), 2:111–12; Curt Meine, *Aldo Leopold: His Life and Work* (Madison: University of Wisconsin Press, 1988), 177–78; Roderick Nash, "Arthur Carhart: Wildland Advocate," *Living Wilderness* 44 (December 1980): 32–34; Nash, *Wilderness and the American Mind,* 3d ed. (New Haven: Yale University Press, 1982), 185–87; Donald N. Baldwin, *The Quiet Revolution: Grass Roots of Today's Wilderness Preservation Movement* (Boulder, Colo.: Pruett, 1972), 29–36; and Susan L. Flader, review of Baldwin's *Quiet Revolution,* in *Journal of Forest History* 18 (April 1974): 36.
2. Carhart, "This Way to Wilderness," 61.
3. Carhart, "Memorandum for Mr. Leopold, District 3," Dec. 10, 1919, in AHC Papers, CONS 88, Box 2:100, Folder: "Biography: Wilderness Chronology with Historic Memos, 1919–1955."
4. Carhart, "Historical Development of Outdoor Recreation," 116.
5. Carhart, *Timber in your Life,* 140–48.

6. Meine, *Aldo Leopold,* 178.

7. Louis J. Halle Jr., *Spring in Washington* (New York: William Sloane, 1947), 129.

8. Bernhard Fernow, *A Brief History of Forestry in Europe, the United States, and Other Countries,* 2d ed. (Toronto: University of Toronto Press, 1909), 21–140, 390–438.

9. Richard W. Behan, *Plundered Promise: Capitalism, Politics, and the Fate of the Federal Lands* (Washington, D.C.: Island Press, 2001), 95–97, 111; Ralph S. Hosmer, "Fernow Hall," *American Forestry* 28 (November 1922): 670–72; and *National Cyclopaedia of American Biography,* s.v. "Fernow, Bernhard Eduard."

10. Fernow, *Brief History of Forestry,* 410–11.

11. William B. Greeley, *Forests and Men* (Garden City, N.Y.: Doubleday, 1951), 81–82.

12. On Pinchot's relations with his "fellow crusaders," see *Journal of Forestry* 43 (August 1945), a special issue honoring Pinchot on his eightieth birthday, with recollections by Henry S. Graves, Ralph S. Hosmer, and others.

13. Char Miller, *Gifford Pinchot and the Making of Modern Environmentalism* (Washington, D.C.: Island Press/Shearwater Books, 2001), 119–44.

14. Gifford Pinchot, *Breaking New Ground* (New York: Harcourt, Brace, 1947), 103.

15. Ibid., 89–104; Frederick Turner, *Rediscovering America: John Muir in His Time and Ours* (San Francisco: Sierra Club Books, 1985), 300–313; Michael P. Cohen, *The Pathless Way: John Muir and American Wilderness* (Madison: University of Wisconsin Press, 1984), 286–94; Stephen Fox, *The American Conservation Movement: John Muir and His Legacy* (1981; Madison: University of Wisconsin Press, 1985), 112–15; and Linnie Marsh Wolfe, *Son of the Wilderness: The Life of John Muir* (New York: Knopf, 1945), 270–74. The other national forestry commissioners were General Henry L. Abbot, an Army engineer; Alexander Agassiz, curator of the Museum of Comparative Zoology at Harvard; William H. Brewer, professor of agriculture at Yale; Wolcott Gibbs, a chemist and physicist; and Arnold Hague, a geologist.

16. John Muir, "National Parks and Forest Reservations," *Harper's Weekly,* June 5, 1897, 563–67; "The American Forests," *Atlantic Monthly,* August 1897, 145–57; and "The Wild Parks and Forest Reservations of the West," *Atlantic Monthly,* January 1898, 15–28. The *Atlantic Monthly* articles reappeared in Muir, *Our National Parks* (1901; Boston: Houghton Mifflin, 1916).

17. Gifford Pinchot, "Government Forestry Abroad," and Edward A. Bowers, "The Present Condition of the Forests on the Public Lands," both in *Publications of the American Economic Association,* vol. 6 (Washington, D.C., 1891), 191–238, 241–58.

18. Pinchot, *Breaking New Ground,* 171.

19. Gifford Pinchot, *The Training of a Forester,* 3d ed. (Philadelphia: Lippincott, 1917), 65–66. Wolfe, in *Son of the Wilderness,* 262, noted that Muir had given this advice to young Pinchot himself in 1893.

20. See H. W. S. Cleveland, *Landscape Architecture as Applied to the Wants of the West* (1873; Pittsburgh: University of Pittsburgh Press, 1965).

21. David N. Livingstone, *Nathaniel Southgate Shaler and the Culture of American Science* (Tuscaloosa: University of Alabama Press, 1987), 198.

22. Ibid., 195.

23. David Lowenthal, introduction to George Perkins Marsh, *Man and Nature*, ed. Lowenthal (Cambridge: Belknap/Harvard University Press, 1965), x. See also Lowenthal, *George Perkins Marsh: Prophet of Conservation* (Seattle: University of Washington Press, 2000).

24. Nathaniel S. Shaler, "Forests of North America," *Scribner's* 1 (May 1887): 561.

25. Nathaniel S. Shaler, "The Landscape as a Means of Culture," *Atlantic Monthly*, December 1898, 777–85.

26. Nathaniel S. Shaler, *Man and the Earth* (New York: Fox, Duffield, 1905), 181–83.

27. Ibid., 189.

28. Henry S. Graves and Cedric H. Guise, *Forest Education* (New Haven: Yale University Press, 1932).

29. Livingstone, *Nathaniel Southgate Shaler*, 208.

30. J. S. Pray, "The Department of Landscape Architecture in Harvard University" (1911), in *Landscape Architectural Education*, ed. Gary O. Robinette, 2 vols. (Dubuque: Kendall/Hunt, 1973), 1:39–44. See also Arthur A. Shurtleff (later Shurcliff), "Landscape Architecture: Notes of Lectures Given during the Year 1900 at Robinson Hall," ms, two vols. in FLL/SC, Rare NAB 280 Sh 562.

31. Charles W. Eliot, *Charles Eliot, Landscape Architect* (1902; Amherst: Library of American Landscape History/University of Massachusetts Press, 1999).

32. Keith N. Morgan, Introduction, ibid., xli.

33. Charles Eliot, review of Charles A. Platt's *Italian Gardens*, ibid., 547–49.

34. Charles Eliot, "The Coast of Maine," ibid., 308–15.

35. Charles Eliot, "Landscape Forestry in the Metropolitan Reservations," ibid., 709–14.

36. Pinchot, *Breaking New Ground*, 32, 96. Pinchot greatly admired Olmsted Sr., who had first interviewed him in 1891 for the forester's position at Biltmore, the G. W. Vanderbilt estate in North Carolina. See Laura Wood Roper, *FLO: A Biography of Frederick Law Olmsted* (Baltimore: Johns Hopkins University Press, 1973), 418–19; and chapter 6 below.

37. F. L. Olmsted to F. L. Olmsted Jr., Sept. 5, 1890, in Roper, *FLO*, 423. The other writers the elder Olmsted counted on to defend the profession of landscape architecture were J. C. Olmsted, Henry S. Codman, Charles Eliot, the architect Charles A. Coolidge, Charles S. Sargent, William A. Stiles, and, in time, F. L. Olmsted Jr. On Olmsted's views of the art of landscape architecture, shared with Van Rensselaer and others, see also Charles E. Beveridge and Paul Rocheleau, *Frederick Law Olmsted: Designing the American Landscape* (New York: Rizzoli, 1995), 32–34.

38. Mariana Griswold Van Rensselaer, *Accents as Well as Broad Effects: Writings on Architecture, Landscape, and the Environment, 1876–1925,* ed. David Gebhard (Berkeley: University of California Press, 1996); Van Rensselaer, *Henry Hobson Richardson and His Works* (Boston: Houghton Mifflin, 1888); and Van Rensselaer, "Frederick Law Olmsted" (1893), in *Accents as Well as Broad Effects.*

39. Eliot, *Charles Eliot, Landscape Architect*, 546–47.

40. Shaler, "Landscape as a Means of Culture," 781.

41. Mariana Griswold Van Rensselaer, "A Glimpse of Nantucket" (1888), in her *Accents as Well as Broad Effects*, 345.

42. Graves and Guise, *Forest Education*, 102.

43. Henry S. Graves, "Education in Forestry," *Journal of Forestry* 23, February 1925, 108–25.

44. Aldo Leopold, "The Role of Wildlife in a Liberal Education," *Transactions of the Seventh North American Wildlife Conference* (Washington, D.C.: American Wildlife Institute, 1942), in TWS Papers, CONS 130, Box 3: 103, Folder: "Aldo Leopold, articles, 1921–1953."

45. J. Baird Callicott and Michael P. Nelson, eds., *The Great New Wilderness Debate* (Athens: University of Georgia Press, 1998).

46. William Cronon, "The Trouble with Wilderness; or, Getting Back to the Wrong Nature," in *Uncommon Ground: Rethinking the Human Place in Nature,* ed. Cronon (New York: Norton, 1995), 69–90.

47. Daniel B. Botkin, *No Man's Garden: Thoreau and a New Vision for Civilization and Nature* (Washington, D.C.: Island Press/Shearwater Books, 2001).

48. On the desert as a "waste," see Cheryll Glotfelty, "Literary Place Bashing, Test Site Nevada," in *Beyond Nature Writing: Expanding the Boundaries of Ecocriticism,* ed. Karla Armbruster and Kathleen R. Wallace (Charlottesville: University Press of Virginia, 2001), 233–47.

ONE **Desert**

1. John C. Van Dyke, *Nature for Its Own Sake,* 5th ed. (New York: Scribner, 1908), 203. This "edition" seems to be identical with the first one, published in 1898.

2. My account of Van Dyke in the desert is drawn largely from John C. Van Dyke, *The Desert: Further Studies in Natural Appearances* (New York: Scribner, 1901); Van Dyke, *The Open Spaces: Incidents of Nights and Days under the Blue Sky* (1922; rpt. Salt Lake City: University of Utah Press, 1991); *The Autobiography of John C. Van Dyke: A Personal Narrative of American Life, 1861–1931,* ed. Peter Wild (Salt Lake City: University of Utah Press, 1993); Lawrence Clark Powell, "The Desert Odyssey of John C. Van Dyke," *Arizona Highways* 58 (October 1982): 5–29; and Peter Wild's forewords to several reprints of Van Dyke's works. According to Powell, Van Dyke's first summer in the desert was that of 1898. I accept Wild's date, 1899, as it is based on more recent, extensive research.

3. Powell, "Desert Odyssey"; and Peter Wild, "The Desert as Art," in *The Desert Reader,* ed. Wild (Salt Lake City: University of Utah Press, 1991), 111–13.

4. Van Dyke, *The Desert,* 58–59.

5. Ibid., 79–88.

6. Ibid., 59.

7. Peter Wild, introduction to *Autobiography of John C. Van Dyke,* xxxii.

8. Van Dyke, *The Desert,* 16–22.

9. Van Dyke, *Nature for Its Own Sake,* Preface.

10. Van Dyke, *The Mountain: Renewed Studies in Impressions and Appearances* (1916; Salt Lake City: University of Utah Press, 1992), 17.

11. Van Dyke, *The Desert,* 231, 13, 150.

12. Ibid., 233. In "Desert Odyssey," Powell identifies the mountain as San Jacinto.

13. Mary Austin, *Land of Journey's Ending* (1924; New York: AMS Press, 1969), 437.

14. Mary Austin, *Land of Little Rain* (1903; Albuquerque: University of New Mexico Press, 1974), 40.

15. Ibid., 171.

16. Charles Dudley Warner, *Our Italy* (New York: Harper, 1891), 175.

17. Ibid., 169.

18. Mary Austin, *California: The Land of the Sun* (New York: Macmillan, 1914), 17.

19. Mary Austin, *Earth Horizon* (New York: Literary Guild, 1932), 182.

20. Ibid., 71.

21. Carl Van Doren, introduction to Austin, *Land of Little Rain* (Boston: Houghton Mifflin, 1950), xiv–xv.

22. Carl Sandburg, "Jack London: A Common Man," *Tomorrow* 2, no. 4 (April 1906): 35–39, excerpted in Jack London, *The Jack London Reader* (Philadelphia: Courage Books/Running Press, 1994), 271.

23. Austin, *Land of Little Rain,* 14.

24. In 1908 President Theodore Roosevelt named the Grand Canyon a national monument. It 1919 it became a national park.

25. Austin, *Land of Journey's Ending,* 119, 140.

26. Quoted in Ansel Adams, with Mary Street Alinder, *An Autobiography* (Boston: New York Graphic Society/Little, Brown, 1985), 91. The quotation is from Austin's text in *Taos Pueblo* (1930; Boston: New York Graphic Society/Little, Brown, 1977). See also Ansel and Virginia Adams to Mary Austin, Dec. 22, 1930, in *Literary America, 1903–1934: The Mary Austin Letters,* ed. T. M. Pearce (Westport, Conn.: Greenwood Press, 1979), 218.

27. Mary Austin discusses the diversion of water from the Owens River in *Earth Horizon,* 307–8. See also T. M. Pearce, *Mary Hunter Austin* (New York: Twayne, 1965), 37–39; William L. Kahrl, *Water and Power: The Conflict over Los Angeles' Water Supply in the Owens Valley* (Berkeley: University of California Press, 1982); Marc Reisner, *Cadillac Desert: The American West and Its Disappearing Water* (New York: Viking, 1986); and Kevin Starr, *Material Dreams: Southern California through the 1920s* (New York: Oxford University Press, 1990). On Austin's experience in the Owens Valley and for interpretations of both Austin and Van Dyke (which diverge from those offered here), see Donald Worster, *Rivers of Empire: Water, Aridity, and the Growth of the American West* (New York: Pantheon, 1985), 69–74.

28. Mary Austin, "The Colorado River Controversy," *Nation* 125, no. 3253 (Nov. 9, 1927): 510–12. T. M. Pearce discusses the Second Colorado River Conference and Austin's novel *The Ford* (1917) in *Mary Hunter Austin,* 56–57, 75–77;

29. Austin, *California,* 85–103.

30. See Mary Austin, "Regionalism in American Fiction" (1932), in *Beyond Borders: The Selected Essays of Mary Austin,* ed. Reuben J. Ellis (Carbondale: Southern Illinois University Press, 1996), 130–40.

31. Austin, *Land of Journey's Ending,* 438.

32. John L. Stoddard, *Lectures: Southern California,* vol. 10 (Boston: Balch, 1905), 172–73. See also George Wharton James, *The Grand Canyon of Arizona: How to See It* (Boston: Little, Brown, 1910). Essays on the Grand Canyon by Warner, Monroe, Muir, Burroughs, and others appear in *The Grand Canyon: Early Impressions,* ed. Paul Schullery (Boulder, Colo.: Pruett, 1989).

33. James, *Grand Canyon of Arizona,* 18.

34. John Muir, "The Grand Canyon of the Colorado" (1902), in Schullery, *Grand Canyon,* 71–72.

35. John C. Van Dyke, *The Grand Canyon of the Colorado: Recurrent Studies in Impressions and Appearances* (1920; Salt Lake City: University of Utah Press, 1992), xxxi.

36. Ibid., 203, 194–95, 218.

37. Ibid., 199.

38. Ethan Carr, *Wilderness by Design: Landscape Architecture and the National Park Service* (Lincoln: University of Nebraska Press, 1998), 115–19; and Curt Meine, *Aldo Leopold: His Life and Work* (Madison: University of Wisconsin Press, 1988), 159–60. Waugh acknowledges assistance from Leopold, Don P. Johnson, and other Forest Service personnel in his *Plan for the Development of the Village of Grand Canyon, Arizona* (Washington, D.C.: USGPO, 1918), 3.

39. Meine, *Aldo Leopold,* 159.

40. Ibid., 307.

41. Aldo Leopold, "Wilderness" (1935), draft of a speech before a German audience, in *The River of the Mother of God and Other Essays by Aldo Leopold,* ed. Susan L. Flader and J. Baird Callicott (Madison: University of Wisconsin Press, 1991), 226–29.

42. Aldo Leopold, "Conservationist in Mexico" (1937), ibid., 239–44.

43. Aldo Leopold, "Foreword," dated July 31, 1947, in his manuscript "Great Possessions," in AL Papers, CONS 47, Box 1 (a draft of *A Sand County Almanac* [New York: Oxford University Press, 1949]). The foreword appears in *Companion to "A Sand County Almanac": Interpretive and Critical Essays,* ed. J. Baird Callicott (Madison: University of Wisconsin Press, 1987), 281–88.

44. Susan L. Flader, *Thinking Like a Mountain: Aldo Leopold and the Evolution of an Ecological Attitude toward Deer, Wolves, and Forests* (1974; Madison: University of Wisconsin Press, 1994), 153–54. See also Aldo Leopold, *Game Management* (1933; Madison: University of Wisconsin Press, 1986).

45. Leopold, "Conservationist in Mexico," 242.

46. Aldo Leopold, "The State of the Profession," *Journal of Wildlife Management* 4 (July 1940): 343–46; reprint in AL Papers, CONS 47, Box 1, Folder: "Reprints: Articles, 1940s."

47. Ibid., 343.

T W O **Prairie and Plains**

1. Lora S. La Mance, letter to the editor, *Garden and Forest*, Oct. 20, 1897, 416–17.

2. Jens Jensen, *Siftings* (1939), in Jensen, *"Siftings," "The Major Portion of the Clearing,"* *and Collected Writings* (Chicago: Ralph Fletcher Seymour, 1956), 57.

3. Frederick Jackson Turner, "The West and American Ideals" (1914), in Turner, *Frontier and Section: Selected Essays* (Englewood Cliffs, N.J.: Prentice-Hall, 1961), 100.

4. Frederick Jackson Turner, "The Significance of the Frontier in American History" (1893), in Turner, *The Frontier in American History* (New York: Henry Holt, 1920), 1.

5. Ray Allen Billington, *America's Frontier Heritage* (New York: Holt, Rinehart & Winston, 1966), 6–22.

6. Emerson Hough, *The Passing of the Frontier: A Chronicle of the Old West* (1918; New Haven: Yale University Press, 1920); *Who Was Who in America*, s.v. "Hough, Emerson"; and Paul Schullery, *Searching for Yellowstone: Ecology and Wonder in the Last Wilderness* (Boston: Houghton Mifflin, 1997), 121.

7. Hough, *Passing of the Frontier*, 1, 172–73.

8. Emerson Hough, "The Plains and Prairies," *Country Life in America*, Oct. 1, 1912, 27.

9. Ibid.

10. Sharon O'Brien, *Willa Cather: The Emerging Voice* (New York: Oxford University Press, 1987), 400.

11. Quoted ibid., 63.

12. Willa Cather, "The Enchanted Bluff" (1909), in Cather, *Stories, Poems, and Other Writings*, ed. Sharon O'Brien (New York: Library of America, 1992), 64–73.

13. Jens Jensen, "The Preservation of Our River Courses and Their Natural Setting," in Friends of Our Native Landscape, *Proposed Park Areas in the State of Illinois* (1921); substantial extract in "Preserve Water Courses," *Parks and Recreation* 6 (March–April 1923): 340–42.

14. Ibid., 340.

15. Willa Cather, *O Pioneers!* (1913; Boston: Houghton Mifflin, 1941), 118.

16. Ibid., 15, 307–8. On Cather's tendency to ambivalence, see Janis P. Stout, *Willa Cather: The Writer and Her World* (Charlottesville: University Press of Virginia, 2000).

17. Edith Lewis, *Willa Cather Living* (New York: Knopf, 1953), 80–81.

18. Phyllis C. Robinson, *Willa: The Life of Willa Cather* (Garden City, N.Y.: Doubleday, 1983), 178. Robinson uses the words "benign" and "manageable" in *paraphrasing* Cather's letter to Elsie Sargeant, for Cather's will prohibits publication of her letters.

19. Willa Cather, *My Ántonia* (1918; Boston: Houghton Mifflin, 1954), 7, 18.

20. Ibid., 341, 264.

21. Essays on Simonds by Julia Sniderman Bachrach and on Jensen by Robert E. Grese appear in *Midwestern Landscape Architecture*, ed. William H. Tishler (Urbana: University of Illinois Press/Amherst, Mass.: Library of American Landscape History, 2000). See also Erle O. Blair, "Ossian Cole Simonds," *Landscape Architecture*, April 1932, 235; Mara Gelbloom, "Ossian Simonds: Prairie Spirit in Landscape Gardening,"

Prairie School Review 12, no. 2 (1975): 5–18; Robert E. Grese, introductory essay in O. C. Simonds, *Landscape Gardening* (1920; Amherst: Library of American Landscape History/University of Massachusetts Press, 2000); Leonard K. Eaton, *Landscape Artist in America: The Life and Work of Jens Jensen* (Chicago: University of Chicago Press, 1964); and Robert E. Grese, *Jens Jensen: Maker of Natural Parks and Gardens* (Baltimore: Johns Hopkins University Press, 1992). On Wright, nature, and the environment, see *The Nature of Frank Lloyd Wright,* ed. Carol R. Bolon, Robert S. Nelson, and Linda Seidel (Chicago: University of Chicago Press, 1988); and Anne Spirn, "Frank Lloyd Wright: Architect of Landscape," in *Frank Lloyd Wright: Designs for an American Landscape, 1922–1932,* ed. David G. De Long (Montreal: Canadian Centre for Architecture/New York: Harry N. Abrams, 1996).

22. Carl Sandburg, "Prairie" (1918), in Sandburg, *Complete Poems* (New York: Harcourt, Brace, 1950), 79–85.

23. Grese, *Jens Jensen,* 99–100. On the "Chicago Renaissance," see J. Ronald Engel, *Sacred Sands: The Struggle for Community in the Indiana Dunes* (Middletown, Conn.: Wesleyan University Press, 1983).

24. Grese, *Jens Jensen;* Engel, *Sacred Sands;* and Kay Franklin and Norma Schaeffer, *Duel for the Dunes: Land Use Conflict on the Shores of Lake Michigan* (Urbana: University of Illinois Press, 1983).

25. Engel, *Sacred Sands,* 235–36.

26. Wilhelm Miller, "What Is the Matter with Our Water Gardens?" *Country Life in America,* June 15, 1912, 23–26, 54.

27. Wilhelm Miller, *The Prairie Spirit in Landscape Gardening* (Urbana: University of Illinois College of Agriculture/Illinois Agricultural Experiment Station, 1915). See also Christopher Vernon, "Wilhelm Miller: Prairie Spirit in Landscape Gardening," in Tishler, *Midwestern Landscape Architecture*; Vernon, "Wilhelm Miller and *The Prairie Spirit in Landscape Gardening,*" in *Regional Garden Design in the United States,* ed. Therese O'Malley and Marc Treib (Washington, D.C.: Dumbarton Oaks, 1995); and Vernon, introductory essay in Wilhelm Miller, *The Prairie Spirit in Landscape Gardening* (1915), ed. Robin Karson (Amherst: University of Massachusetts Press/Library of American Landscape History, in press).

28. Wilhelm Miller, *What England Can Teach Us about Gardening* (Garden City, N.Y.: Doubleday, Page, 1911) x, 55–62; and William Robinson, *The Wild Garden* (1870), facs. of 4th ed. (London: Scolar Press, 1977).

29. O. C. Simonds to Wilhelm Miller, July 20, 1915, quoted in Robert Grese, "The Prairie Gardens of O. C. Simonds and Jens Jensen," in O'Malley and Treib, *Regional Garden Design,* 122; Frank Lloyd Wright to Wilhelm Miller, Feb. 24, 1915, in Frank Lloyd Wright, *Letters to Architects,* ed. Bruce B. Pfeiffer (Fresno: Press at California State University, 1984), 50–52; and Donald Hoffman, "Meeting Nature Face to Face," in Bolon et al., *Nature of Frank Lloyd Wright,* 94.

30. Frank Lloyd Wright, "In the Cause of Architecture" (1908), in *Frank Lloyd Wright on Architecture,* ed. Frederick Gutheim (New York: Grosset & Dunlap, 1941), 31–45.

31. Frank Lloyd Wright, "In the Cause of Architecture, II" (1914), ibid., 46–58.

32. O. C. Simonds, *Landscape Gardening* (New York: Macmillan, 1920), 180.

33. Ibid., 184.

34. Frank Lloyd Wright, *An Autobiography,* 2d rev. ed. (New York: Horizon Press, 1977). Wright's son took issue with some points in his father's *Autobiography;* see John Lloyd Wright, *My Father Who Is on Earth,* new ed., ed. Narciso G. Menocal (Carbondale: Southern Illinois University Press, 1994). Works that contest parts of Wright's *Autobiography* include Meryle Secrest, *Frank Lloyd Wright* (New York: Knopf, 1993); Herbert Muschamp, *Man about Town: Frank Lloyd Wright in New York City* (Cambridge: MIT Press, 1983); and Brendan Gill, *Many Masks: A Life of Frank Lloyd Wright* (New York: Putnam, 1987). On Taliesin in Wisconsin and Taliesin West, in Scottsdale, Arizona, see Spirn, "Frank Lloyd Wright."

35. Wright, *Autobiography,* 23–24.

36. William C. Gannet[t], *The House Beautiful: In a Setting designed by Frank Lloyd Wright and Printed by Hand at the Auvergne Press in River Forest by William Herman Winslow and Frank Lloyd Wright During the Winter Months of the Year Eighteen Hundred Ninety Six and Seven;* based on the original edition printed in 1898, with an introduction by John Arthur (Rohnert Park, Calif.: Pomegranate Artbooks, 1996).

37. See Wright to Louis Sullivan, Apr. 2, 1923, and Wright's several letters to Jensen, in his *Letters to Architects.*

38. John Lloyd Wright, *My Father Who Is on Earth,* 173–77. In 1946 Frank Lloyd Wright wrote in the margin of this book's first edition, at the end of John's chapter on Isaiah and the *Autobiography,* "O.K.—John."

39. Wright, *Autobiography,* 27. Wright's quotation came close to the words of the King James Version of the Old Testament, Isa. 40:8: "The grass withereth, the flower fadeth: but the word of our God shall stand forever."

40. Jensen, *Siftings,* 23, 95–96. In *Landscape Artist in America,* 8, Leonard Eaton notes that Jensen was familiar with the writings of Emerson, Thoreau, Muir, and Burroughs.

41. Ibid., 33.

42. Grese, *Jens Jensen;* Eaton, *Landscape Artist in America.*

43. Jensen, *Siftings,* 30.

44. Ibid., 46.

45. See chapters 8 and 9. Any connections among native plants, nativism, fascism, and Nazi Germany are beyond the scope of this book. For an illuminating review (and refutation) of recent scholarship in this area, see Dave Egan and William H. Tishler, "Jens Jensen, Native Plants, and the Concept of Nordic Superiority," *Landscape Journal* 18 (Spring 1999): 11–29.

46. Jensen, *Siftings,* 90–93.

47. Ibid., 95.

48. Donald Culross Peattie, *A Prairie Grove* (New York: Literary Guild, 1938), 3–6, 233; and Peattie, *The Road of a Naturalist* (Boston: Houghton Mifflin, 1941), 109–22.

49. *National Cyclopaedia of American Biography,* s.v. "Peattie, Donald Culross"; and Engel, *Sacred Sands,* 207.

50. Aldo Leopold, "The State of the Profession," *Journal of Wildlife Management* 4 (July 1940): 343–46; reprint in AL Papers, CONS 47, Box 1, Folder: "Reprints: 'Articles, 1940s."

51. Peattie, *Prairie Grove,* 234, 264–65, 239–40, 274.

52. Edwin Way Teale, *Dune Boy* (1943; New York: Dodd, Mead, 1945), 2–3.

53. Edwin Way Teale, *The Lost Woods* (New York: Dodd, Mead, 1945), 1–4.

54. Edwin A. Hunger, "Boyhood reminiscences of his high school classmate Aldo Leopold—written at request of an editor of Audubon Magazine" (ca. 1966–67; photocopy), in TWS Papers, CONS 130, Box 3:103, Folder: "Aldo Leopold, articles, 1954–1968."

55. Ibid.

THREE **Forested Mountains**

1. John Burroughs, in Clara Barrus, *The Life and Letters of John Burroughs* (1925), 2:320, quoted in Stephen Fox, *The American Conservation Movement: John Muir and His Legacy* (1981; Madison: University of Wisconsin Press, 1985), 119.

2. See John Burroughs, journal entry, June 22, 1896, quoted in Edward J. Renehan Jr., *John Burroughs: An American Naturalist* (Post Mills, Vt.: Chelsea Green, 1992), 205; Mary Austin, *Earth Horizon* (New York: Literary Guild, 1932), 298; and Pinchot's comments in Introduction, above.

3. See William Frederic Badè, *The Life and Letters of John Muir,* 2 vols. (Boston: Houghton Mifflin, 1924).

4. John Muir, "Wild Wool" (1875), in Muir, *Wilderness Essays* (Salt Lake City: Peregrine Smith, 1980), 227–42; and Henry David Thoreau, "Wild Apples" (1862), in Thoreau, *The Natural History Essays,* ed. Robert Sattelmeyer (Salt Lake City: Peregrine Smith, 1980), 178–210.

5. Frederick Turner, *Rediscovering America: John Muir in His Time and Ours* (San Francisco: Sierra Club Books, 1985), 230.

6. Michael P. Cohen, *The Pathless Way: John Muir and American Wilderness* (Madison: University of Wisconsin Press, 1984), 350–61.

7. John Muir, *My First Summer in the Sierra* (1911; San Francisco: Yolla Bolly/Sierra Club Books, 1989), 9, 38, 77.

8. Ibid., 89, 143. On the wasteful farming practices of the Muirs and their contemporaries in the Midwest, see Turner, *Rediscovering America,* 48–53.

9. Muir, *My First Summer in the Sierra,* 31.

10. Ibid., 130. See Robert Burns (1759–1796), "For A' That and A' That," in *An Anthology of Famous English and American Poetry,* ed. William Rose Benét and Conrad Aiken (New York: Modern Library, 1945), 194–95. More recently some editors have modernized the Scots vernacular in Burns's poems; see *The Oxford Anthology of English*

Literature, ed. Frank Kermode and John Hollander, 2 vols. (London: Oxford University Press, 1973), 2284–85.

11. On the unity of all life on earth and the world as a living organism, see J. E. Lovelock, *Gaia: A New Look at Life on Earth* (1979; Oxford: Oxford University Press, 1987); William Irwin Thompson, ed., *Gaia, a Way of Knowing: Political Implications of the New Biology* (Great Barrington, Mass.: Lindisfarne Press, 1987); and Thomas Berry, *The Great Work: Our Way into the Future* (New York: Bell Tower, 1999).

12. See Michael P. Cohen, *The History of the Sierra Club, 1892–1970* (San Francisco: Sierra Club Books, 1988).

13. For a full-length biography of Mills, see Alexander Drummond, *Enos Mills: Citizen of Nature* (Niwot: University Press of Colorado, 1995). Details of Mills's meeting with Muir and other biographical information appear in "The Friend of the Rocky Mountains," *Literary Digest* 55 (July 14, 1917): 44–49; Arthur Chapman, "Enos A. Mills, Nature Guide," *Country Life* 38 (May 1920): 61–63; Philip Ashton Rollins, "A Champion of Wild Life," in Enos Mills, *The Rocky Mountain National Park,* rev. ed. (Boston: Houghton Mifflin, 1932), 208–27; Enos Mills, *The Rocky Mountain Wonderland* (1915; Lincoln: University of Nebraska Press, 1991); and *Radiant Days: Writings by Enos Mills,* ed. John Dotson (Salt Lake City: University of Utah Press, 1994).

14. Mills, *Rocky Mountain National Park,* 189–90.

15. Enos Mills, "Trees at Timberline," in his *Radiant Days,* 155–64.

16. In his introduction to *Radiant Days,* John Dotson lists some famous guests at Longs Peak Inn: Edna Ferber, Eugene V. Debs, Gene Stratton-Porter, Clarence Darrow, Charles Evans Hughes, Jane Addams, David Starr Jordan, and Douglas Fairbanks Sr.

17. Quoted in "Friend of the Rocky Mountains," 44.

18. See Mills's stories "Snow-Blinded on the Summit" (1920) and "Racing an Avalanche" (1910), in his *Radiant Days.* On the ecological insights that emerged from Mills's work as a snow inspector, see Drummond, *Enos Mills,* 145–58.

19. Enos Mills, "Story of a Thousand-Year Pine," in his *Radiant Days,* 47–57.

20. Quoted in Rollins, "Champion of Wild Life," 219–20.

21. Mills, *Rocky Mountain National Park,* 159. See also Mills, *Romance of Geology* (Garden City, N.Y.: Doubleday, Page, 1927); and Chapman, "Enos A. Mills."

22. Mills, *Rocky Mountain National Park,* 64. See John Keats, "Ode on a Grecian Urn" (ca. 1820), in Keats, *Poetical Works,* ed. H. Buxton Forman (London: Oxford University Press, 1929), 233–34.

23. See Chapman, "Enos Mills," 63; Enos Mills, *Your National Parks* (Boston: Houghton Mifflin, 1917); and chapter 6 below.

24. Mathilde Edith Holtz and Katharine Isabel Bemis, *Glacier National Park: Its Trails and Treasures* (New York: George H. Doran, 1917).

25. Walter Prichard Eaton, *Skyline Camps: A Notebook of a Wanderer over Our Northwestern Rockies, Cascade Mountains and Crater Lake* (Boston: W. A. Wilde, 1922), 140.

26. Holtz and Bemis, *Glacier National Park,* 86.

27. Ibid., 190. As authorities on Native Americans, Holtz and Bemis cited George Bird

Grinnell, editor of *Forest and Stream*, and J. W. Schultz, author of *My Life as an Indian: The Story of a Red Woman and a White Man in the Lodges of the Blackfeet* (1907; Williamstown, Mass.: Corner House, 1973). For wildlife they referred to William T. Hornaday, author of *Our Vanishing Wildlife: Its Extermination and Preservation* (New York: Scribner, 1913).

28. Walter Prichard Eaton, "Timber Line," in his *Skyline Camps,* 56.

29. Walter Prichard Eaton, "The Literature of Place," *Bookman* 48 (September 1918): 13–20.

30. Walter Prichard Eaton, "To Whom It May Concern," in his *Skyline Camps.*

31. Benton MacKaye, Journal (1897), in MKF Papers, ML/5, Box 197. See also Larry Anderson, "Benton MacKaye and the Art of Roving: An 1897 Excursion in the White Mountains," *Appalachia,* no. 185 (Dec. 15, 1987), 85–102.

32. MacKaye, Journal. The five hikers were MacKaye, James Sturgis Pray, Benjamin Sweetser Pray (James's father), Draper Maury, and Robert P. Mitchell.

33. Percy MacKaye, *Epoch: The Life of Steele MacKaye: Genius of the Theatre,* 2 vols. (New York: Boni & Liveright, 1927), 2:478.

34. Steele MacKaye to Benton MacKaye, Dec. 14, 1893, quoted in Percy MacKaye, *Epoch,* 2:436, 477.

35. Benton MacKaye to Percy MacKaye, July 26, 1914, quoted ibid., 467–69.

36. Benton MacKaye, *Employment and Natural Resources* (Washington, D.C.: USGPO, 1919). A copy of this report, in Dartmouth College Library, Special Collections, contains a handwritten insert, dated June 3, 1924, inscribed to Benton MacKaye, by Louis F. Post, former assistant secretary of labor. As Post explains, Secretary of Labor W. B. Wilson, Secretary of Agriculture Huston, and President Woodrow Wilson all agreed to pursue the recommendations; but without the cooperation of Interior Secretary Franklin K. Lane, no action could be taken.

37. Some of MacKaye's letters of the late 1920s to siblings and Lewis Mumford reveal his desire to live up to his potential and carry out the work his father had expected of him. See especially Benton MacKaye to Percy MacKaye, Mar. 29, 1926, in MKF Papers, ML/5, "Scrapbook, Epoch, A–P."

38. Walter Prichard Eaton, "James Morrison Steele MacKaye," in *Dictionary of American Biography* (1933), 10:76–77. See also Eaton, "Steele MacKaye: Or the Dreamer Delivered," review of Percy MacKaye, *Epoch,* in *Theatre Arts Monthly* 11 (November 1927): 827–37.

39. Quoted in Percy MacKaye, *Epoch,* 2:475–76.

40. Benton MacKaye, *The New Exploration: A Philosophy of Regional Planning* (New York: Harcourt, Brace, 1928).

41. Benton MacKaye, "Progress toward the Appalachian Trail," *Appalachia* 15 (December 1922): 244–52. MacKaye noted that about one-third of his proposed trail already existed in segments among the White Mountains of New Hampshire, along Vermont's Long Trail, and in national forests of the southern states, where the Forest Service maintained some trails.

42. At the Nineteenth Appalachian Trail Conference, at Plymouth State College in Plymouth, New Hampshire, June 16–18, 1972, Chairman Stanley A. Murray read a long message from ninety-three-year-old Benton MacKaye; and MacKaye noted the mountain treks on which the idea of the Appalachian Trail may have occurred to him. See "Message from Benton MacKaye . . . ," TWS Papers, CONS 130, Box 3:104, Folder: "Benton MacKaye, 1920s-1960s." See also Benton MacKaye, "Diary of Vermont Trip, 1900," MKF Papers, ML/5 Box 197; Anderson, "Benton MacKaye"; James R. Hare, ed., *Hiking the Appalachian Trail*, 2 vols. (Emmaus, Pa.: Rodale Press, 1975), 1:6; and W. Storrs Lee, ed., *Footpath in the Wilderness: The Long Trail in the Green Mountains of Vermont* (Middlebury, Vt.: Middlebury College Press, 1941).

43. Benton MacKaye to William B. Moulton, May 10, 1921, in MKF Papers, ML/5 Box 165, Folder: 1921. See also Benton MacKaye, foreword to a biographical sketch of Jessie Hardy MacKaye, ibid., Box 144, Folder 20.

44. Benton MacKaye, "An Appalachian Trail: A Project in Regional Planning," *Journal of the American Institute of Architects,* October 1921, 325–30, and "Progress toward the Appalachian Trail," *Appalachia* 15 (December 1922): 244–52. See also John R. Ross, "Benton MacKaye: The Appalachian Trail," in *The American Planner: Biographies and Recollections,* ed. Donald A. Krueckeberg (New York: Methuen, 1983), 196–207.

45. See Benton MacKaye's correspondence of the 1920s in MKF Papers, including Gifford Pinchot to MacKaye, Dec. 22, 1921, ML/5, Box 165, Folder: "1921, P–R"; Aldo Leopold to MacKaye, Feb. 3, 1926, ML/5, Box 166, Folder: "1926, C–L"; and correspondence with Stein, Mumford, Comey, Torrey, Eaton, Chamberlain, and Pray. See also Lewis Mumford, "Benton MacKaye as Regional Planner," *Living Wilderness* 39 (January/March 1976): 13–17.

46. Raymond H. Torrey to Benton MacKaye, Jan. 31, 1924; and MacKaye to William A. Welch, Sept. 29, 1935 (draft letter), in MKF Papers, ML/5, Box 166:5 and Box 168:3.

47. Myron H. Avery, "The Appalachian Trail," *Mountain Magazine* 8 (February 1930): 3–6; Hare, *Hiking the Appalachian Trail,* 1:25–26; and Carl Sussman, ed., *Planning the Fourth Migration: The Neglected Vision of the Regional Planning Association of America* (Cambridge: MIT Press, 1976).

48. MacKaye, "Progress toward the Appalachian Trail," 248–49.

49. Benton MacKaye, "Outdoor Culture: The Philosophy of Through trails," *Landscape Architecture* 17 (April 1927): 163–71, and "Wilderness Ways," *Landscape Architecture* 19 (July 1929): 237–49.

50. See the series of articles on urban, rural, and primeval environments by Garrett Eckbo, Dan Kiley, and James Rose in *Architectural Record,* May and August 1939 and February 1940; rpt. in *Modern Landscape Architecture: A Critical Review,* ed. Marc Treib (Cambridge: MIT Press, 1993).

51. MacKaye, "Wilderness Ways," 249.

52. Hare, *Hiking the Appalachian Trail,* 1:20–26; and Avery, "Appalachian Trail."

53. Benton MacKaye to Myron H. Avery, Nov. 20, 1935, in MKF Papers, ML/5, Box 168,

Folder: "1935, A–G." See also Avery, "Appalachian Trail"; and Benton MacKaye, "Flank-line vs. Skyline," *Appalachia* 20 (1934): 104–8.

54. Avery to MacKaye, Dec. 19, 1935, in MKF Papers, ML/5, Box 168, Folder "1935, A–G."

55. The Appalachian Trail was declared complete on Aug. 15, 1937 (although some alterations have since been made). In 1968 the A.T. and the Pacific Crest Trail were established as national scenic trails. See Hare, *Hiking the Appalachian Trail*, 1:1–4. In 1980 the Benton MacKaye Trail Association was formed to help create the Benton Mac-Kaye Trail, some seventy-eight miles long, in a remote wilderness in northern Georgia, along a route similar to MacKaye's original route for the A.T. in that region. See Jane R. McCauley, "The Southeast," in *Pathways to Discovery: Exploring America's National Trails* (Washington, D.C.: National Geographic Society, 1991), 30–31.

56. Benton MacKaye, copy of statement sent to Seventh Appalachian Trail Conference, Shenandoah National Park, May 1935, in MKF Papers, ML/5, Box 168, Folder 1. Nearly all of this statement was reproduced in Benton MacKaye, "Why the Appalachian Trail?" in *Living Wilderness* 1 (September 1935): 7–8.

57. Raymond H. Torrey to MacKaye, May 5, 1935; and MacKaye to Arno B. Cammerer, Aug. 31, 1934, in MKF Papers, ML/5, Box 168:3, Box 167:21.

58. The A.T. and the Wilderness Society are also discussed in chapters 6 and 10.

59. Benton MacKaye, "The Appalachian Trail: A Guide to the Study of Nature," *Scientific Monthly*, April 1932, 330–42. For another reading of the A.T., see Ian Marshall, *Story Line: Exploring the Literature of the Appalachian Trail* (Charlottesville: University Press of Virginia, 1998).

FOUR San Francisco Bay Area

1. Charles Keeler, *Bird Notes Afield*, 2d ed., rev. and enl. (San Francisco: Paul Elder, 1907), 1.

2. George Santayana, "The Genteel Tradition in American Philosophy" (1911), in *The Genteel Tradition: Nine Essays by George Santayana*, ed. Douglas L. Wilson (Cambridge: Harvard University Press, 1967), 62–64.

3. Charles Eliot, review of Charles Platt, *Italian Gardens*, in Charles W. Eliot, *Charles Eliot, Landscape Architect* (1902; Amherst: University of Massachusetts Press/Library of American Landscape History, 1999), 547–49.

4. "On the Edge of the World" was the title of an article in *Sunset Magazine*, August 1902, cited in Richard Longstreth, *On the Edge of the World: Four Architects in San Francisco at the Turn of the Century* (Cambridge: Architectural History Foundation/MIT Press, 1983), 1.

5. Michael Laurie, with David Streatfield, *75 Years of Landscape Architecture at Berkeley: An Informal History* (Berkeley: University of California, College of Environmental Design [ca. 1988]), 5–6; and Michael L. Smith, *Pacific Visions: California Scientists and the Environment, 1850–1915* (New Haven: Yale University Press, 1987), 189.

6. The architect Louis Christian Mullgardt considered the exposition a "phantom kingdom" in his book *The Architecture and Landscape Gardening of the Exposition* (San

Francisco: Paul Elder, 1915), v, 12. Marjorie M. Dobkin and Gray Brechin cite San Francisco's epithet, "the Paris of America," in their essays in Burton Benedict, *The Anthropology of World's Fairs: San Francisco's Panama Pacific International Exposition of 1915* (Berkeley: Lowie Museum of Anthropology/Scolar Press, 1983).

7. Keeler, *Bird Notes Afield*, 49–58. See also Keeler, *San Francisco and Thereabout* (San Francisco: California Promotion Committee, 1902). For alterations to this bay shore, see Mel Scott, *The San Francisco Bay Area: A Metropolis in Perspective*, 2d ed. (Berkeley: University of California Press, 1985); and Paolo Polledri, ed., *Visionary San Francisco* (San Francisco: San Francisco Museum of Modern Art, 1990).

8. Keeler, *San Francisco and Thereabout*, 28, 83.

9. Keeler, *Bird Notes Afield*, 53.

10. Ibid., 55–56.

11. Dimitri Shipounoff, introduction to Charles Keeler, *The Simple Home* (Santa Barbara: Peregrine Smith, 1979), xxix–xxxi; and *Who Was Who in America*, s.v. "Keeler, Charles."

12. See Charles Keeler, "Recollections of John Muir" (1916), in *John Muir: His Life and Letters and Other Writings*, ed. Terry Gifford (Seattle: Mountaineers/London: Bâton Wicks, 1996), 878–80; and Keeler, "Friends Bearing Torches," unpublished ms., Bancroft Library, University of California, Berkeley, quoted in Shipounoff, introduction to Keeler, *Simple Home*, xix.

13. Charles Keeler, "On Science," in Keeler, *A Light through the Storm* (San Francisco: William Doxey, 1894), 93.

14. Keeler, *Bird Notes Afield*, 87–88.

15. Keeler, *San Francisco and Thereabout*, 83–85.

16. Keeler, *Simple Home*, xlv.

17. See, for example, David Ottewill, "The Arts and Crafts Garden," in Ottewill, *The Edwardian Garden* (New Haven: Yale University Press, 1989); David C. Streatfield, "Arts and Crafts Gardens," in Streatfield, *California Gardens: Creating a New Eden* (New York: Abbeville Press, 1994); and Judith B. Tankard and Martin A. Wood, *Gertrude Jekyll at Munstead Wood* (Godalming, Surrey: Bramley Books, 1996).

18. Keeler, *Simple Home*, 15.

19. Ibid., 16.

20. *Journal of the American Institute of Architects* 16 (July 1951): 6.

21. Quoted in Frederick D. Nichols, "A Visit with Bernard Maybeck," *Journal of the Society of Architectural Historians* 11 (October 1952): 31.

22. Kenneth H. Cardwell, *Bernard Maybeck: Artisan, Architect, Artist* (Santa Barbara: Peregrine Smith, 1977). Other biographical sources include Esther McCoy, *Five California Architects* (1960; New York: Praeger, 1975); and Sally Woodbridge, *Bernard Maybeck: Visionary Architect* (New York: Abbeville Press, 1992).

23. Quoted in "'Programme for the Development of a Hillside Community,' by Bernard Ralph Maybeck, as written for the Bulletin of the Hillside Club, 1906–07, by Annie White Maybeck (unsigned)"; excerpted in *Journal of the American Institute of Architects* 15 (May 1951): 226–28.

24. For Maybeck's authorship of the Hillside Club booklet, see, for example, William H. Jordy, *American Buildings and Their Architects*, 4 vols. (Garden City, N.Y.: Anchor/ Doubleday, 1976), 3:284; and Longstreth, *On the Edge of the World*, 314.

25. Shipounoff, introduction to Keeler, *Simple Home*; and Diane Harris, "Maybeck's Landscapes," *Journal of Garden History* 10, no. 3 (1990): 145–61.

26. Raymond H. Clary, *The Making of Golden Gate Park*, 2 vols. (San Francisco: Don't Call It Frisco Press, 1987), 1:1–13, 76–77; 2:1–14. See also Charles E. Beveridge, "Introduction to the Landscape Design Reports: San Francisco Pleasure Grounds," in *The Papers of Frederick Law Olmsted*, vol. 5, *The California Frontier (1863–1865)*, ed. Victoria Post Ranney et al. (Baltimore: Johns Hopkins University Press, 1990), 461–64.

27. Clary, *Making of Golden Gate Park*, 2:12.

28. John McLaren, *Gardening in California: Landscape and Flower*, 3d ed. (San Francisco: A. M. Robertson, 1924). / ɩ ୨౦ 8

29. For discussions of Knight and Price, with excerpts from their writings, see *The Genius of the Place: The English Landscape Garden, 1620–1820*, ed. John Dixon Hunt and Peter Willis (New York: Harper & Row, 1975); and Melanie Louise Simo, *Loudon and the Landscape: From Country Seat to Metropolis, 1783–1843* (New Haven: Yale University Press, 1988).

30. McLaren, *Gardening in California*, 8–11.

31. Mary Austin, *California: Land of the Sun* (New York: Macmillan, 1914), opposite 107; Austin, "Art Influence in the West," *Century* 89, no. 6 (April 1915): 829–33; and Kevin Starr, *Americans and the California Dream, 1850–1915* (New York: Oxford University Press, 1973), 300. Starr notes that Austin served on the Pageantry Commission of the exposition.

32. See photographs of the site in Frank Morton Todd, *The Story of the Exposition*, 5 vols. (New York: Putnam, 1921), opposite 1:302; and in John D. Barry, *The City of Domes* (San Francisco: John J. Newbegin, 1915), opposite 6.

33. For Aitken's *Earth*, see Elizabeth N. Armstrong, "Hercules and the Muses: Public Art at the Fair," in Benedict, *Anthropology of World's Fairs*, 117. For *The End of the Trail*, see Eugen Neuhaus, *The Art of the Exposition* (San Francisco: Paul Elder, 1915), opposite 32.

34. For Mathews's *Victorious Spirit*, see Harvey L. Jones, *Mathews: Masterpieces of the California Decorative Style* (Santa Barbara: Peregrine Smith, 1980), 28; and Neuhaus, *Art of the Exposition*, opposite 60. Born in Markesan, Wisconsin, in 1860, Mathews was taken by his family to California six years later; they settled in Oakland. Charles Keeler notes the "notorious graft" involved in building the old city hall and includes an image of the city hall in ruins in his *San Francisco through Earthquake and Fire* (San Francisco: Paul Elder, 1906), 2 and opposite 28.

35. Barry, *City of Domes*, 75. See also Neuhaus, *Art of the Exposition*, 58.

36. Woodbridge, *Bernard Maybeck*, 101.

37. Quoted in Mullgardt, *Architecture and Landscape Gardening*, 156.

38. Bernard Maybeck, *Palace of Fine Arts and Lagoon* (San Francisco: Paul Elder, 1915).

Copies of this rare pamphlet can be found in FLL/SC and in the library of the College of Environmental Design, University of California, Berkeley.

39. John E. D. Trask, from his verses alongside the frontispiece to Maybeck's *Palace of Fine Arts and Lagoon*. Before his appointment as the exposition's director of fine arts, Trask had served as director of the Pennsylvania Academy of Fine Arts. See Barry, *City of Domes*, 22.

40. *New Larousse Encyclopedia of Mythology*, trans. Richard Aldington and Delano Ames (London: Prometheus Press/Hamlyn, 1968), 198.

41. Barry, *City of Domes*, 21–26.

42. Maybeck is quoted in Gray Brechin, "Sailing to Byzantium: The Architecture of the Fair," in Benedict, *Anthropology of World's Fairs*, 106–7. Brechin's source is Ruth Waldo Newhall, *San Francisco's Enchanted Palace* (Berkeley: Privately printed, 1967), 75.

43. "Walter Johnson gives $2 million to save San Francisco's Palace of Fine Arts," *Architectural Forum* 111, no. 1 (July 1959): 14; and "The Dream Made Permanent," *Progressive Architecture* 49 (February 1968): 120–23.

44. Quoted in Longstreth, *On the Edge of the World*, 347.

45. Todd, *Story of the Exposition*, 1:311.

46. William Jordy discusses Maybeck's praise of McLaren's work in *American Buildings and Their Architects*, 3:285 and n. 5. His source is Ben Macomber, *The Jewel City* (San Francisco and Tacoma: J. H. Williams, 1915), 102.

47. Barry, *City of Domes*, 12.

48. Jules Guérin, "The Magic City of the Pacific: Architects, Painters, and Sculptors Offer Their Best to the Panama-Pacific Exposition," *Craftsman* 26, no. 5 (August 1914): 465–80; and Guérin, quoted in Elmer Grey, "The Panama-Pacific International Exposition," *Scribner's* 54, no. 1 (July 1913): 48.

49. Austin, "Art Influence in the West," 829–33.

50. Maybeck, *Palace of Fine Arts and Lagoon*, 13.

51. See Sally Woodbridge, ed., *Bay Area Houses*, new ed. (Salt Lake City: Peregrine Smith, 1988); and Longstreth, *On the Edge of the World*.

F I V E **Around New York and Boston**

1. Mariana Griswold Van Rensselaer, "A Glimpse of Nantucket" (1888), in Van Rensselaer, *Accents as Well as Broad Effects: Writings on Architecture, Landscape, and the Environment, 1876–1925*, ed. David Gebhard (Berkeley: University of California Press, 1996), 341–45.

2. Mariana Griswold Van Rensselaer, "Early Autumn near Cape Cod" (1892) and "Wood Roads on Cape Cod" (1892), both ibid., 330–37.

3. Mariana Griswold Van Rensselaer, *Art Out-of-Doors: Hints on Good Taste in Gardening*, 2d ed., enl. (New York: Scribner, 1925), 35–39. These pages remained unaltered from the 1st ed., of 1893.

4. Ibid., 389–429.

5. See Virginia Tuttle Clayton, ed., *The Once and Future Gardener: Garden Writing from the Golden Age of Magazines: 1900–1940* (Boston: David R. Godine, 2000).

6. James Sturgis Pray taught this introductory course. See Pray, Course Record Books, HUA, UAV 510.214, Boxes 1 and 2.

7. Henry Vincent Hubbard and Theodora Kimball, *Introduction to the Study of Landscape Design* (New York: Macmillan, 1917), 364.

8. Van Rensselaer, *Art Out-of-Doors,* 475–76.

9. Hubbard and Kimball, *Introduction to Landscape Design,* 66–68.

10. *National Cyclopaedia of American Biography,* s.v. "Hubbard, Theodora Kimball." See also "Theodora Kimball Hubbard: A Biographical Minute," *Landscape Architecture* 26 (January 1936): 53–55; and June R. Donnelly, "Theodora Kimball Hubbard, 1887–1935," *Simmons Review,* January 1936, 44–45.

11. Henry Vincent Hubbard, Harvard College *Class Record* (Class of 1897), Twenty-fifth Anniversary Report (1922), 285–88, HUA.

12. Howard K. Menhinick, "Editor and School Head," in "Henry Vincent Hubbard: An Official Minute on his Professional Life and Work," *Landscape Architecture* 38 (January 1948): 53.

13. Hubbard and Kimball, *Introduction to Landscape Design,* 74.

14. In 1987–88 Garrett Eckbo lent the author his copy of Hubbard and Kimball's *Introduction to Landscape Design.* See Melanie Louise Simo, "The Education of a Modern Landscape Designer" (on Garrett Eckbo), *Pacific Horticulture* 49 (Summer 1988): 19–30.

15. Garrett Eckbo, taped conversation with the author in Berkeley, Feb. 26, 1987. See Marc Treib and Dorothée Imbert, *Garrett Eckbo: Modern Landscapes for Living* (Berkeley: University of California Press, 1997).

16. Hubbard and Kimball, *Introduction to Landscape Design,* 75.

17. See *The Papers of Frederick Law Olmsted,* especially vol. 5, *The California Frontier, 1863–1865,* ed. Victoria Post Ranney (Baltimore: Johns Hopkins University Press, 1990), for Olmsted's "Preliminary Report upon the Yosemite and Big Tree Grove" (August 1865), 488–516.

18. Henry David Thoreau, "Walking" (1862), in Thoreau, *The Natural History Essays,* ed. Robert Sattelmeyer (Salt Lake City: Peregrine Smith, 1980), 112. This quotation is sometimes rendered, ". . . in *wilderness* is the preservation of the world." See, for example, Sherman Paul, *The Shores of America: Thoreau's Inward Exploration* (1958; Urbana: University of Illinois Press, 1972), 415.

19. Henry Vincent Hubbard, Harvard College *Class Record* (Class of 1897), Twenty-fifth Anniversary Report (1922), 285–88; and "Course data, problems and miscellaneous records of B. W. Pond, 1917–1930," HUA, UAV 510.20.5 hd.

20. See, for instance, James Sturgis Pray, "The Department of Landscape Architecture in Harvard University," *Landscape Architecture,* January 1911; rpt. in *Landscape Architectural Education,* ed. Gary O. Robinette, 2 vols. (Dubuque: Kendall/Hunt, 1973), 1:39–44; and Melanie L. Simo, *The Coalescing of Different Forces and Ideas: A History of*

Landscape Architecture at Harvard, 1900–1999 (Cambridge: Harvard University Graduate School of Design, 2000).

21. Charles W. Eliot, "Welfare and Happiness in Works of Landscape Architecture," *Landscape Architecture,* April 1911, 146.

22. Charles W. Eliot, "The Need of Conserving the Beauty and Freedom of Nature in Modern Life," *National Geographic,* July 1914, 67–73.

23. Henry Vincent Hubbard, editorial, *Landscape Architecture,* October 1910, 49.

24. Frederick Law Olmsted, "A Consideration of the Justifying Value of a Public Park" (1880), in Olmsted, *Public Parks* (Brookline, Mass.: Privately printed, 1902), 110–14, cited in Hubbard and Kimball, *Introduction to Landscape Design,* 74.

25. See, for instance, Harold Caparn, "Central Park, New York: A Work of Art," *Landscape Architecture,* July 1912, 167–76; and Van Rensselaer, *Art Out-of-Doors,* 387–429.

26. Benton MacKaye, Journal (1897), in MKF Papers, Ms. ML/5, Box 197.

27. See Allen Chamberlain, "The Club's Reservations," *Appalachia* (journal of the Appalachian Mountain Club) 10 (1902–4): 303–14; Mark Primack, "Charles Eliot: Genius of the Massachusetts Landscape," *Appalachia,* June 1982, 80–88; and Charles W. Eliot, *Charles Eliot, Landscape Architect* (1902; Amherst: University of Massachusetts Press/ Library of American Landscape History, 1999).

28. James Sturgis Pray, "Improvements," in "Reports of the Councillors . . . " (Autumn 1902, Autumn 1903), *Appalachia* 10 (1902–4): 211–22, 336–44.

29. See, for instance, J. S. Pray, "The Italian Garden," *American Architect and Building News,* Feb. 10 and 17, Mar. 7 and 24, 1900. A typed copy of this four-part article is kept in FLL. See also J. S. Pray and Theodora Kimball, *A City-Planning Classification: Preliminary Outline* (Cambridge: Harvard University Press, 1913); and Pray to Charles W. Eliot II, Apr. 19, 1924, in HUA, UAV 322.148, subser. II, Box 4, Folder: "Charles W. Eliot, II."

30. Pray to Benton MacKaye, Aug. 10, 1902, in MKF Papers, ML/5, Box 165, Folder: "1902."

31. Pray, Course Record Books, HUA, UAV 510.214, Boxes 1 and 2.

32. Bremer Pond, "Teacher of Landscape Architecture," in "Henry Vincent Hubbard: An Official Minute on His Professional Life and Work," *Landscape Architecture* 38 (January 1948): 52.

33. Theodore Roosevelt, *The Strenuous Life: Essays and Addresses* (New York: Century, 1901).

34. Beatrix Farrand, "The Debt of Landscape Art to a Museum of Trees," *Architectural Record,* November 1918, 407–8.

35. Eleanor McPeck, "Beatrix Jones Farrand: The Formative Years, 1890–1920," in *Beatrix Jones Farrand (1872–1959): Fifty Years of American Landscape Architecture* (Washington, D.C.: Dumbarton Oaks, 1982).

36. See, for instance, Diana Balmori, Diane Kostial McGuire, and Eleanor M. McPeck, *Beatrix Farrand's American Landscapes: Her Gardens and Campuses* (Sagaponack, N.Y.: Sagapress, 1985); and Jane Brown, *Beatrix: The Gardening Life of Beatrix Jones Farrand, 1872–1959* (New York: Viking, 1995).

37. See three works by Mabel Osgood Wright: *Flowers and Ferns in Their Haunts* (New York: Macmillan, 1901); *My New York* (New York: Macmillan, 1930); and *The Garden of a Commuter's Wife* (New York: Macmillan, 1901).

38. Wright, *My New York*, 84–85, 209–10, 151–55.

39. Charles M. Skinner, *Nature in a City Yard* (New York: Century, 1897), 166–69.

40. John C. Van Dyke, *The New New York* (New York: Macmillan, 1909), 18.

41. Ibid., 259. See Jacob A. Riis, *How the Other Half Lives* (1901; New York: Dover, 1971).

42. Van Dyke, *New New York*, 346–54.

43. Alfred Kazin, *A Walker in the City* (New York: Harcourt, Brace & World, 1951), 5–12, 173–76.

44. Lewis Gannett, "The Wildness of New York," *Century* 110 (July 1925): 299–304.

45. Dallas Lore Sharp, "The Wildness of Boston," *Century* 110 (August 1925): 406–14; rpt. in Sharp, *Sanctuary! Sanctuary!* (New York: Harper, 1926), 61–85.

46. Charles Downing Lay, "My Country Kingdom," *Country Life* 46 (July 1924): 45–47; Lay, "The Freedom of the City," *North American Review* 222 (September 1925): 123–34; and Lay, *The Freedom of the City* (New York: Duffield, 1926).

47. Robert Wheelwright, "Charles Downing Lay: A Biographical Minute," *Landscape Architecture,* April 1956, 162–64.

48. Eugene O'Neill to Beatrice Ashe, Mar. 2, 1915, in O'Neill, *Selected Letters,* ed. Travis Bogard and Jackson R. Bryer (New Haven: Yale University Press, 1988), 61.

49. Walter Prichard Eaton, "Wild Life in New York," *Outlook,* Apr. 2, 1910; rpt. in Eaton, *Barn Doors and Byways* (Boston: Small, Maynard, 1913), 115–33.

50. Walter Prichard Eaton, *A Bucolic Attitude* (New York: Duffield, 1926), 65.

51. Ibid., 74.

s i x Park Makers and Forest Managers

1. F. L. Olmsted Sr. to F. L. Olmsted Jr., n.d. (1895), quoted in Susan L. Klaus, "Such Inheritance as I Can Give You: The Apprenticeship of Frederick Law Olmsted, Junior," *Journal of the New England Garden History Society* 3 (Fall 1993): 6. After his father's death, the younger Olmsted dropped "Jr." from his name.

2. Klaus, "Such Inheritance," 1–7. See also Laura Wood Roper, *FLO: A Biography of Frederick Law Olmsted* (Baltimore: Johns Hopkins University Press, 1973), 422–24, 430–31, 461–62, 471.

3. Frederick Law Olmsted, "A Consideration of the Justifying Value of a Public Park" (1880), in Olmsted, *Public Parks* (Brookline, Mass.: Privately printed, 1902). This paper also appears in *The Papers of Frederick Law Olmsted,* supp. ser., vol. 1, *Writings on Public Parks, Parkways, and Park Systems,* ed. Charles E. Beveridge and Carolyn F. Hoffman (Baltimore: Johns Hopkins University Press, 1997), 332–46.

4. Frederick Law Olmsted, "The Distinction between National Parks and National Forests," *Landscape Architecture* 6 (April 1916): 114.

5. Horace M. Albright, *The Birth of the National Park Service: The Founding Years,*

1913–33, as told to Robert Cahn (Salt Lake City: Howe, 1985), 32–43. See also Robert Shankland, *Steve Mather and the National Parks* (New York: Knopf, 1954), 100–104.

6. Public Law 235, 64th Congress, as quoted in Albright, *Birth of the National Park Service,* 36. See also Shankland, *Steve Mather,* 100–104; and Ethan Carr, *Wilderness by Design: Landscape Architecture and the National Park Service* (Lincoln: University of Nebraska Press, 1998), 71–79.

7. Olmsted, Harvard College *Class Record* (Class of 1894), Fiftieth Anniversary Report (1944), 407, in HUA. See also Klaus, "Such Inheritance"; E. C. Whiting and W. L. Phillips, "Frederick Law Olmsted—1870–1957: An Appreciation of the Man and His Achievements," *Landscape Architecture* 48 (April 1958): 145–57; and other reports by Olmsted in Harvard *Class Record.*

8. Gifford Pinchot, *Breaking New Ground* (New York: Harcourt, Brace, 1947), 48.

9. Gifford Pinchot, *Biltmore Forest: The Property of Mr. George W. Vanderbilt: An Account of Its Treatment, and the Results of the First Year's Work* (Chicago: Lakeside Press/R. R. Donnelley, 1893), 5. See also Roper, *FLO,* 418–19.

10. Pinchot, *Breaking New Ground,* 71. On the "forever wild" Adirondack Park, see David Dobbs and Richard Ober, *The Northern Forest* (White River Junction, Vt.: Chelsea Green, 1995); and Samuel P. Hays, *Conservation and the Gospel of Efficiency: The Progressive Conservation Movement, 1890–1920* (Cambridge: Harvard University Press, 1959), 189–92.

11. James Wilson, "What Forestry Means to the United States," *Forester* 5 (December 1899): 271.

12. "Park Management and Forestry," *Forester* 4 (April 1898): 73–74. On the American Forestry Association, see Henry Clepper, "Crusade for Conservation: The Centennial History of the American Forestry Association," *American Forests* 81 (October 1975), n.p. On the American Park and Outdoor Art Association, see Carr, *Wilderness by Design,* 65–66.

13. *Transactions,* American Society of Landscape Architects, vol. 1, 1899–1908 (Harrisburg, Penn.: Mt. Pleasant Press/J. Horace McFarland, 1908); Bremer Pond, "Fifty Years in Retrospect: Brief Account of the Origin and Development of the ASLA," *Landscape Architecture* 40 (January 1950): 59–66; and Melanie Simo, *100 Years of Landscape Architecture: Some Patterns of a Century* (Washington, D.C.: ASLA Press/ Spacemaker Press, 1999). The founders were O. C. Simonds, Charles N. Lowrie, J. C. Olmsted, Samuel Parsons Jr., Warren H. Manning, Nathan F. Barrett, Beatrix Jones, Downing Vaux, George F. Pentecost Jr., Daniel W. Langton, and F. L. Olmsted Jr. (The two Olmsteds were half brothers.)

14. Ralph S. Hosmer, "The Society of American Foresters: An Historical Summary," *Journal of Forestry,* November 1950, 756–77. The founding members were Gifford Pinchot, Henry S. Graves, Overton W. Price, Edward T. Allen, William L. Hall, Ralph S. Hosmer, and Thomas H. Sherrard.

15. Pinchot, *Breaking New Ground,* 150.

16. "By-Laws," *Transactions,* American Society of Landscape Architects, vol. 2, 1909–21 (Amsterdam, N.Y.: Recorder Press, 1922), 10.

17. *Garden and Forest,* no. 514 (Dec. 29, 1897), 518.

18. Bernhard E. Fernow, *Economics of Forestry* (New York: Crowell, 1902), 506–7; "Announcement," *Forester* 4 (January 1898): 1; and Ralph S. Hosmer, "Fernow Hall," *American Forestry* 28 (November 1922): 670–72.

19. Editorial, *Landscape Architecture* 10 (July 1920): 210.

20. Robert Wheelwright, "Charles Downing Lay, September 3, 1877–February 15, 1956: A Biographical Minute," *Landscape Architecture* 46 (April 1956): 162–64; and Wheelwright, letter to the editor, *Landscape Architecture* 50 (Winter 1959–60): 110. See also Bruce K. Ferguson, "The History of *Landscape Architecture* Magazine," *Landscape Architecture* 89 (November 1999): 86–91, 110–13.

21. Ralph S. Hosmer, "Some Recollections of Gifford Pinchot, 1898–1904," *Journal of Forestry,* August 1945, 558–62. See also David A. Clary, *Timber and the Forest Service* (Lawrence: University Press of Kansas, 1986), 5–28.

22. J. S. Pray to Arthur H. Carhart, July 19, 1921, in AHC Papers, CONS 88, Box 1:100, Folder: "1921, Correspondence."

23. See Suzanne B. Riess, ed., "Thomas Church, Landscape Architect" (1978), Regional Oral History Office, Bancroft Library, University of California, Berkeley; Thomas D. Church, *Gardens Are for People* (New York: Reinhold, 1955); and Peter Walker and Melanie Simo, *Invisible Gardens: The Search for Modernism in the American Landscape* (Cambridge: MIT Press, 1994), 92–115.

24. Henry Vincent Hubbard, "The Bureau and the Landscape Designer," *Landscape Architecture* 31 (January 1941): 68–69. On landscape architects in the government and the military, see "War Records of Those Who Were Fellows and Members during the Years 1917 and 1918," *Transactions,* American Society of Landscape Architects, vol. 2, 1909–1921, 75–80; B. W. Pond, "A Report to the Committee of Chairmen, Graduate School of Design, Regarding the Curriculum for Instruction in Landscape Architecture," Mar. 17, 1943, HUA, UAV 510.120; Norman T. Newton, *Design on the Land* (Cambridge: Harvard University Press, 1971), 517–619; and Phoebe Cutler, *The Public Landscape of the New Deal* (New Haven: Yale University Press, 1985), 83–89.

25. Hosmer, "Some Recollections of Gifford Pinchot," 561.

26. Pinchot, *Breaking New Ground,* 55.

27. Pinchot, *Biltmore Forest,* 7–14.

28. Pinchot, *Breaking New Ground,* 49–50. On the Biltmore arboretum project, see Roper, *FLO,* 465–66, 477.

29. Pinchot, *Biltmore Forest,* 44–45. Some of the forest lands that Pinchot managed for Vanderbilt were later given to the federal government; they now form part of Pisgah National Forest. See Michael Frome, *Whose Woods These Are: The Story of the National Forests* (Garden City, N.Y.: Doubleday, 1962), 104.

30. G. Frederick Schwarz, *Forest Trees and Forest Scenery* (New York: Grafton Press, 1901).

31. Ibid., 12–15, vii.

32. Ibid., 145–46.

33. See Charles Eliot, "Vegetation and Scenery in the Metropolitan Reservations" (1897), in *Charles Eliot, Landscape Architect*, ed. Charles W. Eliot (Boston: Houghton Mifflin, 1902), 721–26; and Schwarz, *Forest Trees*, 150–53.

34. Schwarz, *Forest Trees*, 156–60.

35. Hosmer, "Some Recollections of Gifford Pinchot," 559–60.

36. Schwarz, *Forest Trees*, 65, 165–69.

37. G. Frederick Schwarz, "Forestry and Scenery," *Outlook* 92 (May 8, 1909): 72–73.

38. Schwarz, Harvard College *Class Record* (Class of 1895), Twenty-fifth Anniversary Report (1920), 431, in HUA.

39. *National Cyclopaedia of American Biography*, s.v. "Schwarz, George Frederick."

40. See, for instance, Roderick Nash, *Wilderness and the American Mind*, 3d ed. (New Haven: Yale University Press, 1982); Michael P. Cohen, *The History of the Sierra Club, 1892–1970* (San Francisco: Sierra Club Books, 1988); Stephen Fox, *The American Conservation Movement: John Muir and His Legacy* (1981; Madison: University of Wisconsin Press, 1985); and Hays, *Conservation.*

41. John Muir, "Hetch Hetchy Valley" (1912), in Muir, *Nature Writings*, ed. William Cronon (New York: Library of America, 1997), 817.

42. Quoted in Nash, *Wilderness and the American Mind*, 171.

43. Hays, *Conservation*, 197.

44. Frederick Law Olmsted, "Hetch-Hetchy, the San Francisco Water Supply Controversy," *Boston Evening Transcript*, Nov. 19, 1913; rpt. in *Landscape Architecture* 4 (January 1914): 37–46. In 1864 Yosemite became a public park, to be administered by the state of California. When Yosemite reverted to federal control as a forest reservation in 1890, its boundaries were redrawn to include Hetch Hetchy Valley. In 1905 this entire enlarged area became Yosemite National Park.

45. Nash, *Wilderness and the American Mind*, 170.

46. For debates over control of the national parks and national forests, see Henry S. Graves, "A Crisis in National Recreation," *American Forestry* 26 (July 1920): 391–400; Charles P. Punchard Jr., "Hands Off the National Parks," *Landscape Architecture* 11 (January 1921): 53–57; Harold K. Steen, *The U.S. Forest Service: A History* (Seattle: University of Washington Press, 1976); William C. Everhart, *The National Park Service* (Boulder, Colo.: Westview Press, 1983); Clary, *Timber and the Forest Service;* and Carr, *Wilderness by Design.*

47. Arthur H. Carhart, "This Way to Wilderness," unpublished ms., AHC Papers, CONS 88, Box 2:100, Folder: "Manuscripts—Biography: This Way to Wilderness." Details of Carhart's life are also found in Carhart, *Water—or Your Life* (Philadelphia: Lippincott, 1951), 78–79; and Carhart, *The National Forests* (New York: Knopf, 1959), 101–6.

48. Arthur H. Carhart, "Historical Development of Outdoor Recreation," vol. 2 of *Outdoor Recreation Literature: A Survey*, Report to the Outdoor Recreation Resources Review Commission by the Librarian of Congress (Washington, D.C., 1962), 110;

Carhart, *Timber in Your Life* (Philadelphia: Lippincott, 1955), 136; and Carhart, *National Forests*, 120–25.

49. Carhart to Will W. Blakeman, Feb. 4, 1924, AHC Papers, CONS 88, Box 1:100, Folder: "1924–25, Correspondence"; and Carhart, *Timber in Your Life*, 89. See also Carhart, "The First Ranger," *American Forests* 62 (February 1956): 26–27, 55–56.

50. Carhart, "A Federation of Outdoor Clubs," ca. 1921–22, AHC Papers, CONS 88, Box 1:100, Folder: "1921." See also Carhart to E. A. Sherman, Feb. 12, 1919, AHC Papers, CONS 88, Box 1:100, Folder: "1918–1919, Correspondence"; and Carhart, "The Superior Forest: Why It Is Important to the National Recreation System," *Parks and Recreation* 6 (July–August 1923): 502–4.

51. Frank Hamilton Culley, born in Marshalltown, Iowa, received a B.S. in landscape architecture from Massachusetts Agricultural College (now University of Massachusetts, Amherst) and an M.L.A. from Harvard in 1914. See Carhart, "This Way to Wilderness." Carhart was a member of the Denver firm McCrary, Culley & Carhart, landscape architects and city planners, from 1923 to 1931, before he turned to freelance writing and conservation. In 1960 he and John T. Eastlick, the Denver city librarian, began the Conservation Collection at the Denver Public Library. See Andrew G. Kirk, *The Gentle Science: A History of the Conservation Library* (Denver: Denver Public Library, 1995).

52. J. S. Pray to Carhart, Oct. 11, 1921, AHC Papers, CONS 88, Box 1:100, Folder: "Correspondence, 1921."

53. F. L. Olmsted, "Vacation in the National Parks and Forests," *Landscape Architecture* 12 (January 1922): 107–11.

54. Ibid., 108.

55. "The Cult of the Wilderness," editorial, *Journal of Forestry* 33 (December 1935): 955–57.

56. Aldo Leopold, letter to the editor, *Journal of Forestry* 34 (April 1936): 446.

57. Aldo Leopold, *A Sand County Almanac* (1949; New York: Oxford University Press, 1970), 224–25.

58. Ibid., 224. On Leopold's growing interest in the scientific value of wilderness, see his "Why the Wilderness Society?" *Living Wilderness*, September 1935, 6; and Curt Meine, *Aldo Leopold: His Life and Work* (Madison: University of Wisconsin Press, 1988), 342–46.

59. On the Wilderness Society, see also chapter 10.

60. Walter Prichard Eaton, "To Appreciate the Wilderness One Must Have Seen It," *Living Wilderness*, March 1939, 9–10.

61. Ibid.

62. Benton MacKaye, "A Wilderness Philosophy," *Living Wilderness*, March 1946, 1–4.

63. MacKaye to F. L. Olmsted, Sept. 2, 1947, in TWS Papers, CONS 130, Box 3:106, Folder: "F. L. Olmsted, 1947–1949."

64. F. L. Olmsted to Howard Zahniser, Oct. 29, 1949, in TWS Papers, CONS 130, Box 3:106, Folder: "F. L. Olmsted, 1947–1949."

65. F. L. Olmsted to L. Cabot Briggs, Nov. 9, 1949 (copy), ibid.

66. At the Registry of Deeds, Cheshire County, Keene, N.H., are records of several property transactions by Sarah Sharples Olmsted and her siblings. See, for instance, 473:452 (Apr. 29, 1937), and 797:27 (June 10, 1969).

67. On the history of both Spoonwood Pond and nearby Lake Nubanusit, see Francelia Mason Clark and David S. Robinson, with Alison Rossiter, *Lake Nubanusit (Long Pond/Great Pond): Its History and Its People* (Nelson and Hancock, N.H.: Nubanusit Lake Assn., 2000). See also Ethel Durham, ed., *An Ecological Survey of the Louis Cabot Preserve*, Nature Conservancy Ecological Studies leaflet no. 6 (March 1965).

S E V E N **Layers of Human Habitations and Wildness**

1. Lewis Mumford, *The Golden Day: A Study in American Experience and Culture* (New York: Boni & Liveright, 1926), 279; and Mumford, *The Brown Decades: A Study of the Arts in America, 1865–1895* (New York: Harcourt, Brace, 1931), 59.

2. Lewis Mumford, *Sticks and Stones: A Study of American Architecture and Civilization* (Boni & Liveright, 1924), 95; and Donald Miller, *Lewis Mumford: A Life* (New York: Weidenfeld & Nicolson, 1989), 26, 35, 205, 476.

3. Mumford, *Brown Decades*, 59.

4. Mumford, *Golden Day*, 80.

5. Ibid., 69.

6. Mumford, *Brown Decades*, 66.

7. Frederick Jackson Turner, "The Significance of the Frontier in American History" (1893), in Turner, *The Frontier in American History* (New York: Henry Holt, 1920), 14–16. See also Ray Allen Billington, *America's Frontier Heritage* (New York: Holt, Rinehart & Winston, 1966) and foreword to Turner, *Frontier in American History* (1920; New York: Robert E. Krieger, 1976).

8. Harvey Broome, journal entry of Jan. 27, 1950, in *Out under the Sky of the Great Smokies: A Personal Journal* (1975; Knoxville: University of Tennessee Press, 2001), 82.

9. Turner, "Significance of the Frontier," 11.

10. John Burroughs, "In Green Alaska" (1901), in Burroughs, *Far and Near* (Boston: Houghton Mifflin, 1904), 92. See also John Muir, *Edward Henry Harriman* (New York: Doubleday, Page, 1912); Edward J. Renehan Jr., *John Burroughs: An American Naturalist* (Post Mills, Vt.: Chelsea Green, 1992); and Patrick Wasley, "John Burroughs's (Re)Presentations of Alaska in His 'Narrative' for the Harriman Alaska Expedition," in *Sharp Eyes: John Burroughs and American Nature Writing*, ed. Charlotte Z. Walker (Syracuse, N.Y.: Syracuse University Press, 2000), 105–19.

11. Burroughs, "In Green Alaska," 19.

12. John Burroughs, "A River View," in Burroughs, *Signs and Seasons* (Boston: Houghton Mifflin, 1897), 183.

13. Charles Keeler, "Recollections of John Muir" (1916), in *John Muir: His Life and Letters and Other Writings*, ed. Terry Gifford (Seattle: Mountaineers/London: Bâton Wicks, 1996), 878–80.

14. John Muir, "Notes on the Pacific Coast Glaciers," in *The Harriman Alaska Expedition,* ed. C. Hart Merriam (New York: Doubleday, Page, 1901), 1:119–35.

15. John Muir, *Travels in Alaska* (1915; Boston: Houghton Mifflin, 1979), 70–75.

16. On the adventure with Stickeen, see Muir, *Travels in Alaska,* 250–57.

17. Robert Marshall, *Arctic Village* (New York: Literary Guild, 1933). See also James M. Glover, *A Wilderness Original: The Life of Bob Marshall* (Seattle: Mountaineers, 1986).

18. On Marshall's reasons for the Alaska sojourn, see Robert Marshall, *Alaska Wilderness: Exploring the Central Brooks Range,* 2d ed. (Berkeley: University of California Press, 1970), 1–3.

19. H. L. Mencken, "Utopia in Little," *American Mercury,* May 1933, 124–26. *Arctic Village* was widely reviewed and sold fairly well (3,500 copies in two years) despite the Depression; see Glover, *Wilderness Original,* 151–58.

20. Marshall, *Arctic Village,* 379.

21. Willa Cather, *Death Comes for the Archbishop* (New York: Knopf, 1927), 38.

22. Ibid., 30.

23. Ibid., 276–77.

24. On ambivalence in Cather's *Death Comes for the Archbishop,* see Janis P. Stout, *Willa Cather: The Writer and Her World* (Charlottesville: University Press of Virginia, 2000). Stout's focus is not, however, on ambivalence between cultivation and wildness or between civilization and wilderness.

25. James Maurice Thompson, *My Winter Garden: A Nature-Lover under Southern Skies* (New York: Century, 1900), 6–7, 15–16.

26. Ibid., 170, 83–84.

27. Henry Hazlitt Kopman, *Wild Acres: A Book of the Gulf Coast Country* (New York: Dutton, 1946). See also *Dictionary of American Biography,* s.v. "Thompson, James Maurice." Rachel Carson's early writings are discussed in chapter 9.

28. Kopman, *Wild Acres,* 93–95.

29. Ibid., 76.

30. Ibid., 124–28.

31. On the Army Corps of Engineers' more recent attempts to control the direction of the Mississippi's mainstream, see John McPhee, *The Control of Nature* (New York: Farrar Straus Giroux, 1989).

32. Kopman, *Wild Acres,* 90.

33. Herbert Ravenel Sass, *Adventures in Green Places* (New York: Putnam, 1935), 261, 134–42.

34. See Charles M. Skinner, *Nature in a City Yard* (New York: Century, 1897); Mabel Osgood Wright, *People of the Whirlpool* (New York: Macmillan, 1903) and *My New York* (New York: Macmillan, 1930); Margaret McKenny, *Birds in the Garden* (New York: Grosset & Dunlap, 1939); Lewis S. Gannett, "The Wildness of New York," *Century* 110 (July 1925): 299–304; Walter Prichard Eaton, *Barn Doors and Byways* (Boston: Small, Maynard, 1913); Charles Downing Lay, "Tidal Marshes," *Landscape Architecture,* April 1912, 101–8; John C. Van Dyke, *The New New York* (New York: Macmillan,

1909); Donald Culross Peattie, *The Road of a Naturalist* (Boston: Houghton Mifflin, 1941); John Kieran, *Footnotes on Nature* (Garden City, N.Y.: Doubleday, 1947); and Katharine S. White, *Onward and Upward in the Garden,* ed. E. B. White (New York: Farrar Straus Giroux, 1979).

35. E. B. White, *Here Is New York* (New York: Harper, 1949). See also Scott Elledge, *E. B. White: A Biography* (New York: Norton, 1984).

36. Sarah Orne Jewett, "A Dunnet Shepherdess," in Jewett, *The Queen's Twin and Other Stories* (Boston: Houghton Mifflin, 1899). This story is reprinted in Jewett, *The Country of the Pointed Firs and Other Stories,* ed. Mary Ellen Chase (New York: Norton, 1981). See also F. O. Matthiessen, *Sarah Orne Jewett* (Boston: Houghton Mifflin, 1929).

37. Edith Wharton, *A Backward Glance* (1933; New York: Scribner, 1985), 293.

38. Ibid., 294–96.

39. William S. Annin, "Our Berkshires," *Berkshire Eagle* (Pittsfield, Mass.), Mar. 5, 1957. For this and other biographical accounts, see the Walter Prichard Eaton file in the Berkshire Athenaeum, Local History File, Pittsfield, Mass.

40. Walter Prichard Eaton, "The Little Town on the Hill," in Eaton, *Green Trails and Upland Pastures* (Garden City, N.Y.: Doubleday, Page, 1917), 184.

41. Walter Prichard Eaton, *Skyline Camps* (Boston: W. A. Wilde, 1922), 81–104. I discuss the Appalachian Trail in chapters 3 and 10.

42. Walter Prichard Eaton, *On Yankee Hilltops* (Boston: W. A. Wilde, 1933), 99.

43. William A. Babson, *Modern Wilderness* (New York: Doubleday, Doran, 1940), foreword, by Frank M. Chapman, and 3.

44. Ibid., 259–61.

45. Louis J. Halle Jr., *Spring in Washington* (New York: William Sloane, 1947), 62.

46. A foreword by the ornithologist Roger Tory Peterson and an epilogue by Halle appeared in the 2d ed. of *Spring in Washington* (1957) and also in the paperback ed. (New York: Atheneum, 1963).

47. Halle, *Spring in Washington* (1947), 38.

48. Ibid., 129.

E I G H T **Ecology along the Roadside, by the Water, and in the Garden**

1. Henry C. Cowles, *The Plant Societies of Chicago and Vicinity* (Chicago: Geographic Society of Chicago, 1901); and Mabel Osgood Wright, *Flowers and Ferns in Their Haunts* (New York: Macmillan, 1901).

2. Henry C. Cowles, "The Ecological Relations of the Vegetation on the Sand Dunes of Lake Michigan," *Botanical Gazette* 27 (February–May 1899): 95–117, 167–202, 281–308, 361–91. In the segment published in March 1899, the sand reed shown in fig. 2, p. 178, is identified as *Ammophila arundinacea.*

3. Cowles, *Plant Societies.*

4. Ibid., 7. The scientists Cowles mentioned were Eugenius Warming and Andreas Schimper.

5. Donald Worster, *Nature's Economy: The Roots of Ecology* (San Francisco: Sierra Club Books, 1977), 206.

6. Cowles, *Plant Societies,* 9.

7. Dallas Lore Sharp, "The Nature-Writer," in Sharp, *The Face of the Fields* (Boston: Houghton Mifflin, 1911), 117–21.

8. Wright, *Flowers and Ferns,* 4–10.

9. Cowles, *Plant Societies,* 7; and Eugenius Warming, *The Oecology of Plants,* trans. Percy Groom and Isaac Bayley Balfour (London: H. Milford [1929]). As Cowles noted, hydrophytes grow in water or wet places; xerophytes grow in dry habitats; mesophytes grow in areas of medium moisture; halophytes grow in saltwater or alkaline soil.

10. Henry David Thoreau, quoted in Bradford Torrey, "Thoreau's Attitude toward Nature," *Atlantic Monthly,* November 1899, 706–10.

11. Bradford Torrey, *Friends on the Shelf* (Boston: Houghton Mifflin, 1906), 106, 120. See also *The Journal of Henry Thoreau,* ed. Bradford Torrey and Francis H. Allen, 14 vols. (Boston: Houghton Mifflin, 1906).

12. See Bradford Torrey, *Footing It in Franconia* (Boston: Houghton Mifflin, 1902); Torrey, *Field Days in California* (Boston: Houghton Mifflin, 1913); and *National Cyclopaedia of American Biography,* s.v. "Torrey, Bradford."

13. Bradford Torrey, *Nature's Invitation* (Boston: Houghton Mifflin, 1904), 115–16.

14. Torrey, *Field Days in California,* 23.

15. Jeanette Porter Meehan, *Lady of the Limberlost: The Life and Letters of Gene Stratton Porter* (1927; Port Washington, N.Y.: Kennikat Press/Amereon House Mattituck [ca. 1977]), 11–20.

16. Gene Stratton Porter, excerpt from *Moths of the Limberlost* (1912), in *Coming through the Swamp: The Nature Writings of Gene Stratton Porter,* ed. Sydney Landon Plum (Salt Lake City: University of Utah Press: 1996), 90–91.

17. Deborah Dahlke-Scott and Michael Prewitt, "A Writer's Crusade to Portray Spirit of the Limberlost," *Smithsonian* 7 (April 1976): 64–68.

18. Meehan, *Lady of the Limberlost,* 118.

19. William Lyon Phelps, "The Why of the Best Seller," *Bookman,* December 1921, 298–302.

20. Meehan, *Lady of the Limberlost,* 152–53; and Dahlke-Scott and Prewitt, "Writer's Crusade," 68.

21. Torrey, *Field Days in California,* 15.

22. Gene Stratton Porter, "Shall We Save Natural Beauty?" excerpt from *Let Us Highly Resolve* (1927), in Stratton Porter, *Coming through the Swamp,* 105–8.

23. Walter Prichard Eaton, *The Actor's Heritage* (Boston: Atlantic Monthly Press, 1924), 3–6; and Eaton, biographical file, HUA, HUD 300.505, Box 617.

24. Walter Prichard Eaton, "The Dismal Swamp" (1910), in his *Barn Doors and Byways* (Boston: Small, Maynard, 1913), 178–80.

25. Ibid., 201.

26. Ibid., 204–5. See N. S. Shaler, "General Account of the Fresh-Water Morasses of the United States with a Description of the Dismal Swamp District of Virginia and North Carolina," in J. W. Powell, *Tenth Annual Report of the United States Geological Survey, 1888–89* (Washington, D.C.: USGPO, 1890), 255–339. In 1973 the Union Camp Corporation donated 49,100 acres of land to the Nature Conservancy, which in turn conveyed it to the U.S. Department of the Interior. In 1974 that gift became the Great Dismal Swamp National Wildlife Refuge. See also Paul W. Kirk Jr., ed., *The Great Dismal Swamp* (Charlottesville: University Press of Virginia/Old Dominion University Research Foundation, 1979); and Jack Temple Kirby, *Poquosin: A Study of Rural Landscape and Society* (Chapel Hill: University of North Carolina Press, 1995).

27. John Burroughs, "Scientific Faith," in Burroughs, *Time and Change* (Boston: Houghton Mifflin, 1912), 175.

28. John Burroughs, "Scientific Faith Once More," in Burroughs, *Under the Apple Trees* (Boston: Houghton Mifflin, 1916), 175.

29. John Burroughs, "Literature and Science," ibid., 196.

30. Burroughs, "Scientific Faith," 177.

31. On Burroughs and Bergson's élan vital, see also Justin Askins, "Thankfully, the Center Cannot Hold," in *Sharp Eyes: John Burroughs and American Nature Writing*, ed. Charlotte Z. Walker (Syracuse, N.Y.: Syracuse University Press, 2000), 251–64.

32. John Burroughs, "Life and Chance," in Burroughs, *Under the Apple Trees*, 256.

33. John Burroughs, "Nature and Natural History," in Burroughs, *Field and Study* (Boston: Houghton Mifflin, 1919), 316.

34. Walt Whitman, *Leaves of Grass,* quoted ibid., 318.

35. On Sargent's place, see "Artificial Water," *Garden and Forest* 1 (Feb. 29, 1888): 8; Wilhelm Miller, "The Sargent Home Near Boston," *Country Life in America* 3 (March 1903): 199–208; and Miller, "A Spring Garden of Lilacs, Irises, and Peonies," *Country Life in America* 21 (Feb. 15, 1912): 35–40. After Sargent's death, Holm Lea was sold and subdivided; see S. B. Sutton, *Charles Sprague Sargent and the Arnold Arboretum* (Cambridge: Harvard University Press, 1970), 17.

36. Editorial, *Garden and Forest* 1 (Aug. 1, 1888): 266.

37. Ibid.; E. J. Hill, "Oecological Notes upon the White Pine," *Garden and Forest* 10 (Aug. 25, 1897): 331–32; and William Trelease, "The Swamps of South-eastern Missouri," ibid. (Sept. 22, 1897): 370–71.

38. Editorial, ibid. (Sept. 8, 1897): 349–50; and M. G. Van Rensselaer, "Native Plants for Ornamental Planting," ibid. (Sept. 22, 1897): 376.

39. William Grundmann, "Warren Manning," in *American Landscape Architecture: Designers and Places,* ed. William H. Tishler (Washington, D.C.: Preservation Press/National Trust for Historic Preservation, 1989), 56. See also Robin Karson, "Warren H. Manning: Pragmatist in the Wild Garden," in *Nature and Ideology: Natural Garden Design in the Twentieth Century,* ed. Joachim Wolschke-Bulmahn (Washington, D.C.: Dumbarton Oaks, 1997), 113–30; and Lance M. Neckar, "Warren H. Manning and His Minnesota Clients: Developing a National Practice in a Landscape of Re-

sources, 1898–1919," in *Midwestern Landscape Architecture*, ed. William H. Tishler (Urbana: University of Illinois Press/Amherst, Mass.: Library of American Landscape History, 2000), 142–58.

40. Warren H. Manning, "The Two Kinds of Bog Garden," *Country Life in America* 14 (August 1908): 379–80. On his home at North Billerica, Massachusetts, see also Manning, "Bringing in the Offscape," ibid. (July 1908): 290–91, and "Framing of Home Pictures," ibid. (May 1908): 52–53.

41. Manning, "Two Kinds of Bog Garden," 380.

42. Dan Kiley, quoted in Peter Walker and Melanie Simo, *Invisible Gardens: The Search for Modernism in the American Landscape* (Cambridge: MIT Press, 1994), 180.

43. Stephen F. Christy, "The Metamorphosis of an Artist," *Landscape Architecture* 66 (January 1976): 60–66. On Jensen as an artist, see also *Alfred Caldwell: The Life and Work of a Prairie School Landscape Architect*, ed. Dennis Domer (Baltimore: Johns Hopkins University Press, 1997); Robert Grese, *Jens Jensen: Maker of Natural Parks and Gardens* (Baltimore: Johns Hopkins University Press, 1992); and Leonard K. Eaton, *Landscape Artist in America: The Life and Work of Jens Jensen* (Chicago: University of Chicago Press, 1964).

44. Jens Jensen, "Beauty and Fitness in Park Concrete Work," *Park and Cemetery* 18 (November 1908): 435–37.

45. Jens Jensen, "Original Designs for Bulb Beds," *Garden Magazine* 2 (October 1905): 122–24.

46. Jens Jensen, "Landscape Gardening in the Middle West," *Park and Cemetery* 22 (February 1913): 303.

47. Quoted in Mertha Fulkerson, "Jens Jensen and 'The Clearing,'" *Parks and Recreation* 25 (November 1941): 100.

48. Ibid., 97. For the swimming hole as recently built, see Ruth Dean, "The New Swimming Hole," *House and Garden* 41 (April 1922): 44–45, 112, 114, 116. Jensen's attitude toward garden restoration is discussed at the end of chapter 2.

49. On Jensen's desire to idealize nature, not copy it, see his "Natural Parks and Gardens," as told to Ragna B. Eskil, *Saturday Evening Post*, Mar. 8, 1930, 169.

50. Edith A. Roberts and Elsa Rehmann, "Plant Ecology," a series of articles in *House Beautiful*, June 1927–May 1928, in their *American Plants for American Gardens: Plant Ecology—The Study of Plants in Relation to Their Environment* (New York: Macmillan, 1929). See also Robert Wheelwright, letter to the editor, *Landscape Architecture* 45 (April 1955): 139–40. Here Wheelwright, formerly a coeditor of that magazine, noted that the science of ecology had not yet been developed when he was a student (at Harvard, 1902–8). Yet the influence of nineteenth-century naturalists, particularly Burroughs and Thoreau, was still strong; and it was reflected in the mature landscape design work of Andrew Jackson Downing and Frederick Law Olmsted. "A definite understanding of the relation of plants to environment and site, an appreciation of the beauty in natural plant associations, was acknowledged without attempt at scientific explanation," he added.

51. On changes in the profession, see Darrel G. Morrison, foreword to Roberts and Reh-mann, *American Plants for American Gardens* (1929; Athens: University of Georgia Press, 1996); Norman T. Newton, *Design on the Land* (Cambridge: Harvard University Press, 1971); Phoebe Cutler, *The Public Landscape of the New Deal* (New Haven: Yale University Press, 1985); and Melanie Simo, *100 Years of Landscape Architecture* (Washington, D.C.: American Society of Landscape Architects/Spacemaker Press, 1999).

52. Elsa Rehmann, "An Ecological Approach," *Landscape Architecture* 23 (July 1933): 239–45.

53. Early works on "human ecology" include Jaquetta Hawkes, *A Land* (New York: Random House, 1951); May Theilgaard Watts, *Reading the Landscape: An Adventure in Ecology* (New York: Macmillan, 1957); and Paul Shepard, *Man in the Landscape* (New York: Knopf, 1967).

54. Henry Beston, *The Outermost House* (1928; New York: Henry Holt, 1992).

55. Henry Beston Sheahan, Harvard College *Class Record* (Class of 1909), Twenty-fifth Anniversary Report (1934), 566–71, HUA. After his first book, *A Volunteer Poilu*, appeared in 1916, he wrote under the name of his paternal grandmother, Beston.

56. Beston, *Outermost House*, 164.

57. Ibid., 154–57.

58. Henry Beston, "Original manuscript of the Outermost House, Presented to the Library of Dartmouth College by the author, March 21st 1949," in HB Papers, MS 90: Box 2, Folder 10, pp. 5–6. Beston was probably referring to the British nature writer W. H. Hudson (1841–1922), one of his favorite authors.

59. Ibid., 11–12.

60. Henry Beston, *The Outermost House* (Garden City, N.Y.: Doubleday, Doran, 1928), foreword.

61. Henry Beston Sheahan, Harvard College *Class Record* (Class of 1909), Twenty-fifth Anniversary Report (1934), 567, HUA. Beston began, "I am a writer by profession, and I was going to add 'a naturalist by avocation' when it occurred to me that I was really nothing of the kind."

62. Beston, *Outermost House* (1992 ed.), 217.

N I N E **Spirit of the Landscape, Humanized and Wild**

1. Robert Marshall, *Alaska Wilderness: Exploring the Central Brooks Range,* ed. George Marshall, 2d ed. (Berkeley: University of California Press, 1970), 22, 85. Marshall's first Alaskan journey is described in chapter 7 above.

2. John Kauffmann, formerly of the National Park Service, quoted in Devereux Butcher, *Exploring Our National Parks and Monuments,* 9th ed. (Boulder, Colo.: Roberts Rinehart/National Parks and Conservation Assn., 1995), 59.

3. Kenneth Harvey, quoted in George Marshall, "Postscript to the Second Edition," in Robert Marshall, *Alaska Wilderness,* 167.

4. Robert Marshall, journal entry, quoted in James M. Glover, *A Wilderness Original: The Life of Bob Marshall* (Seattle: Mountaineers, 1986), 109.

5. Excerpts from reviews by Lewis Mumford and Bertrand Russell on the back cover of the paperback edition of Joseph Wood Krutch, *The Modern Temper: A Study and a Confession* (New York: Harcourt, Brace & World, 1956); and John D. Margolis, *Joseph Wood Krutch: A Writer's Life* (Knoxville: University of Tennessee Press, 1980), 67–92.

6. George Marshall, "Introduction to the First Edition," in Robert Marshall, *Alaska Wilderness* (1970), xxxi; and Robert Marshall, "The Problem of the Wilderness," *Scientific Monthly* 30 (February 1930): 141–48. This article was reprinted in *Sierra Club Bulletin* 32 (May 1947): 43–52 and in *The Great New Wilderness Debate*, ed. J. Baird Callicott and Michael P. Nelson (Athens: University of Georgia Press, 1998), 85–96.

7. Krutch, *Modern Temper*, 160–61, 169; and Marshall, "Problem of the Wilderness," 143. The phrases "too absorbed in living to feel the need for thought" and "animal rejuvenation" are Krutch's.

8. On the Wilderness Society's debt to Marshall and his " Problem of the Wilderness," see Harvey Broome, "Origins of the Wilderness Society," *Living Wilderness*, July 1940, 13–15; Stephen Fox, "'We Want No Straddlers,'" *Wilderness*, Winter 1984; Roderick Nash, *Wilderness and the American Mind*, 3d ed. (New Haven: Yale University Press, 1982), 200–208; and chapter 10 below.

9. Benjamin M. Cardozo to Robert Marshall, Nov. 28, 1930, quoted in George Marshall, "Introduction to the First Edition," in Robert Marshall, *Alaska Wilderness* (1970), xxviii–xxix.

10. Krutch, *Modern Temper*, 12.

11. Joseph Wood Krutch, *More Lives than One* (New York: William Sloane, 1962), 3–56; and Margolis, *Joseph Wood Krutch*, 3–23.

12. Krutch, *Modern Temper*, 169.

13. Krutch, *More Lives than One*, 210.

14. John C. Van Dyke, *The Meadows* (New York: Scribner, 1926), 73, 144.

15. Ibid., 245.

16. Charles Downing Lay, "Tidal Marshes," *Landscape Architecture* 2 (April 1912): 101–8. For another perspective on Lay and salt marshes, see John R. Stilgoe, *Alongshore* (New Haven: Yale University Press, 1994), 123–24.

17. Charles Downing Lay, *The Freedom of the City* (New York: Duffield, 1926). See chapter 5 above.

18. Charles Downing Lay, *A Garden Book for Autumn and Winter* (New York: Duffield, 1924), 16.

19. Charles Downing Lay, "Space Composition," *Landscape Architecture* 8 (January 1918): 77–86.

20. Lay, *Garden Book*, 38–39.

21. Ibid., 33.

22. Elsa Rehmann, *The Small Place: Its Landscape Architecture* (New York: Putnam, 1918).

23. Lay, *Garden Book*, 33.

24. Ibid., 15–18.

25. Ibid., 23–30. See also E. S. Draper, "Shall the ASLA Undertake Publicity?" *Landscape Architecture* 19 (January 1929): 126–28.

26. Charles Keeler, *The Simple Home* (1904; Santa Barbara: Peregrine Smith, 1979), 1–16; see chapter 4 above.

27. Mrs. Theodore Thomas, *Our Mountain Garden* (New York: Macmillan, 1904), 23–24, 170; and *Dictionary of American Biography*, s.v. "Thomas, Christian Friedrich Theodore." Mrs. Thomas (also known as Rose Fay) did not name her reference books, which may have included Robinson's *Wild Garden* (1870) and a volume of Bailey's *Cyclopedia of American Horticulture* or his editorials and essays in *Country Life in America*.

28. Lay, *Garden Book*, 233–37; and Lay, "Tidal Marshes."

29. Lay, *Garden Book*, 30–31.

30. Charles Downing Lay, "Art and the Landscape Architect," *Landscape Architecture* 13 (April 1923): 161–67.

31. Lay, *Garden Book*, 238–52.

32. Henry Beston, "Original manuscript of the Outermost House, Presented to the Library of Dartmouth College by the author, March 21st 1949," in HB Papers, MS 90: Box 2, Folder 10, pp. 35–37.

33. Robert Finch, introduction to Beston, *Outermost House* (1928; New York: Henry Holt, 1992), xxxii.

34. Nancy Kober, *With Paintbrush and Shovel: Preserving Virginia's Wildflowers* (Charlottesville: University Press of Virginia/Petersburg Garden Club, 2000).

35. Ibid., 9.

36. Donna M. E. Ware, personal communications to the author, May 24 and July 22, 2001. Among the 295 species represented in the herbarium collection, nearly 50% of those recently found growing in Lee Memorial Park are not located in the sanctuary (which is now nearly all forested) but are found beyond its original territory, in what are now open, sunny habitats in the park. Ware has learned that some wildflowers were originally transplanted to areas along the roadway that enters Lee Park, not within the sanctuary itself.

37. Arthur A. Shurcliff, "City Plan and Landscaping Problems," *Architectural Record*, December 1935, 383–86; and Shurcliff, *Autobiography* (Cambridge, Mass.: Privately printed, 1981), 54–55, in FLL/SC.

38. Shurcliff, *Autobiography*, 45–47; and Melanie L. Simo, *An Interview with Sidney N. Shurcliff* (Watertown, Mass.: Hubbard Educational Trust, 1992), 22–24.

39. Simo, *Interview with Shurcliff*, 24.

40. Arthur A. Shurtleff, "Annual Report of the President," *Landscape Architecture* 20 (April 1930): 229–31. Shurtleff changed his name to Shurcliff on Apr. 17, 1930. See his *Autobiography*, 1.

41. Arthur A. Shurcliff, *New England Journal* (Boston: Houghton Mifflin, 1931), 8.

42. Jens Jensen, *Siftings* (1939), in his *"Siftings," "The Major Portion of the Clearing,"* and *Collected Writings* (Chicago: Ralph Fletcher Seymour, 1956), 95.

43. Leonard K. Eaton, *Landscape Artist in America: The Life and Work of Jens Jensen* (Chicago: University of Chicago Press, 1964), 42–45, and selected letters by Jensen in Eaton's unpaginated photo essay of Lincoln Memorial Garden, ibid.

44. Robert E. Grese, *Jens Jensen: Maker of Natural Parks and Gardens* (Baltimore: Johns Hopkins University Press, 1992), 195.

45. Frank A. Waugh, *The Natural Style in Landscape Gardening* (Boston: Richard G. Badger, 1917), 58–59.

46. Unsigned review of Waugh, *Natural Style in Landscape Gardening*, in *Landscape Architecture* 8 (January 1918): 102–4.

47. Otto G. Schaffer, review of Jensen, *Siftings* (1939), in *Landscape Architecture* 30 (April 1940): 153–54. On Waugh's enthusiasm for Jensen's work, see Waugh, *The Landscape Beautiful* (New York: Orange Judd, 1910), 174, 198–99.

48. On Waugh's formative years, see Waugh, *Landscape Beautiful*, 31, 51. See also Linda F. McClelland, "Frank Albert Waugh," in *Pioneers of American Landscape Design*, ed. Charles A. Birnbaum and Robin Karson (New York: McGraw-Hill, 2000), 434–36; and A. Donald Taylor, "Frank Albert Waugh: A Biographical Minute" (1943), in *Landscape Architectural Education*, ed. Gary O. Robinette, 2 vols. (Dubuque: Kendall/Hunt, 1973), 1:133–34.

49. Arthur Carhart, "Historical Development of Outdoor Recreation," in *Outdoor Recreation Literature: A Survey*, Report to the Outdoor Recreation Resources Review Commission by the Librarian of Congress, 2 vols. (Washington, D.C.: 1962), 2:109; Frank A. Waugh, *Recreation Uses on the National Forests* (Washington, D.C.: USGPO, 1918); and Waugh, *Landscape Engineering in the National Forests* (Washington, D.C.: USGPO, 1918).

50. Frank A. Waugh, "The Forest Margin," *Journal of Forestry* 32 (January 1934): 11–14; and Waugh, "Ecology of the Roadside," *Landscape Architecture* 21 (January 1931): 81–92. The roadside study was the first of Waugh's articles on plant ecology and physiography in *Landscape Architecture*.

51. Waugh, *Landscape Beautiful*, 33–34.

52. Frank A. Waugh, *Book of Landscape Gardening*, 3d ed., rev. (New York: Orange Judd, 1926), 7.

53. R. L. Carson, "Undersea," *Atlantic Monthly*, September 1937, 322–25; and Linda Lear, *Rachel Carson: Witness for Nature* (New York: Henry Holt, 1997), 81–87. Lear relates that Carson had originally written "The World of Waters" as an introduction to a government brochure, but her division chief suggested it would be more appropriate for the *Atlantic*.

54. Carson, "Undersea," 325. "Undersea" was reprinted in Paul Brooks, *The House of Life: Rachel Carson at Work* (Boston: Houghton Mifflin, 1972) and in *Lost Woods: The Discovered Writings of Rachel Carson*, ed. Linda Lear (Boston: Beacon, 1998).

55. Carson to Henry Beston, May 14, 1954, quoted in Lear, *Rachel Carson*, 535, n. 49.

56. Rachel Carson, "Road of the Hawks" (October 1945), field notes printed in *Lost Woods*, 30–32.

TEN **A Land Ethic for a Plundered Planet**

1. Aldo Leopold, *A Sand County Almanac and Sketches Here and There* (1949; New York: Oxford University Press, 1968), vii.

2. Fairfield Osborn, *Our Plundered Planet* (Boston: Little, Brown, 1948), 194.

3. Nathaniel Southgate Shaler, *Man and the Earth* (New York: Fox, Duffield, 1905), preface.

4. Ibid., 228.

5. Ibid., 232.

6. Ibid., 188.

7. David N. Livingstone, *Nathaniel Southgate Shaler and the Culture of American Science* (Tuscaloosa: University of Alabama Press, 1987), 192–214.

8. Shaler, *Man and the Earth*, 188, 31, 87–100.

9. John Burroughs, "Grist of the Gods," in Burroughs, *Leaf and Tendril* (Boston: Houghton Mifflin, 1908), 201. See also Frank Bergon, "'Sensitive to the Verge of the Horizon': The Environmentalism of John Burroughs," in *Sharp Eyes: John Burroughs and American Nature Writing*, ed. Charlotte Zoë Walker (Syracuse, N.Y.: Syracuse University Press, 2000), 19–25.

10. William T. Hornaday, *Thirty Years War for Wild Life* (Stamford, Conn.: Permanent Wild Life Protection Fund, 1931), preface; and Hornaday, *Our Vanishing Wild Life: Its Extermination and Preservation* (New York: Scribner, 1913). See also Stephen Fox, *The American Conservation Movement: John Muir and His Legacy* (1981; Madison: University of Wisconsin Press, 1985), 148–67.

11. Henry Fairfield Osborn, foreword to Hornaday, *Our Vanishing Wildlife*, vii.

12. See "Parks, Playgrounds, and Beaches for the Los Angeles Region: A Report Submitted to the Citizens' Committee on Parks, Playgrounds, and Beaches by Olmsted Brothers and Bartholomew and Associates, Consultants" (1930), in Greg Hise and William Deverell, *Eden by Design: The 1930 Olmsted-Bartholomew Plan for the Los Angeles Region* (Berkeley: University of California Press, 2000).

13. Dallas Lore Sharp, "The Little Foxes," in Sharp, *The Hills of Hingham* (Boston: Houghton Mifflin, 1916), 153–54.

14. Dallas Lore Sharp, "Mere Beans," in *Hills of Hingham*, 100.

15. Sharp, "Little Foxes," 165.

16. Walter Prichard Eaton, "The Literature of Place," *Bookman* 48 (September 1918): 13–20.

17. Walter Prichard Eaton, "The Harvest of the Wild Places" (1914), in Eaton, *Green Trails and Upland Pastures* (Garden City, N.Y.: Doubleday, Page, 1917), 116.

18. Walter Prichard Eaton, Harvard College *Class Record* (Class of 1900), Fifth Report (1921), HUA.

19. Walter Prichard Eaton, *In Berkshire Fields* (New York: Harper, 1920), 25–26.

20. *Proceedings of the National Conference on Outdoor Recreation, . . . Washington, D.C., May 22, 23, and 24, 1924* (Washington, D.C.: USGPO, 1924), 74 (hereafter *Proceedings*).

21. Ibid., 2.

22. Arthur H. Carhart, "Historical Development of Outdoor Recreation," in *Outdoor Recreation Literature: A Survey,* Report to the Outdoor Recreation Resources Review Commission by the Librarian of Congress (Washington, D.C.: 1962), 2:116.

23. *Proceedings,* 12–14.

24. Fox, *American Conservation Movement,* 167–69.

25. *Proceedings,* 32–35, 38–41, 17–21.

26. Ibid., 58–61, 144–47.

27. Quoted in Edward Elwell Whiting, *President Coolidge: A Contemporary Estimate* (Boston: Atlantic Monthly Press, 1923), 15.

28. *Proceedings,* 2, 11–14.

29. Carhart, "Historical Development of Outdoor Recreation," 117.

30. *Proceedings,* 122–24, 29–31, 124–27.

31. Alfred North Whitehead, *Science and the Modern World* (1925; New York: Free Press, 1967), 58–59.

32. Ibid., 206.

33. Ibid., 207.

34. Walter Prichard Eaton to Carlton F. Wells, Mar. 25 and Apr. 11, 1929, in WPE Collection (no. 10290). Wells was a professor of English at the University of Michigan, Ann Arbor; his correspondence with Eaton continued through the period when Eaton served as a professor of playwriting in Yale's Department of Drama, from 1933 to 1947.

35. Joseph Wood Krutch, *More Lives than One* (New York: William Sloane, 1962), 210.

36. Ibid., 288–90; Krutch, *Henry David Thoreau* (New York: William Sloane, 1948); and John D. Margolis, *Joseph Wood Krutch: A Writer's Life* (Knoxville: University of Tennessee Press, 1980), 90–92.

37. Aldo Leopold, "Wilderness as a Form of Land Use" (1925), in Leopold, *The River of the Mother of God and Other Essays,* ed. Susan L. Flader and J. Baird Callicott (Madison: University of Wisconsin Press, 1991), 134–42; and Leopold, "The Last Stand of the Wilderness," *American Forests and Forest Life,* October 1925.

38. Robert Marshall, "The Problem of the Wilderness," *Scientific Monthly* 30 (February 1930): 141–48.

39. H[arold] C. Anderson to Benton MacKaye, Apr. 3, 1930, in MKF Papers, ML-5, Box 167: 1.

40. Benton MacKaye, "Flankline vs. Skyline," *Appalachia* 29 (1934): 104–8.

41. "Concerning the Wilderness Society," *Living Wilderness,* December 1937, n.p.; "A Summons to Save the Wilderness," ibid., September 1935, 1; and Harvey Broome, "Origins of the Wilderness Society," ibid., July 1940, 13–15. Broome concluded, "If any organization has been overwhelmingly indebted to a single individual, the Wilderness Society has been, and remains so, to Robert Marshall."

42. Stephen Fox, "'We Want No Straddlers,'" *Wilderness,* Winter 1984, 5–19. See also Po-

tomac Appalachian Trail Club, *Appalachian Trail Guide: Shenandoah National Park, with Side Trails* (Washington, D.C., 1977), 21–23; H. C. Anderson, "What Price Skyline Drives," draft copy, in MKF Papers, ML-5, Box 168: 1; Arno B. Cammerer to Benton MacKaye, Sept. 14, 1934, in MKF Papers, ML-5, Box 167: 21; and Harvey Broome, "The Last Decade, 1935–1945," *Living Wilderness,* December 1945, 13–17.

43. Aldo Leopold, "Why the Wilderness Society?" and Benton MacKaye, "Why the Appalachian Trail?" *Living Wilderness,* September 1935, 6–7.

44. Benton MacKaye to Anne Broome (Mrs. Harvey Broome), Jan. 18, 1965, in TWS Papers, CONS 130, Box 3: 104, Folder: "MacKaye, Writings, 1920s–1960s."

45. Bernard DeVoto, "The West: A Plundered Province," *Harper's,* August 1934, 356.

46. Ibid., 364.

47. Bernard DeVoto, "The National Parks," *Fortune* 35 (June 1947): 120–21. See also Wallace Stegner, *The Uneasy Chair: A Biography of Bernard DeVoto* (Garden City, N.Y.: Doubleday, 1974).

48. Bernard DeVoto, "The West against Itself," *Harper's* 194 (January 1947): 1–13; and Arthur H. Carhart, "Who Says—Sell Our Public Lands in the West?" *American Forests,* April 1947, 152–55. Stegner notes that De Voto "planted" another of Carhart's conservation articles in the *Atlantic,* July 1948, and the *Pacific Spectator;* see Stegner, *Uneasy Chair,* 308 and 437, n. 17. For another reading of DeVoto's "West against Itself" and a more sympathetic view of the stockmen's goals generally, see Karl Hess Jr., *Visions upon the Land: Man and Nature on the Western Range* (Washington, D.C.: Island Press, 1992).

49. Aldo Leopold, "Summary of the Twelfth North American Wildlife Conference" (in San Antonio, Tex., Feb. 3–5, 1947), typed copy on stationary of Wildlife Management Institute, Washington, D.C., in AL Papers, CONS 47, Box 1.

50. Aldo Leopold, foreword (dated July 31, 1947) to "Great Possessions" (manuscript), in *Companion to "A Sand County Almanac": Interpretive and Critical Essays,* ed. J. Baird Callicott (Madison: University of Wisconsin Press, 1987), 281–88. See also Dennis Ribbens, "The Making of 'A Sand County Almanac,'" ibid., 91–109.

51. Curt Meine, *Aldo Leopold: His Life and Work* (Madison: University of Wisconsin Press, 1988), 504.

52. Roderick Nash, "Aldo Leopold's Intellectual Heritage," in Callicott, *Companion to "A Sand County Almanac,"* 84.

53. See note 50.

54. Louis J. Halle Jr., *Spring in Washington* (New York: William Sloane, 1947), 38–40.

55. Sally Carrighar, *One Day on Beetle Rock* (New York: Knopf, 1944). In her autobiography, *Home to the Wilderness* (Boston: Houghton Mifflin, 1973), Carrighar tells of her early years when she worked as a writer/receptionist, an editor, and a writer of commercial radio scripts, before illness and her chance discoveries about wild creatures in San Francisco led her to write about them in the Sierra and elsewhere. Margaret McFadden-Gerber listed the date of Carrighar's birth as "ca. 1905" in *American Women Writers: A Critical Reference Guide from Colonial Times to the Present,* vol. 1

(New York: Frederick Ungar, 1979). But the Social Security Death Index notes that Carrighar was born Feb. 10, 1898, and died in October 1985. See http://ssdi.genealogy .rootsweb.com/cgi-bin/ssdi.cgi.

56. Sally Carrighar, untitled notes on *One Day on Beetle Rock,* perhaps written as a prospectus for a series of books on animal habitats, and a hand-ruled graph of animal activities she had observed, in SC Papers, MS 147, Box 1: "Beetle Rock," Folder 11.

57. Ribbens, "Making of *A Sand County Almanac*," 92–102.

58. Leopold, two draft forewords, dated Dec. 5, 1947, and Mar. 4, 1948 (copies), in AL Papers, CONS 47, Box 1, Folder: "Manuscript of *Sand County Almanac.*"

59. Of the two forewords cited in note 58, the one dated Mar. 4, 1948, and published virtually as written in 1949 reveals some pruning and tightening of the prose as well as a clearer articulation of three concepts to be "welded into one" in the course of the book: the ecology, ethics, and aesthetics of the land.

60. Jens Jensen, *The Clearing* (1949), in *"Siftings," the Major Portion of "The Clearing," and Collected Writings* (Chicago: Ralph Fletcher Seymour, 1956), 114.

61. Jens Jensen, *The Clearing: "A Way of Life"* (Chicago: Ralph Fletcher Seymour, 1949), 73. A copy of this rare first edition is kept in FLL/SC. For comparison, see Jensen, *The Clearing,* in *Siftings,* 134.

62. Leopold, "Why the Wilderness Society?" 6.

EPILOGUE

1. Maurice Thompson, *My Winter Garden* (New York: Century, 1900), 84; Edward Howe Forbush, *Useful Birds and Their Protection* (Boston: Massachusetts State Board of Agriculture, 1907), 156–59; and Frank M. Chapman, *Handbook of Birds of Eastern North America,* 6th ed. (New York: D. Appleton, 1903), 394–97.

2. Louis J. Halle Jr., *Spring in Washington* (New York: William Sloane, 1947); Aldo Leopold, *A Sand County Almanac* (1949; New York: Oxford University Press, 1968), 30–32; and Benton MacKaye, "The Appalachian Trail: A Guide to the Study of Nature," *Scientific Monthly,* April 1932, 342.

3. E. B. White, *Here Is New York* (New York: Harper, 1949), 53–54; and Rachel Carson, *Mattamuskeet: A National Wildlife Refuge,* Conservation in Action no. 4 (Washington, D.C.: USGPO, 1947).

4. See Peter J. Schmitt, *Back to Nature: The Arcadian Myth in Urban America,* (1969; Baltimore: Johns Hopkins University Press, 1990); Ralph H. Lutts, *The Nature Fakers: Wildlife, Science, and Sentiment* (1990; Charlottesville: University Press of Virginia, 2001); and Lewis Mumford, *In the Name of Sanity* (New York: Harcourt, Brace, 1954).

5. Walter Prichard Eaton, "The Literature of Place," *Bookman* 48 (September 1918): 13–20.

6. Colin Woodard, *Ocean's End: Travels through Endangered Seas* (New York: Basic Books, 2000); and Mark Hertsgaard, *Earth Odyssey: Around the World in Search of Our Environmental Future* (New York: Broadway Books/Random House, 1998).

7. Richard W. Behan, *Plundered Promise: Capitalism, Politics, and the Fate of the Federal*

Lands (Washington, D.C.: Island Press, 2001); and Gary Snyder, "Coming into the Watershed" (1992), in Snyder, *A Place in Space* (Washington, D.C.: Counterpoint, 1995), 219–35. Snyder identified Daniel Kemmis as mayor of Missoula, Mont. See Kemmis, *Community and the Politics of Place* (Norman: University of Oklahoma Press, 1990).

8. Fletcher Steele, *Gardens and People* (Boston: Houghton Mifflin, 1964), 221.

9. Malcolm Cowley, *Exile's Return* (1951; New York: Viking/Penguin, 1982), 27, 4–5, 9.

10. Helena Norberg-Hodge, "The Pressure to Modernize," in *The Future of Progress: Reflections on Environment and Development,* rev. ed., ed. Helena Norberg-Hodge, Peter Goering, and Steven Gorelic (Foxhole, Dartington Totnes, Devon: Green Books/International Society for Ecology and Culture, 1995), 91–108; and Norberg-Hodge, *Ancient Futures: Learning from Ladakh* (San Francisco: Sierra Club Books, 1991).

11. E. O. Wilson, *Biophilia* (Cambridge: Harvard University Press, 1984); E. O. Wilson, ed., *Biodiversity* (Washington, D.C.: National Academy Press, 1988); and Stephen R. Kellert, *Kinship to Mastery: Biophilia in Human Evolution and Development* (Washington, D.C.: Island Press, 1997).

12. Bill McKibben, *Hope, Human and Wild: True Stories of Living Lightly on the Earth* (Boston: Little, Brown, 1995).

13. T. S. Eliot, *Notes towards the Definition of Culture* (London: Faber & Faber, 1948), 52–58.

Index

Italicized page numbers refer to illustrations

Forbush, Edward Howe, 199, 230, 245
Forest and Stream, 44
Forester, 4, 141
foresters, education of, 4, 11, 15, 91
Forest Reserve Act (1891), 4–5
forestry, aesthetics of, 144–46
Forestry, Division of (U.S. Department of Agriculture), 3, 11, 139, 142, 145
forestry, profession of, 3–5, 12–13, 15, 138, 139, 154; and public relations, 140–41
Forestry Quarterly, 4, 141
Forest Service, 1–5, 38, 81, 82, 139, 154, 164, 237; and landscape architects, 1–3, 37, 142, 149–51, 219
Fox, Stephen, 238
Frank, Bernard, 238
Fraser, James Earle, 104
Friends of Our Native Landscape, 47, 53
frontier, 158–60, 163, 172–76; Chapman on, 175; Hough on, 44–46; Turner on, 43–44, 159
Fulkerson, Mertha, 194

Gannett, Lewis, 126–27, 171
Garden and Forest, xi–xii, 12, 14, 141, 247; and native plants, 42, 190–92
Geological Survey (U.S. Department of the Interior), 9
Gila National Forest, 2
Gillette, Genevieve, 193
Glacier National Park, 77–79
Grand Canyon, 5, 30, 33, 38, 50, 65; Van Dyke at, 35, 36–37
Graves, Henry S., 15, 140, 141, 147
Great Dismal Swamp, 186–87, *188,* 282 n. 26
Great New Wilderness Debate (Callicott and Nelson), 17
Greeley, William B., 4–5
Green Mountain Club, 84
Grese, Robert, 52, 59, 216
Griffin, Marion Mahony, 52

Griffin, Walter Burley, 52
Grinnell, Joseph, 241
Guérin, Jules, 109
Gulf of Mexico, coast of, 167–71

Hall, William Hammond, 100
Halle, Louis J., Jr., 3, 175–77, 242, 246. Works: *Spring in Washington,* 17, 176–77, 240, 241
Hansen, Anne Marie, 59
Harper's Monthly, 30, 239–40
Harriman, Edward Henry, 161
Harriman Alaska Expedition, 161–63
Harris, Diane, 100
Harrison, Benjamin, 5
Harvard University, xiii, 119, 130, 138, 146, 159, 234, 250; studies in forestry at, 11, 81, 121, 147; studies in landscape architecture at, 11, 113, 116–17, 120–21, 214; studies in natural sciences at, 8–9, 61, 224
health and well-being, human: 16, 17, 147, 151, 174, 204, 243, 247, 251; search for, in Arid West, 21, 23, 24, 30, 37; and stresses of workplace, 84, 175–76, 209, 231–32
health of the land, 24, 37, 38–39, 244
Hertsgaard, Mark, 248
Hetch Hetchy Valley, dam in, 7, 147–49
Hildreth, Horace, 83
Holtz, Mathilde Edith, 77–79
Hoover, Herbert C., 233, 238
Hornaday, William T., 227–28, 232
Hosmer, Ralph S., 140, 142, 145–46
Hough, Emerson, 44–46, 137
House Beautiful, 194, 195
Hubbard, Henry Vincent, 141; as educator, xiii, 121; and government service, 142; and wilderness recreation, 114–16, 233. Works: *Introduction to the Study of Landscape Design* (with Kimball), xiii, 113–14, 115–16, 118–19
Hubbard, Theodora Kimball, xiii, 113–14, 118

Hudson, W. H., 198, 240
Hunger, Edwin A., 63–64
Huxley, Thomas Henry, 189

Illinois: Garden Club of, 216; University of, in Urbana, 54, 232
Indiana Dunes, 53–54
Iowa State College (now Iowa State University), 44, 149, 151

James, George Wharton, 35–36, 154
James, William, 202
Jefferson, Thomas, 204, 237
Jekyll, Gertrude, 96, 207
Jensen, Jens, 8, 46, 51–55, 179, 249; formative years of, 59; and Lincoln Memorial Garden, 216–17, *217;* and native plants, 42–43, 192, 193–94, 216; and prairie spirit, 54–55; on preserving gardens and landscapes, 47–48, 60, 108; and Wright, 57–58, 59. Works: *Clearing,* xv, 223, 243, 247; *Siftings,* 58–60, 215, 218
Jewett, Sarah Orne, 78, 172–73
Johns Hopkins University, 202, 220
Johnson, Robert Underwood, 71
Jones, Beatrix. *See* Farrand, Beatrix
Journal of Forestry, 4, 141, 152–53
Journal of the American Institute of Architects, 84

Kansas Agricultural College, 219
Kazin, Alfred, 125–26
Keats, John, 76, 184
Keeler, Charles, 90–91, 110; on birds of Bay Area, 91–94, 95, 108–9; and Burroughs, 162; on gardens, 96–98, 208–9; and Maybeck, 94–95, 97–98; and Muir, 94, 162. Works: *Simple Home,* 95–98, 208–9
Keeler, Louise Mapes, 94, 96
Keith, William, 94
Kemmis, Daniel, 248
Kent, William, 137

Kephart, Horace, 78
Kieran, John, 171
Kiley, Daniel U., 87, 193
Kimball, Theodora. *See* Hubbard, Theodora Kimball
Knight, Richard Payne, 101
Kober, Nancy, 212–13
Kopman, Henry Hazlitt, 167, 168–71
Koyukuk River Valley (Alaska), 164–65
Krutch, Joseph Wood, 236–37. Works: *Modern Temper,* 201–6, 210, 237

La Mance, Lora S., 42
landscape architects, education of, 11, 91, 113, 116–17, 120–21, 215
landscape architecture: art of, 109, 112–14, 115, 117–18; emphasis on plants in, 55, 56, 60, 121–22, 135, 194–96, 213–14, 216, 219, 236; and natural processes, 60, 179, 194–96, 209–10, 214–17, 219, 236, 283 n. 50; profession of, 3, 8, 12–14, 109, 117, 138, 139, 140, 142, 149, 154; and public relations, 14, 140–41, 208
Landscape Architecture, 136, 137, 141
Lange, Willy, 219
Lay, Charles Downing, 141, 171; on science and the arts, 207, 208, 209–10, 236. Works: *Freedom of the City,* 128–29, 130; *Garden Book for Autumn and Winter,* 207–8
Lear, Linda, 221
Lee, Robert E., 212
Lee Park Wildflower and Bird Sanctuary (Petersburg, Va.), 212–13, *215,* 216
Leopold, Aldo, 17, 61, 85, 87, 141, 202, 235, 237, 246, 247; adolescence of, 63–64; and Carhart, 1–3; at Grand Canyon, 37–38; and health of the land, 38–39; on land ethics and aesthetics, 153, 222–23, 242, 244; on liberal education, 16; and modern science, 40–41, 238, 240, 241; and Waugh, 37, 219; and Wilderness